The Data Modeling Handbook

The Data Modeling Handbook

A Best-Practice Approach to Building Quality Data Models

Michael Reingruber

William W. Gregory

A Wiley–QED Publication

John Wiley & Sons, Inc.

Publisher: Katherine Schowalter
Editor: Rich O'Hanley
Managing Editor: Maureen B. Drexel
Text Design & Composition: Publishers' Design and Production Services, Inc.

Designations used by companies to distinguish their products are often claimed as trademarks. In all instances where John Wiley & Sons, Inc. is aware of a claim, the product names appear in initial capital or all capital letters. Readers, however, should contact the appropriate companies for more complete information regarding trademarks and registration.

This text is printed on acid-free paper.

This publication is designed to provide accurate and authoritative information in regard to this subject matter covered. It is sold with the understanding that the publisher is not engaged in rendering legal, accounting, or other professional service. If legal advice or other expert assistance is required, the services of a competent professional person should be sought.

Library of Congress Cataloging-in-Publication Data:

Reingruber, Michael C.
    The data modeling handbook: a best-practice approach to building
quality data models / Michael C. Reingruber, William W. Gregory.
        p.   cm.
    "A Wiley-QED publication."
    Includes Index
    ISBN 0-471-05290-6 (cloth)
    1. Database design   2. Data structures (Computer science)
I. Gregory, William W.
QA76.9.D26R45   1994
005. 74—dc20   94-12669
                                                              CIP

*To my wife and proofreader, M'liss, my children,
James and Grace, and my parents, Chris and Laima.
Thanks for your support, love, and encouragement.*

—Michael Joseph Reingruber

*To my partner and best friend, Lori, and my family—
Breune, Jack, Jane, Bud, and Bob*

—Bill Gregory

Contents

Preface

Several years ago, as two young consultants working with an East Coast information engineering firm, we paused to review a data model we were preparing for a large financial institution. We had been working diligently on the model for some months. We had applied our best efforts over long hours, used all the modeling skills we had learned, and yet something was not right with the model. To put it in the consulting vernacular, it stunk. It was a data model, but . . . it was definitely not a model of the financial institution that had hired us.

It took us a while to understand that the technical aspects of the modeling we did on that job was okay, if not perfect. We understood normalization and data dependency analysis and subtyping and circular references and mixed domains and all of the other technical nuances of data modeling. But technique alone did not provide the result the client wanted. What was missing was informed, consistent, active participation on the part of the business experts throughout the enterprise. We had the technique, but we lost the context.

This book is about building high-quality data models. It is about blending good technique with business context in a self-regulating modeling process that results in the creation of models that somebody can actually use. This last point is important to us. A good data model has three characteristics: It is built on the consistent application of sound technique; it embodies a business context; and it is used to improve the business. The ability to achieve the last is largely dependent on the other two. We will talk more about utility in Chapter 1. It is central to our concept of quality, and motivates many of the things we do when we build models.

If you go to the information systems bookshelf at your local bookstore, you will find a host of titles covering data modeling, information engineering, and database design. We have been to the bookstore (many, many times), and we have probably read a lot of the same books that you have. What we could not find in any of them was a straightforward, no-nonsense explanation of *how* to build good data models. Every book we have read about data modeling explains the *what* of data modeling, not the *how*. This book is about *how*, and to some extent *why*. It was not written for the novice modeler. If you have never tried to build a data model, then perhaps this book is not for you. If you are an experienced data modeler working in an organization with a well-established data management function, then you may not get a lot out of this book either. But for the vast majority of data modelers laboring without data management guidance, with less training than they really want, with few opportunities to simply talk shop with another analyst, and with pressing deadlines that call for decisions and action, we think this book can provide some ideas.

ACKNOWLEDGMENTS

This book would not have been written without the help of many people. We would like to thank the following individuals who contributed time and talent to this project.

- Mr. Ed Kerr of QED/John Wiley & Sons, Inc., who was willing to listen to our ideas and take a chance on a couple of newcomers. Thanks, Ed, for your enthusiasm, guidance, and confidence in our abilities. We are considerably in your debt.
- Dennis Brennan, our colleague, mentor, and an extraordinary information engineer. Dennis volunteered his time and experience to this effort without hesitation. He kept us on track and to the point, as he has done countless times in the past, and hopefully will be patient enough to continue to do in the future.
- Tim Rinaman, Vice President, Information Engineering Systems Corporation (IESC). Tim has been instrumental in the continuing development of information engineering techniques and CASE tools, and maintains an active presence in the consulting field. He is an excellent teacher, a superior analyst, and quite a sailor.
- Mike Berrier, IESC, who taught an awful lot of information engineers, including us, what it means to do quality work. Mike makes everyone around him better.

- Mike Redman, for his resources and expert review; Keith McCaughin, for his insights on integration and the future of CASE; Patrick Simpers, for his ideas on Object Modeling; Marvin Lerfald for his data modeling expertise; Pat Simes, for her help with best practices; Dave Kahn, Chris Turner, and Steffi Schweigert for their reviews.

We would like to thank our employer, Systems Research and Applications (SRA), who provided us with the time, materials, and atmosphere to prepare this book. In particular, Mr. Emerson Thompson, whose ELITE™ methodology initiatives formed the impetus for our work; Mr. Jerry Yates, who helped us with all of the legal aspects of this venture; and Dr. Matthew Black and Mr. Hal Boylan, who supported us without question or hesitation.

We would like to thank Evergreen CASE Tools, who provided us with the EasyCASE System Designer 4.01 for this project. It is the only CASE product we are aware of that allows an analyst to use his or her favorite notation and provides the rule enforcement behind it. Their new release, 4.1, has received excellent reviews in the trade press.

Finally, we would like to reserve special recognition for Clive Finkelstein, whose ideas on information engineering, strategic planning, and data modeling launched a generation of information engineers and a revolution in systems development.

One final note. We invite comment on any rules readers feel strongly about. Michael Reingruber (reingrum@smtplink.sra.com) and Bill Gregory (gregoryb@smtplink.sra.com) can be reached via the Internet or at Systems Research and Applications (SRA) in Fair Lakes, Virginia. We will try to respond to all inquiries.

Introduction

Data Modeling and Quality

1.1   GOOD NEWS ... AND BAD NEWS

This book is about building good data models. There are a lot of good data models being built these days. They are being used to help managers analyze their business policies and strategies; to help two companies understand each other's data and business practices so they can form an information partnership; to design and build highly complex client/server data architectures; to reengineer aging application systems; to reengineer business processes. The data model is finally being recognized as a tremendously important tool that can be used in many different situations to analyze more than just data requirements. After many years of being overshadowed by process and function modeling, data modeling is moving to its rightful place at the center of application system development efforts. It has been rumored that some systems analysts who cut their teeth on data flow diagrams (DFDs) have been seen doing a little data modeling on the side, even *before* they look at the functional nature of their systems. A revolution is surely at hand. That's the good news.

Now for the bad news. There are a lot of bad data models being built these days. There, we said it up front—bad data models. Not just so-so data models, not just a few questionable relationships here or there, maybe a repeating attribute that wasn't resolved, or a dangling foreign key. We're talking about data models so bad that they are never used after they are completed. We are talking about hours upon hours invested by countless managers, business analysts, data modelers, invoicing agents, payroll clerks, accountants, air crew schedulers, trainers, logisticians, nurses and hospital administrators, and many others from every function in a thousand different kinds of enterprises that sit through joint modeling sessions building a product that will never be used. Why? Because it was "broken" as early as its first day of existence, but no one took the time, had the knowledge, or mustered the courage to say "This is broken. This model is not right." Sometimes the pressure to "just get it done" is so intense that pausing to make it right is simply out of the question. Everyone agrees with the concept of "building it right the first time," but how, they ask, can it be done? And sometimes a modeling team thinks it *is* right.

Understanding the concepts of data modeling is not easy. Actually modeling data under intense time pressures, with limited access to business experts and system users, and with marginal CASE tool support is even more difficult. Becoming excellent at data modeling is something achieved by very few. And it is excellent data models that we strive for, especially now in the Age of the Enterprise Model.

Just because a data model isn't used after it is finished does not mean that it is a bad data model. There are a hundred reasons why a model may be put on a shelf, never to be picked up again. But we suspect that the quality of those models is a contributing factor. Remember when the Apple Macintosh was introduced? Most companies had committed to the IBM PC architecture standard, and to the DOS operating system. But the Mac kept popping up in offices, brought in through the back door, paid for out of departmental funds or out of employees' pockets (Vaskevitch, 1993). Why? Because the Mac had what people wanted. It was a sleek little machine that helped people get their jobs done. It was well designed, easy to use; heck, it was so *useful* that everyone wanted at least one around for those special jobs the IBM PC really didn't handle very well at the time. The Macintosh was a high-quality machine. It was technically sound, handled the software and interfaces that users needed (it met *their* requirements), and it was noted for its utility. Those are characteristics that we believe are important—being technically sound, meeting the users' requirements, and being useful. We also think those qualities can be built into a data model. And we think if you build a model with those qualities, it will become a valued resource.

This book is about building high-quality data models. A data model is obviously not an Apple Macintosh. It is an abstraction of the real things we deal with in our business environment every day. That makes judging quality a little different, but certainly not impossible.

1.2   THE ROOTS OF QUALITY

If you look in *Webster's New World Dictionary* (Guralnik, 1976), you will find the definition of *model* containing two components that are very important to understanding the potential of data modeling to help transform an enterprise, and to building *quality* data models. First, *Webster's* says a model is "a hypothetical or stylized representation"; it attempts to capture in meaningful form some larger, or in some cases smaller, object that exists or will exist.

The model's representation relies on the adoption of a language, a "special set of symbols, letters, numerals, rules, etc." or "any means of expressing or communicating" (Guralnik, 1976). In the case of data models, several languages have evolved, using many similar symbols, but each having unique characteristics. For example, IDEF1X uses rectangular and rounded boxes, solid and dashed lines, little diamonds, and black balls, while James Martin employs rectangular boxes, solid lines, little circles, hash marks, and crow's feet (National Institute of Standards and Technology, 1992; Martin, 1989). Each language has a predefined syntax, which *Webster's* defines as "an orderly or systematic arrangement." In other words, rules govern the way in which the symbols are combined and used. The syntax establishes expectations about the use of the symbols, which allows them to be interpreted consistently and accurately.

Let's return to *Webster's* again, where we find the term *semantic*, which means "the relationships between signs and symbols and the concepts associated with them in the minds of their interpreters." When you attach meaning to the symbols used in the language, you establish the semantics. For example, Figure 1.1 presents a fragment of a data model.

If you have any familiarity with data modeling, you will recognize that this model tells you "a building contains 0 or more equipment items." We have attached meaning to the symbols, and we can express that meaning in the form of a model. Once we know the meaning, we can express the same concept using an alternative language (which employs its own syntax), as we just did when we expressed the concept embodied in the data model fragment using a simple sentence. The advantage with using data modeling symbols, of course, is that they enable us to be very precise. Data modeling languages were developed for a specific purpose—documenting the data, and its characteristics, required to satisfy the needs of a predetermined domain, such as an information system or a business unit. Data modeling languages enable precision out of necessity, because information systems design is a very precise, very demanding process. The language(s) we use to communi-

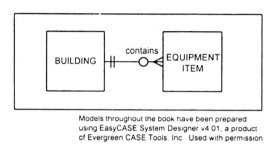

Models throughout the book have been prepared
using EasyCASE System Designer v4 01, a product
of Evergreen CASE Tools, Inc. Used with permission

Figure 1.1 Data model fragment.

cate on an everyday basis must be much more flexible, and as a result, are not as well suited to conveying the complexities of data relationships as precisely or as completely.

Using the right combination of symbols to convey the intended meaning is not always as easy as it first appears, as we shall demonstrate throughout the remainder of this book.

Webster's also defines a model as "a preliminary representation of something, serving as the plan from which the final object is to be constructed." This should be familiar territory. The data model is a blueprint, a plan for building information systems, designing business policies, or changing enterprise strategies (Zachman, 1987). And now the quality imperative begins to be a little clearer. You wouldn't expect to build a house using a blueprint with known errors in it, or that is not complete, or that is drawn using symbols a construction foreman could not understand. What would result from building a house from a flawed plan? What is the value of a data model that is rife with errors or omissions? If the designers and builders have no confidence in the plan (the model), then how can they be expected to follow it? In answering that question, we come to realize how so many data models end up on the shelf. And if systems are built anyway, what does that tell us about the quality of those systems, or the productivity of the development team that has to dig out data requirements all over again during the "design" (now the "requirements again and design") phase?

Before pursuing the quality issue further, let's return briefly to *Webster's* for a look at the definition of *quality*: "1. any of the features that make something what it is; characteristic element; attribute 2. basic nature; character; kind 3. the degree of excellence which a thing possesses." Given the myriad books, articles and speeches made on the topic of quality, the definition seems somewhat underwhelming. However, there are two important ideas represented there. The first idea is that quality includes some aspect of *character*, or *wholeness*. For any thing there is some predefined set of characteristics or features that, when combined, serve to define that thing, to make it whole or complete. If any one feature is missing, then the whole is diminished, or at least not completely discernible. The second idea relates to the concept of "degree of excellence," and goes to the more common notion of quality. When we talk of a "quality product," we are generally referring to its *correctness*, its *suitability for use*, its *adherence to a predetermined set of expectations*, or its *freedom from mistakes or flaws*.

So when we talk about quality, we are talking about two concepts: *completeness* and *correctness*. We are talking about using a language and its syntax correctly and making sure the model is an accurate and complete representation of the thing or concept we are using it to represent.

We have taken these very basic ideas about languages, syntax, semantics, models, and quality and have joined them with a final concept, which we will introduce momentarily, to form what we call the five dimensions of data model quality, as depicted in Figure 1.2. Together these form the scope of our discussions in this book, and should provide a framework on which data analysts can build a comprehensive modeling approach.

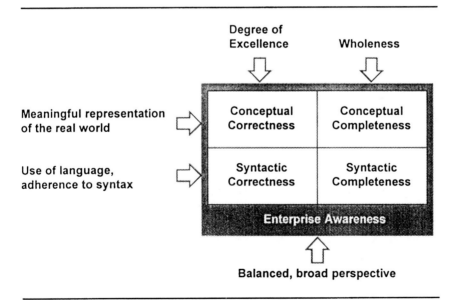

Figure 1.2   Five dimensions of data model quality.

Our five dimensions of data model quality are an extension of early, important work done in this area by Information Engineering Systems Corporation (IESC). IESC was, to our knowledge, one of the first organizations to actively promote a strong data modeling quality program. IESC introduced four characteristics of data model quality: contextual completeness, contextual quality, technical completeness, and technical quality (Information Engineering Systems Corporation, 1991).

1.3   DEFINING THE FIVE DIMENSIONS OF QUALITY

By understanding each dimension, and planning your modeling approach to address each one, you can significantly increase the likelihood that your data models will exhibit characteristics rendering them useful for business analysis and information system design. Each dimension contributes uniquely to the overall quality and utility of the model. You cannot ignore one dimension and expect to make up for it in the other three dimensions. Unfortunately, that is exactly what many modelers do, either consciously or not. They focus on one or two of the dimensions, and neglect the others. The result is a model whose integrity is suspect. It's like building a car while ignoring the realities of the highway system. The car may be a technological marvel and the absolute essence of style, but if it has a two-gallon gas tank, then the integrity of the product is weakened. It simply isn't a practical design for use in the real world. The purpose of this book, particularly Section II, is to present suggestions on a balanced data modeling approach spanning all of the quality dimensions.

Let's define the five dimensions that we presented in Figure 1.2.

Conceptual Correctness

Conceptual correctness implies that the data model accurately reflects the business concepts of the enterprise. These concepts are embodied in the stated and unstated plans, policies, goals, objectives, strategies, and rules by which the enterprise has chosen or is compelled to operate. Conceptual correctness depends on the team's ability to translate the business environment into a semantic language to form a meaningful and accurate representation of the real world. The translation from concept to language must be correct, or the ability of the model to represent the real world is lost. Consider the simple example shown in Figure 1.3. The model fragment appears to represent the stated constraints correctly using the Martin modeling notation.

Business Rule: The enterprise maintains
a set of accounts for managing its financial
activities. A series of transactions may occur
against each account.

Corresponding Model:

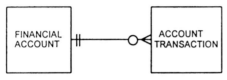

Figure 1.3   A simple example of acceptable conceptual correctness.

Figure 1.4, on the other hand, shows a model fragment that clearly
does not represent the stated business constraints.[1] If we attempt to
understand the enterprise using the model as it is shown, we will gain
an incorrect understanding of the underlying reality.

Of course, we must rely on one or more individuals who have an
understanding of both our language (data models) and the business
domain to judge whether the representation is correct. We will discuss
the role of these individuals, whom we refer to as domain experts or
subject matter experts or business experts, a little later. Determining
conceptual correctness is one of the most difficult aspects of assessing a
model's overall quality. Obviously, it is also the most challenging aspect
of *building* a data model in the first place.

Conceptual Completeness

Conceptual completeness implies that the data model contains objects
(e.g., entities or attributes) adequate to describe the full scope of the
business domain that the model purports to represent. Figure 1.5 portrays a business statement, followed by a model fragment. As you can
see, the model falls short of enabling the airport authorities to record all
of the information they seek about airports. The solution is not as simple

---

[1] We will suspend judgment on the accuracy of the textual business statements'
representation of the real world, and will assume that they are accurate representations.

Business Rule: The enterprise has acquired a fleet of vehicles, each capable of carrying multiple containers at any point in time. A container may be carried by many vehicles over its useful life. It is important to the enterprise to understand which containers a vehicle is carrying, and which vehicles have been used to haul a container.

Corresponding Model:

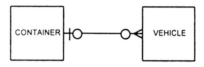

Figure 1.4.   A simple example of poor conceptual correctness.

State Department of Transportation
Airport Information Program Policy

The State Department of Transportation is charged with collection and retention of airport data through physical inspection or by mail solicitation of all proposed, planned, active, closed, and abandoned airports or other landing areas within the borders of this state.

airport identifier (PK)
airport name
activation date
airport abandon date

Attributes do not appear to record entire range of airport status possibilities (e.g., active, planned, proposed, closed, and abandoned).

Figure 1.5   A conceptually incomplete model fragment.

as adding a couple of more attributes to the AIRPORT entity. It will involve issues relating to conceptual correctness, and to some degree syntactic correctness.

As you have probably noticed by now, our ability to judge the quality of a data model is closely tied to things *outside* the data model, like business statements. We will talk about that more in a later section. But you are correct in your observation. You can't build good data models if all you care about or understand in your business environment is data. [Note: We use the term "business" to refer to any enterprise, subject area, or domain of interest, regardless of its actual status as a commercial venture.] Data is always *about* something—it describes something in your business. And if you don't take time to understand all of those "somethings" in your business, then you will never understand data and its interrelationships, and you will never build good data models.

Syntactic Correctness

Syntactic correctness implies that the objects contained in the data model do not violate any of the established syntax rules of the given language. We will assume that the correct set of symbols is being employed. Syntactic correctness implies that the symbols (boxes, lines, crow's feet) are used for their intended purposes, and that the model adheres to generally accepted practices of the methodology. For example, assume that we have a recognized repeating attribute that has not been correctly normalized, or an entity name that violates naming conventions imposed by the enterprise. In both cases, the model may accurately reflect the business environment, but the execution of the modeling techniques is flawed (e.g., we have recorded the fact that the attribute is repeating, but have not normalized it properly by moving it to another entity). The rules we have established for using the language have been broken. Granted, not all of these rules are established as part of the language. There are decisions to be made by each enterprise with regard to using a modeling language. However, once rules are established, then they become part of the enterprise's modeling syntax, and the models must be judged against those rules.

Syntactic Completeness

Syntactic completeness implies that the necessary data model objects are being captured at appropriate points in the modeling process. As an example, assume we have adopted IDEF1X as our modeling technique. IDEF1X is a modeling notation used extensively by agencies and departments of the United States federal government, and to a lesser extent by commercial organizations. In IDEF1X, data models are supposed to be built in three successive phases[2]: an entity-relationship modeling phase, followed by a key-based modeling phase, and finished with a fully attributed modeling phase (National Institute of Standards and Technology, 1992). As the phase names indicate, non-key attributes are not defined until late in the modeling process. Therefore, an IDEF1X model may be considered technically complete without any non-key attributes through the first two phases of modeling. At the end of the third phase, however, the model must contain non-key attributes (*all* necessary non-key attributes in order to be conceptually complete).

Enterprise Awareness

Enterprise awareness is the underlying concept that must be factored into any discussion of data model quality. Each and every data model is really just a view into a much larger set of data requirements and business rules, which has come to be known in common data management parlance as the "enterprise data model." Each time you build a model for a subset of your business (say the inventory management function, or a payroll system), you are actually creating a subset of your enterprise model. Should some other team build a model that documents another subset of the business (say marketing or sales management), there is a high probability that they will touch on many of the same topics modeled in your subset. If both teams choose to model a single concept in different ways, have either of you created high-quality models? Will the differences limit the utility of the model? As you might guess, our position is that a model's ability to be shared and integrated across the enterprise is a tremendously important characteristic of its value, its integrity, and its overall quality.

These five dimensions are not separate and distinct. Resolving quality issues in one dimension thrusts you into another one. Attempts to resolve a conceptual problem may lead to introduction of syntax issues that need to be addressed, which in turn may lead to further conceptual concerns. Data modeling is a dance through all five dimensions simultaneously. A quality assurance review, which we'll discuss in Chapter 2, gives the modeling team a chance to examine each dimension independently and at a point in time. Pausing and focusing, evaluating the model, allows the team to adjust its practices in mid-course, to regulate

---

[2] Please note that the authors do not condone this type of phased modeling approach; we use it here for illustrative purposes only.

its process as it progresses, rather than waiting until the process is complete. So understanding the dimensions is not enough. You have to act willfully on that understanding.

1.4   GENERAL CHARACTERISTICS OF A HIGH-QUALITY DATA MODEL

We have dedicated Section II of this book to discussing specific rules relating to the five dimensions of data model quality. However, the development of these criteria was based on a philosophy of data modeling that transcends the scope of any single rule. The process of building quality data models begins before the first entity is sketched, before the first attribute name is entered into your favorite CASE tool. It begins with an understanding of the big picture of model quality, and the role that data models have in the development of business policies and information systems.

A quality data model has several general characteristics.

Embodies Business Plans, Policies, and Strategies

It embodies the business plans, policies, and strategies of the enterprise. In a high-quality data model, a trained observer can "see the business." This is of utmost importance, of course, if you are "forward engineering" your model, but applies as well to "reverse engineering" efforts. In either case, to build a high-quality data model, you must understand and use business plans and rules to drive your data modeling efforts. The data model becomes a picture of the business, and a tool for visualizing business strategy, for analyzing changes in policy, and for communicating business plans. We'll look more closely at the quality implications of what we term business-driven data modeling a little later. We do not claim invention of the concept, by the way. Clive Finkelstein led the way long before. (Finkelstein, 1989)

Uses Recognized Set of Rules

A quality data model is built according to a recognized set of rules that enable it to be used to greatest effect by the enterprise. We can think of those rules as falling into two groups. First, we have the universal rules, based on relational theory, that have been passed to the new generation of modelers from the early pioneers—Codd, Date, Chen, Fagin, Kent, and others. Normal forms, the semantics of relational modeling, and the widely recognized languages (e.g., Chen, IDEF1X, Martin) all transcend individual enterprises. Essentially every company, government agency, or non-profit association engaged in data modeling draws heavily from the large body of theoretical work forming the foundation for our discipline. Second, within individual enterprises, data administration, data management, systems development, or similar groups add their own enterprise-level rules to the universal ones to make data modeling a practical reality. In some cases, individual enterprises look to an external standards committee for these (e.g., National Institute of Standards and Technology's [NIST] Federal Information Processing Standards [FIPS]). Within this second group of rules we find naming conventions, completeness expectations, integration requirements, and other guidelines without which modeling chaos would surely reign.

The importance of these rules and conventions is not that they *prevent* data modelers from doing what they should. Rather, it is that they *free* the modelers to focus on what is truly important—capturing the data requirements and business rules—while ensuring that the remainder of the enterprise can use their products with some assurance that they will be uniformly understandable, complete to some acceptable standard, integrated with other information architecture products, and relatively consistent regardless of who developed the model, when it was done, or even where it was created. In today's information management environment, products that lack enterprise-wide utility and consistency are measurably less valuable than those that can be readily integrated with other enterprise perspectives.

Involves Domain Experts

Domain experts must be involved directly in the development of a quality data model. A data model is a storehouse of domain-specific requirements and rules. You cannot build a data model without the direct and informed participation of individuals who understand the domain, have an ownership interest in the product, and are empowered to make decisions about changes in business rules. Let us repeat that one more time for effect—if business experts are not involved, your modeling effort will fail. There is no guarantee of success when business experts are involved. But there is no chance of success if they are not. Even models built during the course of reverse engineering projects will require some degree of participation by domain experts for interpretation and clarification of the components of the existing systems.

We recently observed an extensive modeling effort at one of our clients' businesses. The modeling team consisted of half a dozen information systems analysts, all experienced and motivated. They began their efforts with a model that had been under development for more than a year, then set aside due to the emergence of higher priorities. This team was tasked with bringing the model up to date, and validating that it was complete and accurate. The data model was to serve as a foundation for an ambitious system upgrade, involving the use of client/server technologies, off-the-shelf software packages, migration to a new DBMS platform—the works. The final instruction received by the team was "Do not bother the users. They are tired of being asked about their requirements." Understandably so, if they had been participating in the development of a model for more than a year with little or no results. The team proceeded, and after another year of modeling on their own they had progressed no farther than translating the original model into another notation and transferring it to a different CASE tool. Little, if any, real progress had been made on the model.

Can Be Transformed into High-Quality Design

A well-crafted data model is capable of being readily transformed into a high-quality design. The goal of building business-driven models is not contradictory to the need to establish quality criteria ensuring a data model serves its role in driving database and system designs. Ultimately, the characteristics of a high-quality database design will depend on its intended use, and the technology employed to implement the design. Discussion of database design is beyond the scope of this book. However, we will present some ideas about the relationship between requirements and design, and we include a list of things that should be documented as part of the preparation for transitioning to design from requirements analysis.

Is Created in Context of Other Business Architecture Elements

Data models do not stand alone. They must be consistent with other elements of the business architecture, including but not limited to business processes, organizational controls and authorities, and geographic distribution of data and systems (Zachman, 1987). This consistency may take the form of something simple, like using standards or conventions for entity and attribute names or mapping data models to process models. It may require you to build your data model in parallel with process modeling efforts (if your methodology dictates that approach). Awareness of the data model's role as an *integral* element of your business architecture is critical to its quality and utility.

Is Created in Context of Entire Enterprise

We are not suggesting that every model cover all data requirements of the enterprise. We are suggesting that if you build a data model, you should do so only after thinking long and hard about how your model's scope relates to other areas of the enterprise, and what the boundaries of your enterprise really are. If you haven't already, you need to begin thinking about defining data that is shared or readily exchanged with other organizations within the traditional bounds of the enterprise, and with those that have been traditionally viewed as outside the enterprise. If your company has access to a supplier's databases, and you regularly extract information from those for your use, then where is the line drawn that separates your enterprise from your supplier's? On the other hand, if you are building a CASE tool for sale as a commercial product, your enterprise is limited to the methodologies that you intend to support with your tool. It may include requirements imposed by other tools with which you intend to build interfaces for purposes of exchanging information. In our experience, the greatest value to both the data management and business communities is achieved when an enterprise perspective is maintained by each and every modeling team (assuming the enterprise has taken the necessary steps to build an infrastructure that supports true enterprise modeling.)

Is Created in Context of Overall Data Quality Lifecycle

Why emphasize *data quality*, in addition to *data model quality*? Because data modeling is a step in a much larger process (e.g., information systems development) designed to deliver to the key stakeholders of the enterprise a single primary output—high-quality data. Therefore, as we begin our detailed examination of data model quality, we need to retain our perspective. Data models are created as a means of recording as precisely as possible the needs of information users. They are created as a means of assuring that information systems deliver data to users in accordance with their stated needs. When you begin to wonder about the amount of effort put into building quality data models, remember that the ultimate product is data, and the ultimate customer, either directly or indirectly, is everyone in the enterprise.

Depends on Support Infrastructure

Consistent development of high quality models is dependent on the existence of an infrastructure to support data modeling and management. Tools, training, skilled facilitators, model management procedures, integration strategies, configuration management, and quality assurance are all elements of an infrastructure that must be in place to support data modeling efforts. You may succeed temporarily without them, but long-term success in data modeling comes from careful development and active use of a robust infrastructure. We will describe aspects of the infrastructure in the next chapter, and as we move through the rules in Section II.

Involves the Right Stakeholders

The right set of stakeholders needs to be involved in data modeling projects. The mix of participants will vary from project to project. In general, you will need to involve the following people.

Business Experts. These are the people with knowledge of the business domain and the specific subject(s) you are exploring. These individuals must learn how to read and interpret models in order to assure that the proper level of precision has been captured.

Data Modelers and Facilitators. We lump these two together, because quite frankly you can't do one well if you do the other poorly. Building a data model without interacting directly with the users limits its precision, and facilitating joint sessions without excellent data modeling skills will result in missed opportunities for exploring data requirements. A facilitator who does not have sound data modeling skills will not be able to use the model as a tool for eliciting requirements.

Data Management Professionals. In most organizations, these are the individuals charged with establishing data standards, integrating and managing models, operating repositories, and engineering quality data. The modeling team will have significant interaction with the data management group.

Information Systems Developers, and in Particular, Database Administrators. The model will end up in their hands for design, development, and implementation. Ideally, they become involved as the model reaches stability, assisting with completeness checks and helping to ensure a smooth transition.

Business Managers, who are the primary beneficiaries of data modeling efforts. It is always a good idea to keep them informed (you are probably using their people) of the progress and benefits of a data modeling effort. They will be interested in results, and are therefore a key customer for the modeling team.

1.5   SUMMARY

We have introduced our philosophy of data modeling quality. As you can see, there are many factors to consider, and we will explore all of them as we work our way through the remaining chapters. We suggest you come back to this chapter from time to time as you read the detailed rules in Section II. It will help you retain a sense of purpose, and will hopefully allow you to put the individual pieces of the data model quality puzzle into place.

REFERENCES

Finkelstein, Clive. *An Introduction to Information Engineering: From Strategic Planning to Information Systems.* Addison Wesley: Sydney (1989).

Guralnik, David B., editor. *Webster's New World Dictionary of the American Language, Second College Edition.* The World Publishing Company: Cleveland (1976).

Information Engineering Systems Corporation. *Tactical Modeling Workshop* (1991).

Martin, James. *Information Engineering, Book II: Planning and Analysis.* Prentice-Hall: Englewood Cliffs, NJ (1989).

National Institute of Standards and Technology. "Integration Definition for Information Modeling (IDEF1X)." Federal Information Processing Standard Publication. September 9, 1992, Draft.

Vaskevitch, David. *Client/Server Strategies: A Survival Guide for Corporate Reengineers.* IDG Books: San Mateo, CA (1993).

Zachman, John. "A Framework for Information Systems Architecture," *IBM Systems Journal*, 26, No. 3 (1987).

Data Model Quality Assurance Programs

A well-designed process is self-regulating. It contains mechanisms that allow for periodic or continuous identification and correction of out-of-tolerance conditions (Vaskevitch, 1993). Waiting until the end of a process before submitting the product for inspection or test invites trouble. Problems that might have been detected early and corrected with little effort can become compounded as steps later in the process build on errors introduced—and not corrected—in the early stages. Finding all of the problems at the end can be rather shocking, in both magnitude and result. Too many errors and the product may only be good for scrap. Even a moderate number of errors could cause significant rework as the product is sent back through the process for correction. Worse yet, relying on inspection of end products alone limits opportunities for determining which steps are continuously causing out-of-tolerance conditions. The systemic problem, the cause of the errors, goes undetected until the sheer number of bad products causes someone to investigate.

Authors' Note: The materials presented in this chapter, and in portions of Section II, are drawn largely from ideas we developed and practices instituted at Systems Research and Applications (SRA) Corporation. Like many companies with active corporate commitments to quality, SRA has a strong interest in developing quality assurance practices incorporating continuous product assessment and process improvement as an integral part of product development. The authors are deeply indebted to SRA for its permission to present these ideas here.

By evaluating the product periodically, and making small, manageable adjustments, the probability that a quality product will emerge at the end of the process is relatively high. Manufacturing firms have been employing this philosophy for years now, and the service sector is beginning to embrace similar ideas as part of a growing interest in business process reengineering. Data modeling is a process, and you can employ self-regulating mechanisms to help manage the process and improve your product—a high-quality data model. The self-regulating mechanisms for data modeling comprise what we refer to as a data model quality assurance (QA) program. The QA program should be an integral part of any modeling effort, yet must remain somewhat independent of it in order to fulfill its role as a regulating mechanism. It is designed to ensure that data models are evaluated early in their development, then re-evaluated continuously on a regular basis until completed.

We will discuss the exact nature of the relationship between a quality assurance program and modeling teams in this chapter, and explain how a program can be established to help you identify potential quality problems in your data model early in its development. We will also explain how you can use the QA program to get to the root cause of data modeling errors or omissions.

And now for an assertion: You cannot consistently build high-quality models without implementing a rigorous quality assurance program. Any data modeler, regardless of how experienced, how studied, or how naturally gifted, will make mistakes. Data modelers are human, and they are often very harried, overworked, tired, stressed souls who are pushing hard to get a model done in order to maintain a project schedule.

Software developers introduced peer reviews and code walkthroughs long ago in recognition of the fact that people develop bad habits, make mistakes, are rushed, or are just plain stubborn (Yourdon, 1989). The software development community also recognized peer reviews as an opportunity to share ideas and pass along the knowledge of experienced programmers. While a data model quality review is different in many ways for a code walkthrough, there are also many similarities, and some of the same benefits.

2.1 WHAT IS A QUALITY ASSURANCE PROGRAM?

A data modeling quality assurance program consists of the following elements:

• **A set of rules that govern how data models are to be constructed in your organization.** As we have discussed before, you cannot expect to build data models in a consistent, repeatable fashion if you do not establish criteria for their development. The rules constitute the tolerances you will use to test your model and regulate your modeling process. They are boundaries within which the creativity of the modeling team can be exercised. The rules that you establish should be clearly documented, and available to both modeling teams and analysts who serve as independent quality reviewers. And they should form the basis of training programs for your data modelers.

In Section II, we present a series of rules that can be used as the basis for a quality assurance program. You may not agree with every rule in this book. Replace the ones you don't like with ones you are comfortable with. But whatever you decide, we strongly urge you to establish a set of rules (guidelines, if you prefer) for your modelers to use to evaluate the quality of their work.

• **A stable of seasoned data modelers to serve as expert independent reviewers.** Depending on the size of your organization and the number of modeling projects going on at any one time, you may identify one expert reviewer, or several. Our firm is accustomed to having anywhere from five to twenty active modeling projects going on at any time, requiring a substantial number of reviewers. Reviewers need not be held in reserve. They can and probably should be out performing on projects, as long as they can be freed to perform QA duties according to coordinated schedules. They will need to be trained to perform QAs, and equipped with completeness and quality criteria in order to evaluate models consistently.

• **A plan for implementing quality assurance reviews on each data modeling effort.** The objective is to make the reviews an integral part of the modeling process. The implementation plan needs to consider requirements relating to frequency of reviews, use of CASE capabilities, and an approach to conducting the reviews.

• **Someone to coordinate the quality program.** Setting guidelines, scheduling reviews, and managing expert reviewers takes time and effort. If you have a quality assurance group or a data administration function, then they are prime candidates for assuming this role. If not, then you will have to evaluate your organization structure, and identify someone with enough seniority to organize and execute the program.

2.2 WHAT IS A QUALITY ASSURANCE REVIEW?

A data model quality review

•   is an evaluation of the five quality elements discussed in Chapter 1 by an individual or team with expertise in the techniques of data modeling.

•   is a set of activities that is planned and executed as an integral part of the overall data modeling effort. The QA review is a complementary task, designed to fit seamlessly with the ongoing development of the model.

•   provides a means for direct input to the model development process by identifying potential errors, omissions, and opportunities for refinement, then communicating those back to the modeling team. The goal of a QA is not to provide solutions, but rather to raise issues or questions so that the modeling team can devise a proper solution based on business rules.

•   is not a mandate for change; many QA findings (issues or questions) result in no change to the model—the modeling team studies the issue and decides that the model correctly portrays the business concepts. Do not expect all of the QA findings to result in actual changes to the model. Sounds inefficient? Well, think about what having all the problems you do find in your model translates to in terms of user satisfaction.

•   is relatively brief in duration, usually less than one week, and involves a minimum expenditure of resources.

•   is an opportunity to enhance integration of models through reuse, adherence to standards and conventions, and validation of model quality.

•   is an excellent means of identifying systemic problems in the data modeling processes or resources.

•   consists of three major pieces:
  1.   collection of materials
  2.   expert review of models and supporting materials
  3.   resolution of issues raised by the review

Before we dive into a detailed examination of quality assurance programs, let's look at a brief example to illustrate why QA programs are important, and what you should expect a QA program to bring to your modeling efforts. Figure 2.1 shows a policy statement for a fictitious company. Assume that a modeling team constructed a model for the human resources group of the company, and a fragment of that model is shown. It appears to be complete, logical, and correct (although we have not included keys or non-key attributes in the example). Sim-

Human Resources Policy Statement: We will hire promising individuals who have not
yet earned a college diploma. The company encourages them to pursue a degree
by assuming the full cost of tuition, books, and lab fees in degree programs
directly related to their job fields. Individuals who already have a bachelor's degree
will be reimbursed tuition costs for additional degree programs they choose to pursue.

Quality Assurance Review Findings:

1. The relationship between EMPLOYEE and EMPLOYEE COLLEGE DEGREE is
currently modeled as mandatory, suggesting that no one will be hired who does
not yet have a college degree. However, the policy statement suggests otherwise.
Which is correct? Adjust either the policy statement (e.g., the company's hiring
strategy) or the model, based on the modeling team's decision.

2. The policy statement suggests a need to match the individual's degree program
with his or her job field, yet the model does not have adequate components to do so.
Recommend that the modeling team examine this business rule to determine what
additional model objects will be required.

Figure 2.1   Sample business statement, model fragment, and QA finding.

ply looking at the model, you might say that it "looks good." However,
assume that a quality assurance review was undertaken during the
course of the project. Two QA findings are listed at the bottom of the
figure. The findings are typical of the kind of questions or issues raised
during a quality assessment of a model, and they paint a very different
picture of how "good" the model fragment really is. They indicate that
our "good" model may follow the rules of syntax, but is actually a "poor"
representation of our fictitious company's business practices.

Since we want our information systems to support the business,
then either the model must be adjusted (we use the terms "refined" and
"extended"), or the human resources department must re-examine its
policy. This latter point is very important. Models should reflect what
the business users really want. A QA review can reveal the need to go
back and revise business statements in accordance with the future business strategies that have been discovered and decided upon during the
course of a modeling exercise. The model becomes a tool for business

strategy analysis and decision making, rather than simply a passive device for translating statements (requirements) into data structures. We refer the reader to the extensive work of Clive Finkelstein (1989, 1992), one of the pioneers of Information Engineering, for an explanation of strategic planning, business-driven data modeling, and business normal forms (BNF).

Back to our model. If this were a full quality assurance review, the individual charged with performing the review would have looked for problems ("opportunities for refinement" is the term we prefer) across all five of our quality perspectives. He or she would use a set of rules to evaluate syntactic correctness, in accordance with whatever modeling notation we selected (Martin, Finkelstein, IDEF1X, E-R-A, Ross, etc.). The reviewer would evaluate the model using business statements such as objectives, policies, or strategies used by the business as strategic or operating guidelines, and would communicate with the team of business experts and data modelers who worked together to build the model. The reviewer would also assist the team in formulating alternatives for resolving quality problems.

Roles and Responsibilities for QA Reviews

Normally, there are two groups of participants in a QA review—the modeling team that developed the model, and the independent reviewer(s). If you have a quality assurance organization, then they too may participate in a coordinating or managing role, assisting in the scheduling and documentation of the review. The reviewer does most of the work, but the modeling team has a key role to play as well. Figure 2.2 describes the roles each plays in the review process.

2.3   WHO SHOULD PERFORM THE REVIEW?

In order to assure that a QA review achieves its full potential, it needs to be performed by an experienced modeler, preferably one with several years of experience across a wide range of business areas. You can leverage the involvement of your experienced modelers in the quality process if you recognize the opportunities a quality review presents. First, it ensures that the models are being evaluated by someone who knows what to look for and who can bring a broad base of experience to bear. Second, it spreads your experienced people out across all of the modeling projects. This is a tremendous opportunity to provide leadership and specialized training to less experienced data modelers.

Participant	Role
QA Reviewer	• Assists modeling team to plan QA activities, including frequency, duration, scope of reviews
	• Performs reviews of data model correctness and completeness
	• Looks for systemic quality problems—missing or incomplete modeling standards, need for training, poor modeling team structure, etc.
	• Advises modeling team with regard to standards, conventions, and best modeling practices
	• Documents findings and recommendations
	• Meets with modeling team to explain findings, and to develop resolution strategies
	• Coordinates with data management or information systems group to resolve systemic quality problems
Modeling Team	• Plans QA activities in concert with selected reviewer(s)
	• Collects and organizes models and supporting materials; provides them to the reviewer
	• Responds to questions from reviewer during the course of the review
	• Meets with the reviewer to hear findings, and to jointly develop resolution strategies
	• Follows through to resolve model quality problems; maintains issues history for use in future reviews
	• Works to correct any systemic or habitual quality problems within its control

Figure 2.2   QA review participants and their roles.

Selected QA reviewers do not need to have knowledge of a particular business area in order to perform a review. Our experience indicates that it is often an individual's *lack* of area knowledge that allows him or her to be very effective in evaluating the model. A data model should communicate business rules clearly—if a seasoned modeler has difficulty interpreting it, then there is no reason to expect others, including systems developers, to be able to make sense of it either. Furthermore, the quality assurance review is an opportunity to pose questions and raise issues to the team without dictating or suggesting a particular solution. For example, a reviewer examining a financial model might raise questions about the way that financial accounts have been modeled. If the reviewer has considerable background in financial accounting, the tendency may be to strongly suggest or even dictate a solution. The purpose of a QA is not to give solutions, but to raise issues so that the modeling team can work out solutions (with input from the QA reviewer).

If you have more than one modeling team running in parallel, you may want to have each team serve as expert reviewer for one of the other teams, provided the requisite level of expertise exists uniformly across teams. You will get several benefits from this kind of interaction. Teams will find areas of common interest, discover model structures that can be reused, begin the process of integration, gain insight into other areas of the enterprise, and learn from experiences of other teams. Granted, this type of review cycle is much more difficult to manage, but the benefits of cross-fertilization can be substantial.

2.4   LENGTH OF REVIEWS

How long should it take to perform a serious assessment of a data model? It depends greatly on the following factors:

•   **The size of the model.** Big models, obviously, take longer than small models, all other things being equal. But all other things are rarely equal. You will encounter small models (less than 100 entities) that are extremely complex, and larger models that you can sail through very quickly. We do not suggest tackling very large models in a single review. It is preferable to break a large model (say anything larger than 200 entities) into logical subsets, then review those subsets separately. There are simply too many interconnections in a large model to be able to handle them adequately in one review. Our suggestion is that you tackle subsets of a model one at a time, so size is kept under control. We will discuss techniques for subdividing a model later.

•   **How close the model is to completion.** Models that are closer to completion tend to have more things to review.

•   **The business area under consideration.** Some subjects are simply easier to understand and assess than others. For example, human resources models are, in our experience, much easier to review (and build) than models of financial transactions and investments, or manufacturing functions, or transportation activities.

•   **The type of model—whether it is strategic or operational in nature, or somewhere in between.** A strategic model is one that captures a very broad view of the entire enterprise, and contains primarily derived attributes of interest to senior management. An operational model is one focused on a particular area of the business, and involves sticky details, very specific business rules and constraints, and lots of transactional data. Strategic models tend to be less complex from a technical modeling perspective. Operational models tend to take longer to review.

• **The experience of the reviewer.** Like anyone who has worked his or her way down a learning curve, experienced reviewers learn to spot modeling patterns very quickly, tend to have worked out tricks for getting through a model, and generally get to the point with little extra effort.

• **The CASE tool employed.** Some CASE tools are better than others, especially when it comes to enforcing the rules of your selected modeling language. If your tool provides good model analysis features, then much (but not all) of the syntactic quality analysis may be done with the selection of a report in your CASE tool. CASE tools do *not* help you evaluate how well the model represents your business.

Given these variables, Figure 2.3 provides estimates of how long a quality assurance review covering the kinds of rules you will find in later sections of this book will last. The estimate includes kickoff meetings, analysis, and documentation, which we will describe later. It does not include any time required by the expert reviewer or the review team to resolve issues. The estimates assume a single experienced reviewer, a model nearing completeness, no prior QA review of the model, and an operational level of detail. We have used the number of entities as the basis for the estimate for convenience, for universal applicability, and because the numbers in the table are *very rough approximations.* You

Approximate Size of the Model	Estimated Duration of Review
50 entities	1+ days
100 entities	2–3 days
200 entities	5–7 days
300 entities	9–12 days

Figure 2.3   A very rough estimate of expected QA first-time review duration.

should track your own experience with review durations, and use a more appropriate measure if you feel it better suits your needs.

It is important to note that a QA review can be occurring while the modeling team continues to develop the model. The team will not be directly involved in the assessment, except during the early and late stages.

2.5   FREQUENCY OF REVIEWS

Prior to beginning a modeling effort, the designated project manager or technical leader should carefully consider the number of reviews that will be needed, and the frequency of those reviews. Use the following criteria to estimate review requirements:

• **Schedule a minimum of two QA reviews, regardless of the length of the modeling effort.** If the modeling effort is planned to last six weeks, for example, the project team should schedule a review at about the three-week mark, then another near the end of the project. Scheduling a review any earlier than three weeks would probably not be beneficial, since you can expect the model to be undergoing heavy changes; it most likely would not be complete enough for an effective review. The first QA action (at three weeks) would allow plenty of time for the reviewer's findings to influence the development of the model. If the modeling effort is longer than six to eight weeks, consider more than two reviews, evenly spaced over the project duration.

• **Leave enough time after the final review for the team to evaluate the findings, and make necessary corrections to the model prior to their scheduled deadline.** Scheduling a review as the last activity in the model development plan defeats the purpose of the review. There should be time for the team to react to findings, and incorporate changes in a reasonable manner. Coming in at the eleventh hour with new findings will cause considerable turmoil, and could leave you with a list of open issues at the completion of the effort. The reviewer needs to stay close to the team during the final stages of the model development, performing ad hoc reviews of model fragments as the team winds down its efforts.

• **For extended modeling projects, plan to have a review as often as *once per month*.** This will keep the expert reviewer in touch with the modeling team and with the development of the model, and it ensures that the team benefits from regular interaction with the reviewer. It also keeps the reviews reasonably scoped, allowing the team to incorporate issues into its modeling sessions incrementally. Long periods between reviews lead to a larger number of findings, making resolution more difficult to manage.

In order to be accepted as part of the normal sequence of activities, quality assurance reviews must become part of every project plan. This may require development of a written policy or standard for your organization.

2.6   USING CASE TOOL MODEL ANALYSIS CAPABILITIES

CASE tools have come a long way in recent years toward helping data analysts construct sound models. While these tools cannot interpret business policies and compare them to your data model, they can alleviate much of the tedious syntax checks that used to be done by hand. In fact, CASE products have for the most part moved beyond their early role as sophisticated drawing tools; most now have some level of support for methodology rule-checking. Our advice to all modelers: take advantage of whatever capability is available in the tool you are using. If your organization is preparing to go through a CASE evaluation exercise in anticipation of acquiring a new product, make sure that your evaluation criteria include requirements for model analysis features.

Model analysis features are divided into two categories, each fulfilling an important role in an overall quality program:

• **Preventive checking.** These features ensure that only inputs adhering to a predefined configuration are accepted. Depending on the user's ability to tailor options for this kind of checking, it can be either extremely helpful or unnecessarily hindering. For example, some tools *require* a user to supply a name for each relationship. For those who consider relationship names a superfluous characteristic (the authors fall into this group), this is a ridiculous requirement, resulting in the user having to input fictitious names in order to add a relationship. Fortunately, almost all tools that require relationship names also provide the option of not displaying them.

Another common example of preventive checking involves duplicate object names. The user (or system administrator) can establish the rules by which duplicate names will be handled. These typically include: allowing duplicate names; preventing their entry into the tool; asking the user to confirm that the name is a duplicate before proceeding; or automatically renaming the object using a standard prefix or suffix scheme.

• **Corrective checking.** This type of checking is performed on objects in the model encyclopedia, and is therefore much more extensive than the preventive checking performed when an object is first entered. The objective of corrective checking is to verify that each object and the interrelationships between objects come together to create a model following the rules of the selected modeling language, and that the model is complete. Thus, model analysis features of CASE tools use rules established in the product's meta-model.[1]

Consistency checks are methodology-dependent, and may also be dependent on the particular phase in which the modeling occurs. For example, Texas Instruments' Information Engineering Facility™ (IEF™) has a set of rules for each of the five stages of information engineering it supports: Information Strategy Planning, Business Area Analysis, Business System Design, Technical Design, and Construction[2] (Texas Instruments, 1990). The advantage to this type of checking is that it is tightly coupled to the actual stage of the project, ensuring that only those rules applicable to the stage are verified, avoiding generation of warnings or errors that are inappropriate to the expected state of the model.

CASE tool model analysis results in identification and documentation of problems to be used by the modeling team to determine corrective actions.[3] Examples of problems identified by this kind of model analysis include: relationships unsupported by key structure; subtype entity with a different primary key structure than its parent; unimplementable cardinality combination.

2.7   CONDUCTING A QUALITY ASSURANCE REVIEW

The section presents a procedure for conducting a data model review. You should adapt any suggestions presented here to your particular organizational and project needs.

The Review Kit

The modeling team is responsible for supplying a standard set of information to the expert reviewer(s). We'll call this the "review kit" for ease of

---

[1] Products with so-called "extensible" dictionaries have substantially reduced ability to provide model analysis or completeness checking features. Because the meta-model can be modified, rules can only be created on that portion of the model that is not subject to change.

[2] Information Engineering Facility and IEF are registered trademarks of Texas Instruments Incorporated.

[3] Problems are generally grouped into categories (e.g., caution, warning, error) based on relative degree of seriousness.

reference. This kit contains all materials required to perform an adequate model review. Figure 2.4 presents a representative set of materials. The actual contents of the kit will vary depending on the nature of the modeling project (e.g., forward versus reverse engineering), its scope, and the relative functional or organizational level being modeled.

Review Kit Item	Syntax Review	Business Concepts Review
Evaluation criteria, such as those presented in Section II of this handbook, to be used to assess correctness and completeness. These are the expectations that your organization has for data models.	✓	✓
The data model including a diagram (or map), dictionary reports, and other supporting information describing characteristics of the model components	✓	✓
Business statements, such as strategic or operational plans, policies, laws, directives or orders, objectives, critical success factors, performance measures or other statements that guide, constrain, or otherwise affect the enterprise	✓	✓
Business process redesigns, process models, simulations, activity-based costing analyses, or other studies of the business area(s) covered by the data model		✓
Process, activity or data flow diagrams (if available)	✓	✓
Model analysis or validation reports from CASE tool(s) (if available in tool used)	✓	
Session notes from modeling sessions held by modeling team	✓	✓
Project data model development plans and schedules (to provide reviewer with an understanding of relative state of the model related to completion schedules)	✓	✓
Issues list and resolution results from prior QA reviews (to ensure that issues are not continually recycled)	✓	✓

Figure 2.4   Data model review checklist.

Each component of the kit has been marked according to its use in evaluating syntax rules, business concepts, or both. All items may not be readily available, owing to the relative maturity of the model or to project objectives. However, it is important to collect as much of the material as feasible, in order to aid the reviewers in making as complete an assessment as possible. It is *imperative* that the reviewer have access to the business statements (or results of current systems analysis, if appropriate) in order to perform the review. *An assessment of the quality of a model cannot be performed without the documented business statements that the model is being built to support.* We cannot overstate the importance of this point. If the modeling team cannot produce the business statements, then the quality of the model should be immediately called into question.

The Review Kickoff Meeting

The expert reviewer(s) selected to perform a quality assurance review should conduct a brief kickoff meeting with the modeling team prior to commencement of any QA activity. It is a good idea to invite all members of the modeling team to the kickoff, including subject matter experts. The kickoff meeting gives all parties a chance to exchange up-to-date information and to gain an understanding of the purpose and scope of the review. The reviewer should take this opportunity to discuss schedules, and to reinforce his or her role as a member of the team, not as an outside inspector. If this is a first review of the model, the reviewer should be prepared to preempt any resistance from the modeling team, and to openly discuss issues regarding communication of findings, roles for members of the modeling team, and the purpose and focus of the review. At this time, if they haven't already done so, the modeling team hands over the review kit.

The team should take the initiative to discuss several topics that the reviewer will need to understand in order to properly assess the model. Among these are:

- **The items in the QA review kit.** The reviewers will most likely have some preliminary questions, and the kickoff meeting is a good time to address those.
- **A summary of the general state of the model and a discussion of its relative degree of completion.** The team will need to point out areas of the model where there are unresolved issues, or where the model is relatively immature. The team should also identify which areas of the model they believe to be stable, which areas

are undergoing rapid change, and which areas are undeveloped. A written summary of these would be ideal. The description of these items allows the reviewer to judge how much time to spend on different subsets of the model.

- **A description of the continuing modeling activities, and which areas of the model are likely to be undergoing change in the near future.** The reviewer may wish to address those areas first, to unearth potential problems for the facilitator to bring before the modeling participants for timely resolution. This prevents the team from having to revisit areas of the model during the next QA review cycle.

- **Any areas of the model that have been especially sensitive to the participants.** Modeling teams often conduct turbulent and contentious discussions about various topics within their subset of the enterprise. The modeling team should inform the reviewer about these, so that he or she can carefully review the session notes, business plans, or other materials pertaining to those portions of the model, then validate the model's quality. At a practical level, the reviewer must be sensitive when raising additional issues or concerns over topics that have already been painfully hashed out by the team.

- **A description of the relative maturity and degree of activity of the model integration and management functions in place to support model development, if these are not already known to the reviewer.** Was the model initiated using components of a larger enterprise model or a strategic model? Does the project have an active model integration cycle that allows it to identify and resolve issues regarding common objects with other modeling teams across the enterprise? Have any of the model objects (entities or attributes) been standardized in accordance with an enterprise data administration standards program? It is imperative for the reviewer to understand the modeling environment, so that review kit materials can be discussed in proper context, issues are not raised unnecessarily, and findings can be documented correctly.

Location or time constraints may preclude the possibility of a face-to-face meeting between the reviewer and the modeling team. The information we have just described must be conveyed in some manner to the QA reviewer prior to commencement of the review. Obvious alternatives are to provide the information in written form, or to set up a telephone conference.

2.8 REVIEWING A DATA MODEL

This section presents ideas and strategies for conducting the detailed review of the materials provided in the QA review kit. To gain a sense of the subject area(s) covered by the model, we suggest beginning the review by briefly perusing the business statements. The next several subsections are presented in the sequence that they should occur during the review.

Scanning the Model

Briefly scan the entire model to gain a sense of the content and layout. This is best achieved by reviewing the diagram, supplemented by dictionary reports if areas seem unclear. The objective at this point is not to begin an assessment, but rather to become familiar with the scope and major subjects covered.

Studying Business Plans, Policies, and Other Models

Data models are one part of a much larger entity usually referred to as the business architecture. The business architecture typically consists of a data or information model, a functional model, organizational model, system architecture, and the like. All elements of the business architecture should be tightly integrated, mutually supportive, and clearly linked (or mapped) to other logically related elements. Therefore, it is important for the QA reviewer to have an understanding of the overall business architecture in order to conduct a viable review of the model. Assuming the review is for a business-driven ("forward engineered") model, begin by examining the business plans, policies, directives, or other collections of business statements used by the modeling team to develop business rules and identify data requirements. Models should directly reflect the business statements. For example, you should be able to find attributes that are used to capture performance measures, or relationship degrees/ natures that enforce business policies. Business statements provide the only rational basis for judging how well the model represents the business. This assumes, of course, that the statements used to drive the modeling, whether written down or uttered by business experts during interviews or modeling sessions, are themselves accurate representations of the business condition as it is now, or as the enterprise desires it to be in the future. Since this is one of the most important aspects of the quality review, we will review the process for evaluating data models in context of business plans later in this section.

Examine other perspectives, such as those provided by process models or state transition models. If data flow diagrams exist for the area under study, for example, the project team should provide the reviewer with a copy of any current DFDs. The reviewer's job will be to verify that the data model is balanced against the DFDs according to the standards established by the information resource organization, or the methodology used (e.g., every store on the DFD must map to an object type on the data model). Again, use CASE tool facilities to aid in this examination whenever possible, but be sure that you understand the rules used by your CASE tool to do the cross-checking, and that you examine the results carefully to ensure that your standards have been met.

The reviewer should not be limited to posing questions only on the data model. Review of a data model, when coupled with an understanding of the business plans and other models, may spark questions about the latter two products. The QA reviewer should include such questions in the data model review. This is consistent with the view that data modeling serves as an excellent business planning tool, and can provide substantive insight into other aspects of the enterprise architecture as well.

If the review is for a current systems analysis, then the project packet should include system documentation in addition to other models or business statements. The reviewer should start with these, becoming familiar with the scope and content. The process for this type of review will be similar to the forward-engineered model review, but will involve cross-checking to current system documentation during the course of the review.

Reviewing Notes from Interviews and Joint Sessions

Joint session notes are the recorded proceedings of the modeling team's discussions, investigations, and decisions. They are especially important for models being developed through facilitated sessions with users or subject matter experts. Just like a court transcript (although not as detailed) they form a record of the arguments, deliberations, and findings of the team as they work through the many issues and questions arising during the development of a model.

Recording session notes properly requires the use of a designated scribe, an individual who is charged with recording the proceedings of the modeling sessions. The session notes should include:

- **Details of the session or interview, including date, time, location, attendance.**
- **Model sketches and annotated diagrams.** During a modeling session, the facilitator usually draws model diagrams, lists attributes, or sketches value tables on a whiteboard, easel pad, or

some other display device. Any sketches or diagrams created by the team during the session should be included in the session notes.

- **CASE tool reports or diagrams used by the team during discussions.** If the contents of the report are changed or updated by the team, the scribe should include an annotated copy reflecting the agreed upon changes in the session notes.
- **Decisions made by the team.** Many times the facilitator of a modeling team must force the group to come to a consensus on a particularly difficult issue. When such situations are encountered, the alternatives and the team's final decision should be recorded and entered into the session notes for future reference.
- **Key discussion points or statements.** Any important ideas, explanations, or discussions, including identification of new business rules or policy statements, should be captured by the scribe and entered into the session notes. The decision as to what is "important" may be made by the facilitator or the group, and the proceedings of the session should be halted until important concepts are fully recorded by the scribe. Facilitator or group style is a major consideration in how this will be accomplished, but all participants should be aware of the importance of having complete session notes.
- **Completed CASE tool data entry forms (if used), and generated reports from the CASE tool following entry of the session information.** One of the principal failings of many modeling teams is getting the requirements captured in the modeling session completely and accurately recorded in the CASE tool. If the CASE tool is used interactively during the modeling session, then this is less of a concern, although reports showing the session results should still be generated and reviewed. In most cases, the model diagrams and notes are taken away from the session and input later. If so, the scribe's job is to ensure that the CASE tool models completely and accurately represent the results of the modeling session. It is good practice to begin each session with a review of the previous session's results using output from your CASE tool, both as a way to get everyone "warmed up" and as a means of confirming that the "official" model reflects the group's intentions.

If your CASE tool has a feature for recording session notes in the encyclopedia, we suggest you use it. Some tools also allow you to create a session as a separate encyclopedia object, stamp model objects with the session where they were created or modified, then generate a report of the objects created or modified during the session. This gives you a tremendous amount of control over the integrity of your model.

- **Indication of approval by the session leader.** The compiled session notes should be reviewed and approved by the facilitator, leader, or other representative of the group. This provides an immediate check on the completeness of the notes.

The session notes are not simply another piece of documentation to be stacked on a shelf next to unused data flow diagrams. When properly used, they increase model quality by

- **Providing a written record of decisions made by the team.** These can be reviewed when similar issues come up, or when the team needs to refresh its memory about some portion of the model created sometime in the past.
- **Providing a basis for ensuring that decisions made by the team are actually incorporated into the model.** The model can be compared to the joint session notes to determine if all points brought forth in the discussions actually made it into the model. In one review that we performed a couple of years ago for a securities trading association, we found a wealth of requirements carefully documented in interview notes, yet none of the business concepts recorded in those notes made its way into the data model. Little wonder that users say over and over again to analysts, "I already told you guys about this! Why isn't in the model [or system]?"

The quality reviewer assumes two responsibilities with regard to the joint session notes:

- **Quality of the session notes.** The reviewer must determine that the notes and records are orderly, appear to be complete, are clearly marked with date/attendance, and have some sign of approval by the facilitator. The quality of the session notes is generally an indicator of the scribe's experience, training, and capability, and the control with which the session leader runs the modeling team. The reviewer's objective is to gain a sense of how well the notes—in many cases comprising the only record of the requirements elicitation process in which hundreds or perhaps thousands of hours of work have been invested—reflect the actual requirements discussed by the participants.

  If time permits, the QA reviewer may want to attend a modeling session, then evaluate the quality of the session notes in comparison to what actually occurred during the session.
- **Coupling of requirements elicitation and modeling processes.**

As part of the systemic evaluation portion of the review, the reviewer must determine how well the modeling and requirements elicitation processes are coupled. The reviewer must verify that the content of the session notes is reflected in the data models. This is the most important aspect of the verification process. The reviewer's objective is to make sure that there is no loss of vital information between the session notes and the models. If the modeling effort is done interactively, with direct participation of subject matter experts who have some training in data modeling, then the potential for problems from loss of information is dramatically reduced. Unfortunately, many modelers are faced with a cycle of first interviewing, then modeling without direct user input, and finally going back to users to validate models. This kind of decoupled modeling leads to greater potential for slippage between the elicited requirements and the model. We have conducted quality reviews of models that cover several months of effort, only to find that requirements gathered and documented in interviews with subject matter experts never made their way into the model. The modeling team must have a rigorous process for transferring interview or session notes into the models.

Reviewing the Model Management Process

Building high-quality models is considerably easier in a single-project environment than it is in a large-enterprise environment, where several modeling efforts may be going on at the same time. In the latter case, integration, standardization, and cross-fertilization become important aspects of the modeling cycle. For models built in an enterprise context, good model quality is tightly coupled with a model management program that supports the project-level model cycle, yet meets the larger objectives of corporate data management.

The reviewer should evaluate the execution of model management on the project. Model management considerations that the QA reviewer should evaluate include:

- **Use of standard model objects.** These may be drawn from a pool of approved entities or attributes that have undergone an approval process managed by the data administration group, or they may simply be drawn from other models under development. Your data standardization policies will drive the way model objects are created, modified, and approved.
- **Integration cycles.** Building a data model in an organization where a managed enterprise model exists generally requires peri-

odic integration analysis, to assess how well the emerging model fits with the enterprise model. If certain model objects have been "frozen" by the enterprise model team, then the integration cycles are typically the time to address potential changes.

Creation of a model in isolation from other models within the enterprise generally lowers the overall value of that model, and will most likely lead to interoperability or data-sharing problems once the models have been implemented as systems. Development of integrated models as precursors for an integrated systems environment depends on the creation of a model management infrastructure, usually as part of a broader data administration charter. The reviewer should evaluate the project team's efforts to work within whatever current framework exists in order to maximize cross-functional perspectives, to reuse applicable artifacts, and to support system integration. The reviewer should note problems arising from a *lack* of model management infrastructure, and raise these as systemic problems affecting data model quality.

Considering the Skill Level of the Modeling Team

Consider the experience of the modeling team relative to the task at hand. Again, the focus is on doing things right initially, without introducing rework or missed opportunities. Placing an individual (or a team, for that matter) without proper skills or experience in a position requiring the building of complex models introduces risk for the success of the project as well as undue stress for the individual or the team. The quality reviewer should be aware of the modeling team's background, and should apprise the project manager or other appropriate decision maker as early as possible if there are signs that the modeling team's skill set does not match project needs. The modeling team may require additional training or increased support from the reviewer (i.e., more frequent reviews, occasional attendance at modeling sessions to evaluate and provide feedback, or other such activities).

2.9   ASSESSING THE MODEL

After completing the preliminaries, the reviewer turns to the model itself. We now outline a series of activities that should be undertaken to accomplish the actual assessment of the model.

Selecting Subject Areas

If you are serving as an expert reviewer, it is extremely important that you review the model in an orderly progression. Random selection of a starting point leads to difficulties in making correct assessments, and it could lead you back through the same parts of the model over and over again as you try to trace primary key migrations, identify circular references, and the like. To avoid this, break the model down into logically cohesive subsets prior to starting the review. With input from the modeling team, prioritize the subsets. This will help in planning and managing the review by creating a series of relatively independent "mini-reviews" that can be completed in a reasonable time, each dealing with one subject area.

Data dependency analysis (DDA) is one approach for identifying model subsets based on the degree and nature of relationships between entities (McClure, 1993). We will describe one approach to performing data dependency analysis momentarily. DDA is the creation of Clive Finkelstein, who first defined the concept of a data cluster based solely on the relationships between entities. It has been automated in only one CASE tool that we are aware of, **IE: Advantage**™, a product of Information Engineering Systems Corporation. DDA is an extremely effective technique for model management, and has been described in detail in several works (McClure, 1993; Finkelstein, 1989, 1992). Our purpose in describing it here is because few modelers have access to a CASE tool that performs DDA. Therefore, in order to apply the concept when performing a quality review, DDA may have to be done by hand, although with a little practice this can be done relatively quickly.

Ideally, a data dependency analysis is performed on a model meeting the following specifications:

1. All many-to-many relationships have been resolved. Many-to-many relationships are resolved using associative entities.
2. The model is in 4th or 5th normal form.
3. Optional attributes have been moved to subtype entities.

However, quality reviews occur on models under development, and many of these models do not meet the criteria in our list. DDA can be performed on any model, although the rules for doing so become somewhat more complex. Our recommendation is that you at least resolve any many-to-many relationships (into associative entities). Data dependency analysis does not work well for models having a large number of nonspecific (many-to-many) or one-to-one (except supertype-subtype) relationships.

If you have a CASE tool that performs data dependency analysis as described herein, by all means use it. Remember, however, that data dependency analysis is not the same as identifying "neighborhoods" (either complete or immediate) or "path," both of which are available in tools, such as KnowledgeWare's ADW™. Data dependency analysis is more involved, and leads to highly cohesive, tightly structured subsets.

Identifying Data Clusters

A data cluster results from a data dependency analysis. It is a highly cohesive, tightly structured group of entities forming a closed network of relationships. Subsetting the model into data clusters results in the formation of logical groupings of anywhere from 3 to 12 entities (on average), although some clusters are larger. A cluster with less than three entities should be investigated for anomalies in relationship cardinality.

You will gain a better understanding of the nature of a data cluster by working through the dependency analysis steps outlined below.

Step 1 Identify all associative, structure, attributive, and subtype entities that have no children. A "child" entity is one that inherits a key (either as a migrated primary key or as a nonprimary foreign key) from another entity (its parent). Child entities with no children of their own are referred to as endpoints, since they are the last children in a potentially long chain of parental relationships (McClure, 1993). They represent the "end of the family lineage" (see Figure 2.5), and are the means by which separate data clusters are identified.

Step 2 For each endpoint, trace the "family tree" back up through all generations of parental relationships. Determine all entities in the family lineage. Stop only when reaching the entities in the family line that are parents only (i.e., do not inherit any keys from another entity). These are typically referred to as *independent entities*, since they do not inherit keys. Entities that inherit keys, on the other hand, are known as *dependent entities*. Figure 2.6 portrays the tracing of the family tree.

Step 3 Identify any relationships that are mandatory (only!) one-to-many in which a family member is the parent, and include the child entity in the family. The existence of a mandatory relationship indicates a very strong tie to the parent (an instance of the parent cannot exist without at least one instance of the child entity). For each child entity identified in this step, determine all of its parent entities in the same fashion as described in Step 2. Figure 2.6 shows a mandatory one-to-many relationship, and the entities that are pulled into the cluster as a result. Note: A cluster may contain other clusters due to mandatory-many associations.

Figure 2.6 portrays an outline of a data cluster formed through this

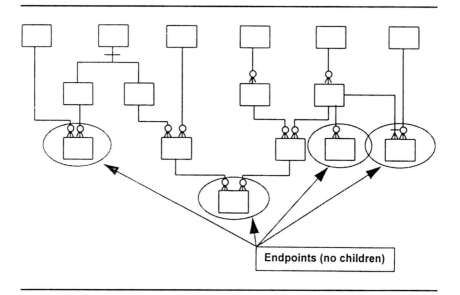

Figure 2.5 Identify endpoints.

method, which can actually be done very quickly and pays dividends when the review begins. There are a total of four clusters in Figure 2.6. We have traced only one. Tracing the other three is left as an exercise for the reader.

Step 4 Identify all derived attributes within the logical data cluster (created in Steps 1 through 3). Trace derivation dependencies to the other (base) attributes in the model (potentially outside of the logical data cluster) involved in the derivation. A derivation dependency extends from a derived attribute to the base attributes used in its derivation (McClure, 1993). Include the base attribute's entity in the data cluster of the derived attribute.

Step 5 Give a name or number to the data cluster that you have formed for ease of reference. The name should represents its business meaning.

Step 7 Select clusters that are closely coupled within the business domain, and organize them into separate groups. For example, if you are modeling a network management system, you may wish to group all of the data clusters dealing with equipment together, and all of the clus-

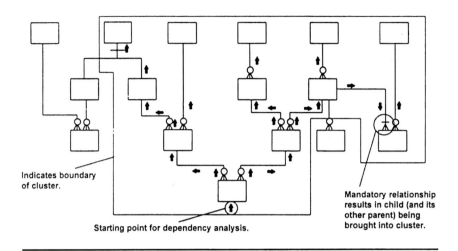

Indicates boundary
of cluster.

Mandatory relationship
results in child (and its
other parent) being
brought into cluster.

Starting point for dependency analysis.

Figure 2.6   Sample model subset.

ters having to do with alarms and event response in another. There will
be overlap among the groups, since entities (except endpoints) typically
belong to more than one data cluster.

Step 8 Determine if there is a preferable progression for working through
the groups of data clusters identified in Step 7. For example, if the model
contains a subject area covering training schedules, then that subject
area is most likely dependent on subject areas covering people (individuals) and training courses. You should work through groups that are relatively independent first, then tackle highly dependent areas.

You can now evaluate a set of model components that have some
natural affinity. And the evaluation can be done on a logically complete
subset of the model that is of reasonable size. As we said before, you will
get a clearer picture of both the model constructs and the business issues
if you subset large, complex models prior to starting your review. You can
use a data cluster to look for questionable patterns as you go through the
model. Evaluating syntax and business concepts will require you to look
at several model components at once, and to be able to identify patterns
that are indicative of potential quality problems. For example, spotting a
circular reference involves at least three entities linked in a parent-child
chain with no endpoint (each child is also a parent).

If the model is relatively small (i.e., less than fifty entities), then the selection of subject areas can be bypassed. However, be aware that even for relatively small models, use of cluster-driven analysis holds benefits.

Beginning the Model Evaluation

The model evaluation activity begins when the analyst sits down with the model and supporting documents to begin the object-by-object review of the model. While individual style, completion state of the model, and the report format may result in variations in the way this step is completed, we offer some suggestions to speed the process and ensure that reviews occur in a methodical, uniform way.

Conducting a Review of Syntax Use If you have access to model analysis reports from your CASE tool, begin your review by looking these over. Obviously, you will want to avoid duplicating efforts that are best left to automated means. Make sure you understand the criteria used by your model analysis tool to assess model objects. Some tools are more robust than others, and you may have to set aside time to conduct a thorough syntax check if your tool does not provide much support. We suggest you use the rules that we have established in Section II of this book as a basis for conducting a syntax review.

Step 1 Independent Entities Begin by reviewing independent entities. As we stated before, an independent entity is one that does not inherit any foreign keys. Therefore, we are starting the actual review of the model at the opposite end of the family tree from cluster endpoints. By starting with independent entities, you can more easily track (and evaluate) the migration of keys through the model. Also, reviewing independent entities first allows you to follow a general-to-specific path through the model, since dependent children inherit characteristics of the parent entity(ies). This aids in understanding the model syntax use, as well as grasping the business concepts implied in the model constructs. As you review the model components, refer to Section II of this book for specific rules, or to evaluation standards that have been established within your organization. We suggest that you go through the following activities one cluster at a time.

> **Activity 1a.** Review each entity and its characteristics (e.g., check the definition, examine the key structure, etc.). Entity rules are documented in Chapter 3.

> **Activity 1b.** Review each attribute that originates in the entity, including both primary keys and non-key attributes. Examine its

characteristics, and evaluate functional dependence to ensure that the entity is in the desired normal form. See Chapter 4 for attribute rules, and Chapter 8 for a discussion of normalization.

Activity 1c. Review each relationship to/from the entity. Relationship rules are presented in Chapter 5.

Step 2 Dependent Entities After reviewing the independent entities, shift your focus to dependent entities. Dependent entities are those with foreign keys (serving as either primary keys or nonprimary foreign keys). Subtype, associative, and attributive entity types are dependent entities. Trace the relationships down from independent entities, then follow parent-child relationship paths through successive dependent entities until you reach the endpoint. You will be following multiple dependency paths, each originating with an independent entity and merging with other dependency paths, as you proceed with this step. This progression allows you to continue tracking key migration and to follow the natural flow of dependencies that exist in the model. Figure 2.7 depicts the flow of the review from independent entities, through dependent entities, to the endpoints.

For each dependent entity, follow Activities 1a through 1c described above. Additionally, perform the following activities:

Activity 2a. Review each attribute that was migrated into the entity, including primary and nonprimary foreign keys. Examine its characteristics in context of the entity it has migrated into, using the rules outlined in Chapter 4.

Activity 2b. Review groups of model components that are closely linked, such as supertype-subtype hierarchies, or associative entities and their parent entities.

Backward Pass The sequence we have just described is known as a forward pass through the model. Now it is time to perform a "backward pass." The backward pass retraces the same paths in the opposite direction, beginning with the endpoints and moving upstream to the independent entities. This pass follows essentially the same path as that depicted in Figure 2.6. The backward pass typically progresses relatively quickly, since most of the issues related to the syntax and business concepts have been already captured. The objective of the backward pass is to ensure that nothing has been overlooked due to a single perspective review.

To prevent reviewing the same objects more than once, mark each

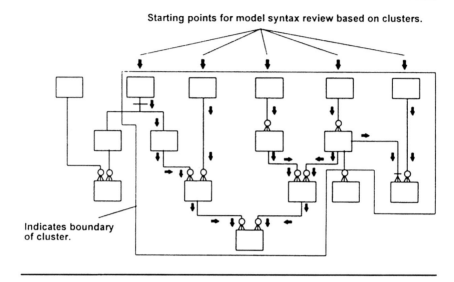

Figure 2.7 Progression of model review from independent entities to endpoints.

entity and attribute as it is reviewed on each pass. Be sure to record issues and make annotations as necessary as you move through the model.

One word of caution before moving on to discuss the business context review. We are not suggesting that you review only one entity at a time. As you move through the model, you will need to look at groups of entities in order to assess syntax compliance and to ensure that business concepts are properly reflected. For example, identifying a circular reference involves at least three entities, as does finding a triad. Quite often, finding subtle problems in the model requires that you step back to absorb the big picture. Again, the progression of the model evaluation as we are describing here is solely to help you work through the model in an organized fashion.

Conducting a Review of Business Concepts A review of business concepts is significantly more difficult to perform than checking syntax and modeling standards compliance. It centers on the modeling team's success in transforming business plans, policies, and rules into data requirements and relationships. The business concept review is used to evaluate the precision with which the model captures business requirements, and to determine if all requirements within the model's scope have been addressed. You should spend the majority of your time on this portion of a quality review. Unlike syntax checks, it is practically impossible to automate the review of business concepts. The former can be handled to a large extent by model analysis features in CASE tools. The latter relies on human faculties of interpretation, comparison, translation, and judgment.

There are some things to keep in mind about a business concept review:

• **The reviewer must have access to the business plans, policies, procedures, functional models, session notes, and other sources that document the business requirements for the model.** If the model has been developed from existing data structures and applications, then these should be collected and used as input to the review. It is important to recognize that a review *cannot* be performed in the absence of these resources. There is simply no way to understand whether the model is correct and complete without them. If they are not available, then you should raise serious questions about the modeling process, and about the utility of the model. In an ideal situation, all requirements in the form of business statements or source data structures will be documented in the CASE tool, and mapped to the data model components supporting them.

• **This part of a quality assurance review takes time and effort.** It cannot be done adequately in someone's spare time, during lunch, or sandwiched between other activities. It requires time to research the business area, to gain an overview of the model, and to work through the business rules and model components in detail, possibly more than once.

• **The goal is not to make judgments, or to identify only things that are unmistakably wrong.** The goal of the business concepts review is to raise questions about the model. Do not assume that the modeling team has looked at all of the alternatives that you might find. If a question pops up as a result of the review, jot it down. It can always be eliminated with just a few moments discussion if it is something the team has already considered.

A typical conceptual review follows the pattern described in Figure 2.8. Individuals are encouraged to develop a style with which they are comfortable. However, the review must cover at least the areas described in this section.

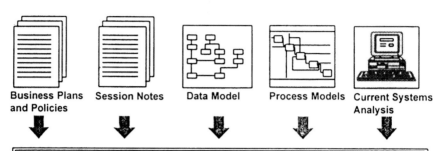

Business Plans   Session Notes   Data Model   Process Models   Current Systems
and Policies   Analysis

Conduct Contextual Review

For forward engineering projects:

Review data model in concert with business plans.

Verify that all statements are reflected

Determine if model accurately reflects business context

Examine data model in context of process or functional models, if available

For reverse engineering projects:

Review data model in concert with systems documentation

Verify that all data structure components are included in data model

Review session notes to determine if key issues and decisions are properly reflected

QA Findings and
Recommendations

Figure 2.8   The conceptual review follows a structured approach.

Conceptual Review Procedures The steps for conducting conceptual reviews, described below, are nonsequential. The conceptual review should proceed using the same model subsets used in assessing the syntax of the model.

Step 1 Verify that the data model supports each and every business statement or stated requirement from other sources (e.g., implied or explicit requirements documented in session notes, or in process models).

Example

The following example (Figure 2.9) illustrates how a reviewer should evaluate plans and models to verify that the latter fully supports the former. At first glance, the model appears to support the Eastern Shore Security Agency's desire to track average response times (note alarm class average response time attribute in ALARM CLASS OPERATING PERIOD). However, the quality reviewer traced the derivation dependency back to individual alarm responses, only to find that the model contained no attribute recording the actual time of response to an alarm following its receipt. The business plan focuses attention on key areas of the model, allowing the reviewer to assess whether it can actually and fully support the plan. In this case, the model will not support performance measurement as originally modeled.

Step 2 Determine if the model accurately reflects the context of the business plans and rules. This is one of the most critical aspects of the QA review. A model that adheres to naming conventions and other superficial constraints is useless unless it also thoroughly captures the rules of the business. The QA reviewer can instigate analysis of these rules from his or her independent perspective.

The project team will need to assess reviewers' findings, and determine the best strategy for resolving them with the work group participants.

Relationships are generally a good place to start when looking for inconsistencies between plans and models. You should consider posing the following questions about each relationship.

- **Does the relationship capture a stated strategy or policy correctly?** Relationships tend to depict the enterprise's strategies or policies. You should document an issue if it is apparent that the model does not contain relationships supporting enterprise plans and policies.

Eastern Shore Security Agency

Planning Statement and Data Model Under Review

Objective Statement: Improve response time for Class I and Class II alarms by 5% per year for the next two years.

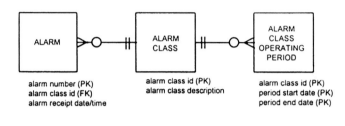

Contextual QA Finding

The data model does not contain attributes that allow the company to calculate average response times.

Modeling Team's Response to QA Finding

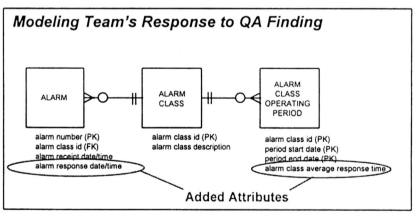

Added Attributes

Figure 2.9   Discovering opportunities for refining a model based on plans.

Planning Statement and Data Model Under Review

Hiring Strategy: We will hire only individuals who have completed a bachelor's degree.

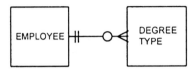

Quality Review Finding

The strategy implies the following rules that are not currently reflected in the model:

1. The firm is interested not only in individuals who are currently employees, but also those that are potential employees ("we will hire...").

2. An employee must have at least one degree. Currently, the relationship between employee and degree type is optional.

Figure 2.10   Example of conceptual analysis and findings.

- **Does the business rule represented by the relationship make sense?** The analyst should look at models that may be structurally correct, but do not properly record the business rules. In particular, look for:

  Reversed relationships. A model may appear to be correct, but actually masks reversed logic.

  Incorrect cardinality or optionality. This situation frequently involves relationships that have been designated mandatory, but should actually be optional. You should carefully

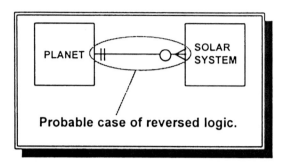

Figure 2.11   Reversing relationships is a common problem.

consider whether two entities must exist together in every possible scenario, and you should rely heavily on business statements to determine correct cardinality. You might also try using known values to test the cardinality.

Does the business rule supported by the relationship make sense when assessed in context of other relationships involving each of the two entities connected by the relationship? By examining these other relationships, the reviewer may find parallel relationships that should be combined, triads, or other improper structures that confuse the logic of the model. See the rules in Section II for specifics regarding these kinds of situations.

Step 3 Review session notes to determine if key issues and decisions have been correctly and completely represented in the model. This step is similar to the review of planning statements, but with the emphasis shifted to discussion points or decisions covered during facilitated sessions or meetings. Quite often these will be added to the business plans as policies, strategies, or goals. However, a review of session notes may turn up clarifications or important assumptions that influence the model. If so, you may also need to note a requirement for the modeling team to extend the plans to include approved decisions of the work group.

Step 4 Examine process models and process-to-data mappings (e.g., matrices). These provide information about how the data will be used, and may unmask additional requirements. Examine definitions of data flows and data stores, as well as process specifications to determine if the data model can fully support them.

Figure 2.12   Compare cardinality/optionality to business rules.

Step 5 Ask a final question: "Does the model make sense to me?" Even if you do not have an extensive background in the subject area, you can apply common sense and good analytical skills to gain a surprising amount of insight into whether the model has captured the essence of the business rules. The purpose of a QA review is to raise questions, not judge the model. You should raise legitimate questions based on your experience or subject knowledge. Quite often, a question posed by a reviewer with little or no subject matter knowledge leads to important discussion when brought forward to the work group participants.

Maintain Continuous Communication during the Review If you are serving as the quality reviewer, it is incumbent upon you to maintain direct, open communication with the modeling team throughout the period of the review. You may need to hold discussions with the team to ensure that you have interpreted certain aspects of the model correctly, or to communicate important findings as early as possible.

Documenting QA Review Findings

Recording Issues Record all issues or questions that have been raised during the review. The case study presented in Appendix C should give you some insight into the manner in which issues are recorded. Be sure to reference any and all model objects involved in your findings, and provide a brief but complete description of the issue.

Recording QA Findings in a CASE Tool Encyclopedia A limited number of CASE tools allow the user to create statements that can be directly and actively linked to entities, attributes, and relationships in a data model. This provides a very effective means for relating planning statements (e.g., policies, objectives, goals) to the model objects that support them. It also can be a very effective means for recording QA findings and their resolution, which provides a readily accessible model development history for use by the modeling team. If agreed upon by both the modeling team and the reviewer, the data model may be transferred in electronic form for review, and the reviewer may then record his or her comments as linked statements directly in the encyclopedia. If you have access to a CASE product with the flexibility to accommodate this kind of documentation, we suggest you take advantage of it.

Maintain a History of QA Reviews Each subsequent review of a model covers many of the objects that were evaluated and refined in prior reviews. Retain a record of findings and resolution strategies for each QA, and refer to it to avoid having to make decisions about the model that have already been put to rest.

Conduct a Close-Out Meeting The reviewer should present the findings (questions and issues) to the full modeling team in a close-out meeting. The meeting provides the modeling team a chance to understand the magnitude of the findings, to pose questions to the reviewer, and to obtain assistance in determining resolution strategies. The reviewer benefits from a chance to summarize the review, to communicate directly and if appropriate, forcefully, on the findings, and to participate in establishing necessary follow-on actions. The close-out meeting helps prevent a defensive response on the part of a modeling team that finds itself with a model with more open issues than they thought possible.

Expert Assistance with QA Issues Resolution The reviewer should not be released from obligation to the modeling team upon completing the documentation of the model review and conducting the close-out meeting. The reviewer, as an active member of the project team, is responsible for aiding the other team members during the resolution of QA findings. This may occur sporadically over the days or weeks following completion of the review, depending on the modeling schedule. The team, or the reviewer, may suggest that assistance from additional subject matter experts be obtained to deal with especially difficult issues.

Regardless of the manner in which it is accomplished, the most important thing is to address and resolve every QA finding, and to record and implement a solution that is agreeable to the modeling team and meets the expectations established for model quality.

REFERENCES

Finkelstein, Clive. *An Introduction to Information Engineering: From Strategic Planning to Information Systems.* Sydney: Addison-Wesley, 1989.

Finkelstein, Clive. *Information Engineering: Strategic Systems Development.* Sydney: Addison-Wesley, 1992.

McClure, Stephen F. "Information Engineering for Client/Server Architectures," *Data Base Newsletter* 21, No. 4 (July/August 1993).

Texas Instruments. *IEF™: A Totally Integrated CASE Environment.* Plano, TX: Texas Instruments, Incorporated, 1990.

Vaskevitch, David. *Client/Server Strategies: A Survival Guide for Corporate Reengineers.* San Mateo, CA: IDG Books, 1993.

Yourdon, E. *Modern Structured Analysis.* Englewood Cliffs, NJ: Yourdon Press, 1989.

Data Modeling Rules

Before you begin to read through the rules (once you start, we're sure you won't be able to stop!), we offer these thoughts:

- **We did not get them all.** There is simply no way to cover *all* of the rules that apply in all of the modeling techniques in use today. We did not try. Instead, we focused our attention on the ones we feel are most important for building a solid foundation for a data model quality program, and the ones we believe are crucial to making data modeling an effective tool for business analysis and information system development. Although we have chosen to depict these using standard information engineering notation, the concepts should translate across most, if not all, relational data modeling techniques popular today.

- **We don't expect you to agree with all of them.** You have probably heard the joke "What is the surest way to bring a data modeling project to a halt? Bring in more than one data modeler." We have encountered this comment in one form or another several times. Data modelers seem to love to argue about technique. We hope that by reviewing the rules in this section you will learn something new (we do all the time), will come to terms with the modeling rules that you do agree on, and will establish a data model quality assurance program using those rules as a foundation.

- **No rule is an island.** You can't make a change to a data model without expecting some sort of ripple effect of other changes. If you change a relationship, then you'll need to look at the key structure of your entities to ensure that they still support the relationship properly. So it is with data modeling rules—a rule about relationships may involve discussion of primary keys, entity definitions, and normalization. The components of a data model are tightly connected. Our "data model for data modeling" (the meta-model) is like any other model, where a change here or an addition there causes a ripple effect. As you read the rules, you will occasionally need to drift over to another rule to read about a related topic.

• **Rules don't build good data models.** Educated, motivated analysts and business experts build good models (and good systems and good business practices). Relying on any kind of standard or criteria without providing necessary training, development, and support will not lead to quality results. Train your data modelers; give them the tools they need to work quickly and productively. Don't set expectations without first giving them the means to meet those expectations.

• **This is the starting point, not the finish.** Our objective is to give you a starting point for building your own data modeling guidelines. Looking around at some pretty large organizations, public and private alike, we are startled by the number lacking even the most rudimentary guidance for systems analysts. Sure, the systems development life cycle standard (or whatever its equivalent is called) might say "Analyze data requirements" or "Develop a logical data model," but few if any follow those statements with specifics of how that is to be done. We hope the level of detail available in these rules gives you and your data administration group a starting point for building a set of guidelines and a training program that improves the quality of data models and increases their utility in your enterprise.

Entity Rules

3.1 ENTITY COMPLETENESS CHECKLIST

The Entity Completeness Checklist presents the set of characteristics that a data modeling team should gather and record to ensure that a complete set of requirements is represented in the data model. Our checklist directly supports the completeness aspect of data model quality.

The list presented here has been made without regard to the limitations or capabilities of any single CASE tool. Rather, it represents those things that we find are data requirements, and are necessary to begin database design. If your CASE tool does not allow you to record some of these requirements, we suggest you contact the vendor and provide some input about your needs (perhaps *their* data model could use some work!).

☑ **Name**

This is the name or "handle" of the entity that meets naming conventions or standards, and that accurately describes the aggregated set of data attributes contained therein. We will describe some of the characteristics an entity name should have later in this chapter.

☑ **Description**

The description, also referred to as the definition or purpose, communicates as precisely as possible *what* the entity represents, and the role it plays in the enterprise. The entity description is vital to sharing and reuse of data model components, and to validation of requirements.

☑ Category

The entity category is methodology-dependent information that classifies entities sharing common characteristics. In particular, individual entity categories can be used to designate rules of behavior and expectations of completeness for metadata, providing a basis for automated quality checks in many CASE tools. For example, subtype entities must have the same primary key as their parent supertype entity. Most CASE tools either prevent the user from adding a primary key attribute to the subtype that does not exist in the supertype, or advises the user that such a condition exists in the model. Commonly used entity categories are listed below.

- *Fundamental entities*, used to represent core or basic concepts that do not fall into one of the other categories.
- *Associative entities*, employed to associate two or more entities in order to reconcile a many-to-many relationship. They are also known as *intersecting entities*. A special type of associative entity, known as a *structure entity*, exists in some methodologies, and is used to associate two occurrences of the same entity (i.e., resolution of recursive relationship) (Finkelstein, 1989).
- *Attributive entities*, used to describe or categorize other entities.
- *Subtype entities*, which represent a subset of occurrences of their parent entity but which have attribute(s) or relationships that apply only to the subset.

☑ Abbreviation(s)

If any abbreviations are used in the entity name (often required due to limitations of CASE tool in use) or in the entity description, then it is important to document the abbreviation and a full definition of it as part of the overall description of the entity. Use of abbreviations should be consistent with any conventions established within the data management community of your organization.

☑ Acronym(s)

We do not recommend using acronyms as a substitute for a full entity name, although their use may be a practical response to limitations on entity name length imposed by most CASE tools. Acronyms suffer from a couple of common problems—they may not be known or understood by parties outside the business domain being modeled, or even by all parties within the domain; and acronyms are often not unique. As with abbreviations, if you use acronyms be sure to document them as part of the entity description.

☑ Current Number of Occurrences

In order to aid database designers and administrators during subsequent phases of information system development, it is important to gather or estimate certain entity statistics, the number of instances of an entity being one. Remember that this must be done for associative entities (e.g., how many potential combinations of two entities do we expect to have), subtypes, and attributive entities, as well as fundamental entities.

☑ Expected Change in Number of Occurrences

In preparation for design and implementation, it is necessary to record the anticipated growth or shrinkage in the current number of occurrences, usually expressed as a percent annual change quantity.

☑ Traceability of Requirements

This is information pertaining to the cause or purpose of the enterprise's interest in the entity. The requirement may have one of several sources, depending on the nature of the data modeling activity (e.g., reverse engineering, strategic information systems planning, etc.). Traceability may be attained through (1) reference to the source of the need (e.g., citation of a statement, clause, paragraph, or section of a regulation, policy or plan; or reference to a physical data structure element, program variable, or human interface component in the case of current systems analysis sources); and, (2) mapping to another metadata object created and managed as part of the system lifecycle, such as a planning statement (e.g., critical success factor, goal, objective) or a physical system or system design element (e.g., file, data element, table, program element). In other words, you need to document where the entity came from, and where it will be used.

☑ Authority

Entity authority is generally defined in two ways. First, metadata authority is established. The individual(s) or organization(s) with metadata authority has responsibility for defining or changing characteristics of the entities, attributes, relationships, model views, or other model components. For example, changing the definition of an entity would require approval by the designated metadata authority. Establishing authority at the metadata level is a vital step in establishing a data management (or data administration) program. A second level of authority may also be identified—data authority. As the term suggests, these are the individuals in the business community that have been given responsibility and authority to create or delete instances of the entity (actually, to create or delete primary keys and attributes whose existence is mandatory upon creation of an instance of the primary key). Establishing authority at the data level is a vital step toward implementation of a data quality program. Every entity should be assigned a steward. The entity steward should be the organization (office) responsible for managing the metadata of the entity.

☑ Primary Key Attribute Name(s)

These are the identifiers (determinants) that have been selected from among the entity's candidate key(s). The candidate key (comprised of one or more attributes) that has been selected to serve as primary key should be designated for each entity. The primary key may be partially or wholly (in the case of a subtype entity or a structure entity) inherited from another entity, or it may originate in the subject entity.

☑ Nonprimary Foreign Key Name(s)

The attributes in the entity whose values are required to match those of the primary key of some other entity in support of a relationship to the other entity are designated as foreign keys. Many entities in the model will have no foreign keys, due to the nature of the relationships they are involved in.

☑ Non-Key Attribute Name(s)

These are the attribute(s) that have been placed in the entity in accordance with the rules of normalization, and whose values are determined by the value of the primary key. These attributes describe a quantitative or qualitative feature or property of the entity but do not serve as the primary key of this or any other entity. A non-key attribute appears in only one entity in the model. It is possible that certain entities will contain no non-key attributes.

☑ **Relationships to Other Entities**

Record the relationships between the subject entity and any other entity in the model. Remember, no entity is an island unto itself—it must have a relationship to at least one other entity in the model. We will discuss this rule in greater detail later in this section.

Obviously you will not have all of the information pertaining to an entity at the moment you identify it. At the very least, you should provide a clear name and description, and you will most likely define one or more attributes, including keys, when you first determine the need for an entity. Our first rule discusses the entity identification process. Other characteristics of the entity will be added as analysis progresses, and as the model stabilizes.

3.2   ENTITY IDENTIFICATION

Each and every entity included in the data model should exhibit the following properties:

- *Lies within the scope of the model*
- *Represents something about which the enterprise wishes to keep information*
- *Represents a single concept, determined by cohesive nature of its attributes*
- *Represents not a single actual thing (instance), but rather a set of like or similar things*
- *Provides an ability to distinguish between occurrences of the entity*
- *Satisfies the rules of normalization*

Discussion

Let's begin our discussion with some of the ways the concept of entity has been defined. We gathered these from some of the most influential writers and thinkers on data modeling:

Definitions of Entity

Thomas Bruce: "Any distinguishable person, place, thing, event, or concept about which information is kept" (1992).

Peter Chen: "A thing which can be distinctly identified" (1976).

C.J. Date: "Any distinguishable object that is to be represented in the database" (1986).

Clive Finkelstein: "A data entity represents some 'thing' that is to be stored for later reference. The term **entity** refers to the *logical* representation of data" (1989).

James Martin: "The word *entity* means anything about which we store information (e.g., a customer, supplier, machine tool, employee, utility pole, airline seat, etc.). For each entity type, certain attributes are stored" (1989).

Themes These definitions contain some common themes that most every data modeler knows by heart.

• An entity is a "thing" or "concept" or "object." Well, most of the time. An entity may also represent the relationship between two or more objects. We call these associative entities. Or it may represent the fact that we need to capture information specific to only a subset of the instances of an entity. We call these subtype (or secondary or category) entities. Both of these types of entities represent refinements to the definition of entity that allow us to build better representations of reality.

• An entity is not a single "thing," but rather a representation of like or similar things that share characteristics or properties. For example, *King Lear* and *Hamlet* are both plays, and have properties such as name, author, cast of characters, and lines of verse. The entity describing these might be PLAY, with *King Lear* and *Hamlet* as examples of instances or occurrences of PLAY. Identification of *Hamlet* as an entity limits the ability to group similar things, and precludes design of efficient information systems.

• Entities involve information. The "things" that entities represent are things about which the enterprise wants or needs to retain information. Therefore, while a data model should be an accurate representation of the business and its rules, we should never forget that data modeling is generally a precursor to design and development of structures intended to collect, store and dispense data.

With these themes in mind, let's refine our view of entities. *Entities are collections of attributes that satisfy a particular set of rules established for relational modeling.* These rules, of course, are known as normal forms (we will discuss normal forms and their role in building quality models in Chapter 8). Normal forms are based on certain types of dependencies among *attributes*. The creation and stabilization of entities should be determined by interattribute dependencies and characteristics. Date (1986) defines the logical database design problem (remember the second of our entity definition themes) as deciding what relations (entities) are needed based on the logical structure of attributes. By adopting an attribute-oriented modeling philosophy early, you will not only improve your ability to understand and portray the business rules, but will position yourself for a smoother transition to database design.

If you use a modeling methodology that prescribes an entity-relationship phase prior to identifying attributes and keys, such as IDEF1X, be aware that the model you build during this phase will most likely undergo heavy changes when you begin identifying attributes. You may find that you have wasted much time, and the patience of your users, by creating models based only on entities. Remember, data and information is held in the attributes, not in the entities.

Finally, the identification of entities involves two practical considerations. First, there must be some mechanism that allows the modeler and database designer to distinguish between instances or occurrences of the entity. This mechanism is known as a primary key. The concept of keys is closely aligned with normal form concepts. In identifying entities, you will necessarily have to deal with definition of a primary key. Second, an entity should lie within the domain you are investigating. In other words, keep in mind the scope of your project, and attempt to draw reasonable boundaries for your model.

3.3   ENTITY NAME

An entity must be labeled with a unique, descriptive name that follows an established set of conventions.

Discussion

Remember that the entity's name is a window into its soul. If you have entities in your model that violate accepted naming conventions, then most likely you have more fundamental problems with your model. Your data administration group should establish a set of naming conventions for entities and attributes. Hopefully, those conventions will follow closely the naming recommendations we make below. We have drawn our rules from many sources, and have adapted them based on our experience and practice.

Above all, do not focus all of your modeling energies, or those of your subject matter experts, on arguing about the correct name for a concept. You will waste time better spent on other aspects of modeling.

Name Characteristics The entity name should exhibit the following characteristics:

- **Descriptive of the real-world objects and information represented by the entity. The name should be meaningful to the business community and accurately reflect the business concept or requirement being recorded.** Do not attempt to be too abstract, or to get cute with names. Assume a conservative, forthright approach, and get the concurrence of your subject matter experts—it has to be meaningful to them.

  Example

  The following entity name was used in the model for a financial services firm we once worked with.

  RESOURCE

  While RESOURCE may seem a reasonable name at first glance, the name actually conveyed little of the essence of what the entity represented, and meant little if anything to the business community. A quality assurance review revealed that the entity actually embodied several concepts, which explained the ambiguity of the name. It was eventually refined into several entities, including EQUIPMENT, PERSON, and FACILITY.

- **Self-explanatory.** Individuals reading a model diagram should be able to gain an immediate sense of what the entity represents.
- **Reflective of the logical nature of the entity, without regard to physical representation, characteristics, or considerations.** For example, the entity PERSONNEL RECORD carries a data file or database table connotation, even though the modeling team may have used the term without thinking about information systems or databases. Nonetheless, the PERSONNEL RECORD entity most likely is describing a PERSON, EMPLOYEE, or another entity containing attributes describing a PERSON, such as EMPLOYEE PERFORMANCE HISTORY. Avoid physical characterizations wherever possible.
- **Containing the minimum set of words necessary to completely and uniquely label the concept.** Focus on the essence of the entity's purpose, based on the attributes contained in it. Economical use of words will assure that the name captures the essence of the entity's concept without limiting or overly constraining it. Too many qualifiers can lead to misrepresentation of an entity. For example, a property management team created an entity called SINGLY MANAGED MATERIAL EQUIPMENT ITEM to describe equipment with individual serial numbers. The redundancy in this

name is apparent. This name also tends to constrain the concept of this type of equipment, introducing the concept of how it is used (i.e., "singly managed"), rather than focusing on what it is. Its use could vary across the organization.

- **In the form of a singular noun, optionally described with modifiers.** A modifier provides additional, differentiating information about the basic concept of the entity. For example, an entity named DAMAGED EQUIPMENT includes a noun "equipment" and a modifier "damaged", the latter serving to differentiate this type of equipment from others. The core concept of the entity is "equipment", as suggested by its primary key (most likely named "equipment code" or something to that effect).

- **Meeting naming convention requirements and limitations.** Most organizations (and many CASE tools) require that entity names be depicted in upper case alphabetic characters (A through Z) only. Hyphens, slashes (/ or \), ampersands or other special characters may be permitted, and could enhance the data modeler's ability to economically describe the entity. However, such special characters may also introduce ambiguity or reflect the fact that the entity actually represents two separate business facts.

Example

MATERIAL/EQUIPMENT

This entity name may appear to cover a single concept. However, a review of the definition revealed that MATERIAL referred to consumable items incorporated into final products, while EQUIPMENT referred to company resources used during the production process.

Length The length of the entity name should comply with existing naming conventions or standards. If none exist, consideration should be given to establishing a de facto standard that is supported by the CASE tool or data dictionary product(s) used in the organization. Many CASE tools support entity names with lengths of greater than 50 characters, which provides the modeling team with important flexibility in establishing meaningful entity names. However, some tools limit the entity name to 32 or 33 characters, which can cause problems in large models, and often require a "workaround" solution. When confronted with the latter situation, we have used abbreviations in the tool's entity name field, supplemented with a full length entity name in the first line of the entity description (or definition) field. This leads to additional overhead in managing models, requires establishing standard abbreviations for naming, and is generally not a good situation in a dynamic modeling environment.

Don'ts An entity name should specifically NOT have the following characteristics:

- **Abbreviations or acronyms, except those approved by the organization's data administrator or other recognized model management agent.** These can lead to misinterpretation or misuse, particularly when models are being created in several different areas of the business and integrated or reused in others.

  Example

  SCI

  Besides the fact that this entity name is very non-communicative, it can also lead to misinterpretation. In this example, the inventory management team has modeled the concept of a SUBSTITUTE CATALOG ITEM (SCI), but has neglected to recognize that the information systems group considers SCI to be a SOFTWARE CONFIGURATION ITEM, and the security department considers an SCI to be a SECURITY CLEARANCE INVESTIGATION.

- **Names of individual organizations, computer or information systems, reports or manuals, publications, forms, or computer screens.** If you have entities with names that include any of these kinds of words, then most likely you have introduced more than a naming problem into the model.

  Example

  EQUIPMENT LOCATED AT XYZ CORP

  This entity contains a reference to a specific organization, XYZ Corporation. This may meet immediate requirements, but what if other equipment locations are needed in the future? Also, make sure that redundant information does not exist elsewhere in the model. Is there an entity EQUIPMENT LOCATED AT ABC CORP in the model also?

- **Information system components, such as tables, files, menus, reports, or entry forms.** This is related to our rule to establish a name that reflects the logical nature of the business fact, not its incarnation in a particular system environment.

Example

EMPLOYEE DATA CAPTURE MENU

The name of the entity at left indicates that physical characteristics or existing system characteristics may have been introduced into the model. Explore the entity definition and attributes to ensure that quality problems do not extend beyond an isolated naming anomaly.

- **Express more than one idea or concept, either explicitly or implicitly.** The rationale for this should be obvious—if you are tempted to introduce more than one concept into the name, then the entity most likely embodies multiple "things" about the business, and the domain of the entity is likely to be mixed. Such a situation, of course, violates our definition of an entity, and leads to subsequent problems in design.

Example

BUILDING OR STRUCTURE

In BUILDING OR STRUCTURE, we have an entity that appears to mix two levels of a generalization hierarchy, a building being only one type of structure. The entity name quickly draws our attention to the problem.

When correcting the situation, make sure that the investigation and resolution carries through the root of the problem. This may require further discussions with users in order to clarify ambiguities.

- **"Garbage" words or phrases that introduce unnecessary or constraining ideas into the entity name.** The list of garbage covers possessive forms, articles (e.g., "a," "an," "the"), conjunctions (e.g., "and," "or," "but"), verbs (an entity is static, not active), or prepositions (e.g., "at," "by," "for," "in," etc.). Not only do garbage words not add value, they can also limit thinking, as illustrated in the example.

Example

THE EQUIPMENT AT A LOCATION

First, this entity is obviously too wordy. EQUIPMENT LOCATION gets the same concept across quite nicely. Second, assuming that the key here includes an identifier for a piece of equipment and an identifier for a location (this is an associative or intersecting entity), then the logical association also supports the inverse concept of THE LOCATION OF EQUIPMENT. In this case, EQUIPMENT LOCATION could serve as an effective entity name that supports the concept of an equipment-location relationship.

Implication

Although we believe that "less is more" when it comes to standards, a good set of naming conventions improves users' ability to read and understand a model quickly We have experienced situations where the naming standards have been quite extreme, resulting in unneeded frustration with little real benefit. The list you see above is relatively simple to follow, and brings enough consistency to allow an organization to manage their models effectively.

Why expend so much effort on naming conventions for entities? Because the entity name (and, as we'll discuss later, the attribute name) is critical in communicating the meaning of the model. Most of the rules we have described seem like common sense, and individually they may seem trivial. However, battling poor naming practices in a model with several hundred or thousand entities can become a needless hindrance that substantially reduces the utility of the model. Naming conventions are less of a necessity in small organizations, those with just a few analysts who work closely together, than in large organizations where multiple teams may be engaged in building complex, overlapping models at different sites. Remember, one success factor in building quality data models is the ability to reuse portions of the model to achieve integration. Naming conventions can go a long way toward achieving success in that endeavor.

3.4   ENTITY DEFINITION

Every entity must be described with a definition, description, or statement of purpose that conforms to a predefined set of rules.

Discussion

We use the terms "definition," "description," and "purpose" synonymously, because we believe that no matter what it is called, a body of text should exist for each entity that allows it to be interpreted consistently across the enterprise, over time, and through each stage of the information systems development cycle. For convenience, we use the term "definition" throughout.

Creating an entity definition is an important step in the data modeling process. It forces the modeling team to describe their requirements, and provides important documentation that will aid future interpretation of the model. Like comments and program headers in software code, succinct definitions increase the utility of the model immeasurably. This may seem like a minor point, but anyone who has attempted to interpret large, complex model can attest to the frustration of dealing with bad definitions.

In order to build good entity definitions, adhere to the following guidelines.

1. **The entity definition should explain what the entity is. Do not limit the definition to quotes from a dictionary, encyclopedia, or other text providing language definitions, although these can be used to supplement the description prepared by the users or analysts.**
2. **Explain why the entity is important to the business. The entity definition must answer the question "Why is this important to the business?"** In other words, what is this entity doing in the model? This forces the modeling team to confront the nature of this particular data requirement. Answering the question serves as a form of requirements validation. If the modeling team cannot succinctly define the importance of the entity, then the team needs to explore the possibility that the data requirement is outside of its scope.
3. **Write clearly and sparingly.** Stick to the point of the definition. The term "utilitarian" springs to mind when thinking of entity definitions. Long rambling prose generally adds little value, and can introduce ideas or concepts not directly related to the entity, leading to ambiguity and the potential for misinterpretation.
4. **If the entity is used across multiple function, process, organization, or system views, then append view-specific definition text clearly marked by the view it applies to.** Entities often span many logical views. While strict definition information may not vary as the entity is reused, the purpose of the entity will vary. Adding all applicable purposes provides important insight to the data management group, and can be very enlightening to others using the entity in their modeling efforts.

5. **Write the definition as soon as the entity is created.** If you are working in a facilitated session, work with the participants to create a draft of the definition on the spot. You can always go back and refine it. However, if you do not capture the essence of the entity definition, and more important its purpose, then you may forget exactly what prompted you to add it in the first place, and subtle nuances of its definition may be lost forever.

6. **Things to AVOID when developing entity definitions:**
    a. **Describing how, where, or when the entity is used, or who uses it.** These are best handled by other analysis tools, such as process-data or location-data matrices.
    b. **Simply restating or rephrasing the name of the entity.** The example should illustrate the weakness of definitions that have this characteristic.

Example

ORDER TYPE

Definition of ORDER TYPE: The possible types of orders.

Obviously, the definition adds little insight into the order types or their role in the business.

    c. **Depending on the definition of another model object.** The entity definition should be written in a manner that provides a complete, independent description of the entity without need for cross-referencing other model objects.
    d. **Restating the list of attributes contained in the entity.** The idea is to provide new information, not a regurgitation of work already documented more effectively elsewhere.
    e. **Using technical jargon, acronyms, or abbreviations that may be unfamiliar to those using the model.** If you must use them, define such terms within the entity definition. Again, the entity definition should stand on its own.
    f. **Including information that should clearly be documented elsewhere, such as process descriptions, derivation formulas, update authority.** Hiding this information in the entity definition almost assures that it will not be readily available to support systems development or data management activities.
    g. **Depending solely on the use of examples.** Examples can be an excellent means of supplementing the definition. However, examples alone do not impart enough of the business meaning necessary for broad, consistent interpretation.

Examples

So what does a "good" definition look like? Several examples are included below. Note the combination of clear description of what the object is with why it is important to the enterprise.

Good Entity Definitions

MARKET

Definition of MARKET: A segment of the general population that shares common characteristics, which in turn influence buying habits. Understanding markets is vital to our company's ability to tailoring advertising, product planning and development, and customer service.

SALES REGION

Definition of SALES REGION: A designated geographical area that has features or characteristics differentiating it in terms of customer expectations, language, customs, or trade regulations or laws, and that requires the company to plan and execute sales and sales support activities consistent with the region's character.

EQUIPMENT TYPE

Definition of EQUIPMENT TYPE: A classification scheme used specifically to organize individual pieces of equipment around common characteristics and use. Classification is necessary to enable management to gain a broad perspective of equipment acquisition, use and retirement, and to accumulate information at a level higher than that of an individual equipment item.

3.5   SINGLE INSTANCE ENTITY

An entity must represent a class or set of things. Entities should not be used to represent single instances of a class.

Description

An entity, by definition, represents a set or class of objects or information needs. It exists at a level of abstraction above that of any single object in an enterprise's domain. The objective of data modeling should be to describe the characteristics of the class, rather than to establish characteristics for a single object or instance.

Violation of this rule leads to two fundamental problems. First, if the problem is prevalent in the model, then the model will be subject to greater instability as new instances are identified and added. Introduction of single instance entities has the potential to lead to redundancy and inconsistency, as similar objects are introduced. Second, the model will not translate well to a database design. Imagine generating a relational design for entities with only one occurrence! As model components are transformed into data structures, the presence of single instance entities will lead to the probability of early and continuous maintenance, or will severely limit the utility and applicability of those structures.

Example

Sometimes the creation of single instance entities is not readily obvious, as in our example. Assume that we are modeling operations of a small hospital. The modeling team builds an initial model for managing operations in the radiology lab, shown in Figure 3.1. The radiology lab needs to track which employees are assigned to work in that area of the hospital, since many different skills are required to operate the lab, and the hospital operates around the clock.

Now assume the modeling activity expands to cover other operations, and the model is updated to reflect new requirements. Our refined model is shown in Figure 3.2, along with the redundancy introduced by the single instance entities. Note that the hospital has only one radiology lab, one emergency room, and one surgery.

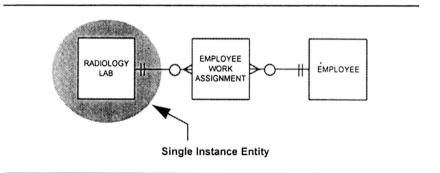

Single Instance Entity

Figure 3.1   Introduction of single instance entity into the model.

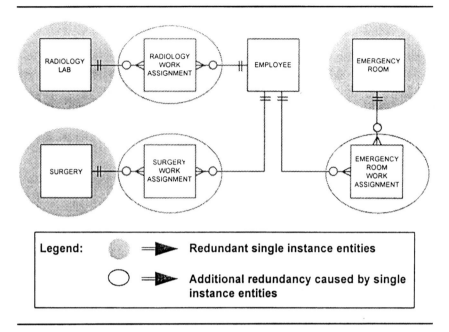

Figure 3.2   Introduction of unnecessary redundancy.

After reviewing the model, the team revised the model as shown in Figure 3.3.

Our simple example was based on the assumption that only one radiology lab, one surgery, and one emergency room exist in the small hospital. But what if there were two of each, say Surgery Room 1 and Surgery Room 2? Would that make the model in Figure 3.2 correct? Not really. We would still have a tremendous amount of redundancy, and the entities

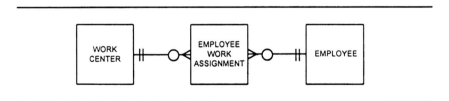

Figure 3.3   One possible resolution of single instance entities.

SURGERY, RADIOLOGY LAB, and EMERGENCY ROOM still represent single instances of a broader concept, that of a *work center type*. We could capture this broader concept by adding an attribute, *work center type*, with an enumerated domain of surgery, radiology lab, and emergency room to WORK CENTER. If necessary, subtype entities for one or more of the work center types can be added to record attributes specific to the subtype. As you can see, our resolution provides us with much greater flexibility and model stability. This rule is related to our rule regarding modeling entities in a single context.

3.6   ENTITY RELATIONSHIP MINIMUM

An entity must have a relationship (a.k.a. association) with at least one other entity in the model, supported by migrated keys.

Discussion

Data is never isolated. Every piece of data is, in some way, connected with at least one other piece of data. Even primitive attributes have some other piece of data that serves to define or describe, which in turn entangles them in a much larger web of data relationships. If you have an entity or attribute in your model that is not related to any other model component, then you are dealing with one of two cases:

*   You are not finished modeling. Go find out how that entity (or attribute) relates to other data model objects in the model that you are working in.
*   The entity (or attribute) is so indirectly related to the subject area that you are currently modeling that it does not belong with the rest of the model components. Your realization of this case should come, of course, after your investigation of the first case. Don't throw away the entity. It was defined to describe some data requirement that exists outside your scope, but most likely within the scope of the enterprise. Put it back in your enterprise entity (or attribute) pool for later use.

Example

The example shows an entity that has not been associated with any other entity(ies). Almost every CASE tool on the market today has some feature to verify that all entities have at least one relationship.

The resolution of our example is relatively simple. In this case, the unconnected entity happens to be in the scope of our model, so we examine the business rules and determine that containers are categorized

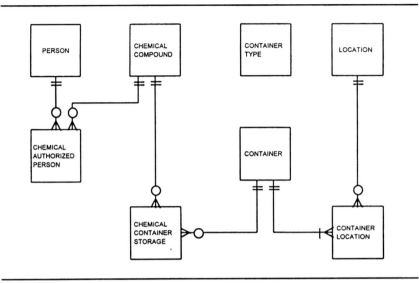

Figure 3.4   Entity with no relationships.

for purposes of assessing their suitability to store certain types of compounds. The corrected model is shown in Figure 3.5.

3.7   MODELING ENTITIES IN A SINGLE CONTEXT

Beware of the temptation to create entities that are limited to a single context, or role, in the model.

Description

One of the most difficult aspects of data modeling is maintaining perspective. It is easy to fall into the trap of listening to subject matter experts, then writing down or mapping their exact words. Business people, like anyone else, tend think about the world in context of their particular roles or jobs. This can lead to potential problems in a data model; the model needs to reflect a stable, broad perspective. How do you recognize when something has been modeled in a single context or role? What if you encountered the model shown in Figure 3.6? Which of these entities would you consider to be entities that fulfill a single role? How would you define them differently?

Note the similarity of the relationships from AIRPORT to OWNER, MANAGER, AIRPORT SERVICES PROVIDER, and REGULATORY

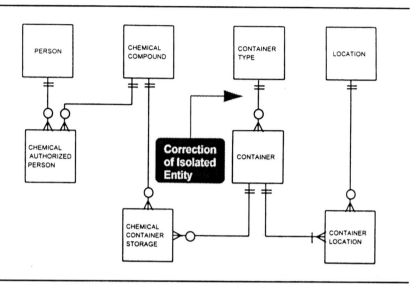

Figure 3.5   Entity with added relationship.

AGENCY. We can assume that each of the four entities related to AIR-PORT are organizations, and that these organizations could assume other roles in context of other parts of the model. Assume XYZ Corporation is an AIRPORT SERVICES PROVIDER. As a provider of services,

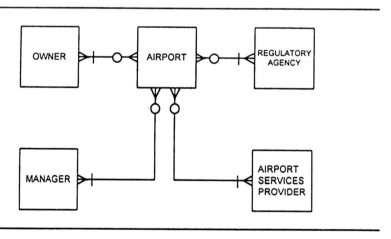

Figure 3.6   Which entities have been modeled in a role play?

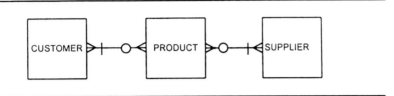

Figure 3.7   XYZ Corporation is now a CUSTOMER!

XYZ must procure supplies in order to sustain its services. How should we model the fact that XYZ procures supplies from other vendors? Let's assume that we model this relationship as shown in Figure 3.7.

Is it reasonable for us to repeat the information about an organization already captured in AIRPORT SERVICES PROVIDER again in CUSTOMER? What happens if XYZ decides to change its name? Assuming we implement the model as shown (there is certainly nothing in the model telling our database design team to do otherwise), the change will have to be performed in both the AIRPORT SERVICES PROVIDER entity and the CUSTOMER entity. Not very efficient, nor very representative of the business reality. Perhaps we should step back from the narrow confines of the airport and product contexts, and attempt to evaluate what XYZ really represents—an ORGANIZATION. We can still capture the role that XYZ plays in relation to airport. One means of doing so is explained in the example at the end of this section.

Why is it important to avoid modeling entities in a single context? For at least three reasons:

- Creation of numerous entities with some underlying commonality will lead to considerable redundancy in the model. These entities will generally have many of the same attributes and relationships. With redundancy, of course, comes the potential for inconsistency.
- The model is relatively inflexible to change. What if other roles are defined in the future, after we have implemented these in separate data structures?
- It will probably be difficult to integrate the model view in which role entities are created with other views. Role play entities tend to be very domain-specific.

The challenge, of course, is to recognize when things are very similar, and when they are different. This rule is closely related to the rules governing homonyms and synonyms, which will be covered next.

Example

In this example, we have an unnormalized model pertaining to the buying and selling of real property (real estate) (Figure 3.8). The CONTRACT covers one or more pieces of REAL PROPERTY, which in turn may be involved in multiple contracts over time as it is bought and sold. We also have a number of "players" in the contract, each having a different role. These are the BUYER, the SELLER, and the AGENT. Let's assume that we capture information such as name, address, telephone number, and other identifiers, about each, plus information specific to their role in the real property transaction (e.g., buyer's credit limit, agent's license number). Now, what if our AGENT wishes to sell his or her property and buy another piece of property? If we stay with our model in Figure 3.8, then we introduce redundant data about the AGENT into the BUYER and SELLER entities. What if another legal party becomes involved in the contract, such as a financial institution or government agency? We'll need to add more entities to describe organizations or individuals, but only in context of a contract.

Figure 3.9 portrays one of many possible revisions to the model. The revised model captures the same set of rules, and enables the modeling team to recognize that BUYER, SELLER, and AGENT share many common properties, including possible relationships not depicted in this model fragment. The LEGAL PARTY CONTRACT ROLE entity is a static table that records the domain of roles for LEGAL PARTYs involved in a CONTRACT. The subtypes BUYER, SELLER, and AGENT exist to contain attributes unique to a LEGAL PARTY as it fulfills a

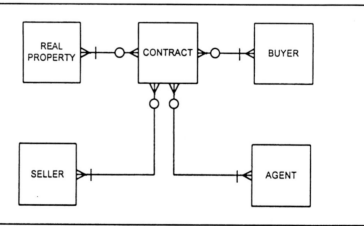

Figure 3.8   Entities modeled in a role play situation.

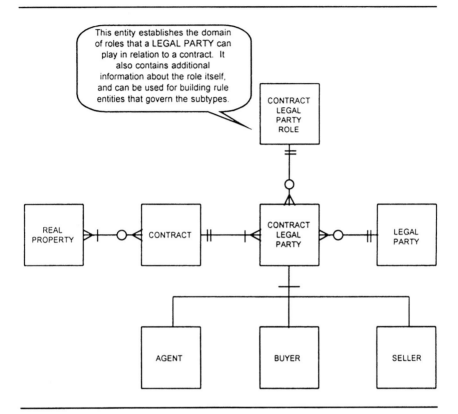

Figure 3.9   Possible resolution of role play problem.

particular role on a CONTRACT. These role playing entities now appear in context of the contract.

Now that you have seen a resolution of the role play problem, try going back to the AIRPORT example we used in our earlier discussion and refining that model.

3.8   HOMONYMS

Homonyms should not be permitted. Identify and eliminate homonyms for both entities and attributes.

Description

A *homonym* is a word or phrase that is either the same or very similar to another in sound or spelling, but which has another meaning altogether. Homonyms creep into data models for many reasons. Whenever two or more groups work on a model, the potential for introducing homonyms increases, particularly if they are from different areas of the enterprise. Our institutions and society at large are full of "overloaded" terms, so it is quite natural to expect them to appear in our logical representation of the business environment. The data processing community is especially guilty of using homonyms; even the terms *entity* and *attribute* have more than one common use.

Unfortunately, homonyms make models less precise, they introduce the potential for confusion, and they may hide important rules or characteristics. Therefore, they must be eliminated from the model. CASE tools can aid modeling teams in this regard, since most products have a feature that either prevents creation of objects with the same name or notifies the user that an object with the same name already exists.

Examples

We present two examples. The first depicts a homonym embodied in a single entity. It demonstrates a case of incomplete analysis, where a modeling team has used a single entity (and a single name) to represent two distinctly different ideas. The second depicts a case where two separate modeling groups created entities that were named the same, but which have different meanings and characteristics.

For our first example, we have the entity MARKET and its definition. Read the definition carefully. You will find that there are two distinctly separate ideas about the common term "market"—geographic markets and demographic markets. If we were looking at an actual model, we would probably find that there were subsets of relationships

Definition: A designated geographical area that has features or characteristics that differentiate it in terms of customer expectations, language, customs, or trade regulations or laws, and that requires separate planning and execution of pricing, advertising, and promotional programs. A market is also defined as a segment of the general population that shares common characteristics, which in turn influence buying habits.

Figure 3.10   Homonyms embodied in a single entity.

and attributes in the entity that belonged to both types of markets, subsets specific to geographic markets only, and those that apply only to demographic markets. Unless these distinct concepts are recognized and handled separately, we limit the precision with which we can model the business rules surrounding marketing.

In our second example, we have a case of two entities that have been modeled simultaneously by different groups within the organization. The groups have very different views of EQUIPMENT, based on their relative positions in the organization (Figure 3.11). The division managers think of *classes* or *categories* of equipment (e.g., short-haul flatbed trucks), while the maintenance crew thinks of individual pieces of equipment (e.g., the same truck that was in the shop last week!). Note the difference in primary key—the maintenance crew is thinking of individual serial numbers, perhaps to keep track of maintenance histories, warranties, and other such information. The challenge for the modeling team will be reconciling and resolving the different requirements for each group, while maintaining the unique requirements of each.

We present one of many possible solutions to this dilemma in Figure 3.12. It involves establishing a hierarchy recognizing the aggregate perspective of the division managers, who have an interest in acquiring

---

EQUIPMENT

Modeled by: Division managers

Definition: A type of durable asset that is owned or otherwise acquired for use either directly or indirectly in creating products or delivering services to our clients. Examples of equipment include drills, stamps, presses, trucks, computers and office furnishings.

Primary key: Equipment id

EQUIPMENT

Modeled by: Maintenance crews

Definition: A mechanical or electronic item or device that is subject to preventive or corrective maintenance action in order to ensure that it is available when required for production or services.

Primary key: Serial number

Figure 3.11   Unreconciled homonyms.

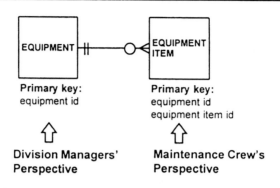

Primary key:
equipment id

⇧

Division Managers'
Perspective

Primary key:
equipment id
equipment item id

⇧

Maintenance Crew's
Perspective

Figure 3.12   One possible resolution of EQUIPMENT homonym.

and managing different types of equipment in their operation but have little or no interest in *individual pieces* of equipment, with the detailed perspective of the maintenance crews, who may need to understand the type of equipment they are working on as well as a maintenance profile for an individual piece (note the composition of the primary keys).

3.9   SYNONYMS

Identify and resolve synonyms for both entities and attributes.

Discussion

A synonym is a word or name with the same or nearly the same meaning as another word or name. In context of data modeling, synonymous entities or attributes are those that represent the same logical concept or requirement, but have been assigned different names. Synonyms occur because, over time, separate functions create their own unique terminology for similar "things" or concepts. For example, the manufacturing and logistics group may use the term "work center" to refer to a group of people and machines that perform a definitive set of value-adding tasks. The manufacturing group is interested in the fact that work is being accomplished that contributes to the creation of a product. The accounting function, referring to the same set of people and machines performing the same set of tasks, may refer to a "cost center." Accounting's interest rests with the fact that those people and machines represent investment, expenses, and work-in-progress.

While the differences for a single such case appear relatively trivial and easy to overcome, imagine dealing with hundreds or thousands of such terms, attempting to resolve each one in order to assure that the real "thing" being referred to by both terms is the same. The problem with synonyms may be further complicated by the fact that homonyms, introduced in our last rule, exist for synonymous terms. Related synonyms and homonyms will have to be resolved at the same time, to avoid cycling back through the same subject.

Confirmation of synonyms requires careful attention to the details of the model. If you suspect that two entities are synonymous, review each of the following, comparing between (or among, as the case may be) entities to determine the level of similarity:

- Definitions
- Relationships to other entities—synonymous entities will often have relationships to the same sets of entities.
- Key structure
- Attributes, although these may have different names as well, based on the entity name (e.g., *person name* in entity PERSON versus *individual name* in entity INDIVIDUAL)

When evaluating potentially synonymous attributes, compare the following characteristics:

- Definitions
- Domain, particularly if the domain for each is enumerated. The same values in an enumerated domain should raise your suspicions immediately.

When identifying and resolving synonymous data objects, remember that these often have characteristics or attributes that remain unique. Therefore, examine all characteristics of the objects to ensure that no metadata is lost during the consolidation. Revise definitions, expand domains, modify relationships to account for any unique characteristics of each synonymous object. Subtype entities represent a special case of synonym, one where it is advantageous to retain both entities in order to ensure that other requirements are met.

Why all the fuss about synonyms? Because they introduce redundancy and imprecision into the model, along with the related implications about consistency and integrity. Resolution of synonyms, like homonyms, is a significant part of the model integration process. Every opportunity, including QA reviews, to identify and resolve synonyms early in model development will lead to less impact than if they are left for resolution during integration or system design. Resolution of synonyms may need to occur in a facilitated model refinement session to ensure that business rules are correctly and completely reflected in the revised model.

Identification and resolution of synonyms is the responsibility of the data administrator, model manager, or other similar function. A search for synonyms should be a standard part of any quality assurance review, and must be included in any periodic model integration exercises. Unlike the case of homonyms, CASE tools do *not* have the capability to recognize synonyms. It is up to the responsible data management party to perform synonym searches.

Examples

In our example, we find an enterprise with several modeling teams running in parallel. During a routine model integration exercise, the model manager discovered the entities shown in Figure 3.13. By examining their definitions, list of attributes, and relationships (not shown), she concluded that they were potentially synonymous. We have ignored the keys throughout this example.

The model manager coordinated an issues resolution meeting, with the result that the three synonymous entities were refined into the model shown in Figure 3.14. Note that INDIVIDUAL and EMPLOYEE were consolidated into EMPLOYEE, but PERSON remains a separate entity, based on the rules of normalization and the requirements of the

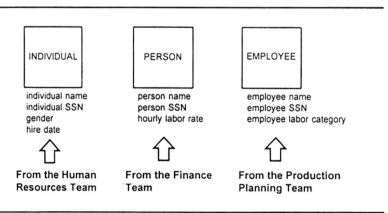

Figure 3.13   Unresolved synonyms.

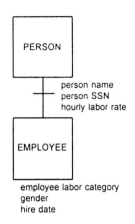

Figure 3.14   Resolved synonyms.

enterprise. However, an EMPLOYEE *is* a PERSON, and therefore is considered a synonym that we retain in order to meet our No Optional Attributes Rule. Note also the placement of attributes. The attribute *hourly labor rate* was not migrated to EMPLOYEE, since the finance team had intended to capture information about employees and non-employees (e.g., contract personnel) when they defined PERSON. The *gender* and *hire date* attributes were migrated to EMPLOYEE, since the enterprise keeps this information only about its employees.

REFERENCES

Bruce, Thomas. *Designing Quality Databases with IDEF1X Information Models*. New York: Dorset House Publishing, 1992.

Chen, Peter. "The Entity-Relationship Model—Toward a Unified View of Data." *ACM TODS 1*, No. 1 (March 1976).

Date, C.J. *An Introduction to Database Systems, Volume I*. Reading, MA: Addison-Wesley, 1986.

Finkelstein, Clive. *An Introduction to Information Engineering: From Strategic Planning to Information Systems*. Sydney: Addison-Wesley, 1989.

Martin, James. *Information Engineering, Book II: Planning and Analysis*. Englewood Cliffs, NJ: Prentice-Hall, 1989.

4

Attribute Rules

4.1   ATTRIBUTE CHECKLIST ITEMS

The Attribute Checklist presents the set of characteristics a data modeling team should gather and record about each attribute to ensure that a complete set of requirements is represented in the data model. Our checklist directly supports the completeness aspect of data model quality.

The list presented here has been made without regard to the limitations or capabilities of any single CASE tool. Rather, it represents those things that we find are essential data requirements, and are necessary to begin database design.

☑ Name

Every attribute shall be given a name that uniquely identifies it. See Attribute Name Rule later in this chapter for further explanation.

☑ Description

Every entity shall have a description that permits it to be correctly interpreted by anyone reviewing the model. The description should be created at the time the attribute is identified and named, and should follow the guidelines established under the Attribute Description Rule found later in this chapter.

☑ Type

An attribute must be categorized as one of two types, either a key attribute or a non-key attribute. This characteristic refers to an attribute's actual use in the model, rather than its potential to serve as a key attribute.

> **Key attributes** serve as primary keys in the entity in which they originate (are first defined), and as either primary or foreign (nonprimary) keys in any entity to which they migrate in support of entity relationships. A primary key is an attribute whose values can be used to uniquely identify occurrences of an entity. Foreign key values are not necessarily unique within the entity. We will discuss primary and foreign keys under the Key Role characteristic a little later. Primary keys are implemented with a unique index to a data structure.

> **Non-key attributes** contain the bulk of the information in a data model. Unlike key attributes, their values do not have to be unique across all occurrences of the entity they have been assigned to through the data modeling process. A non-key attribute can appear in only one entity in the data model. Attributes that are identified as candidate keys (either singularly or in combination with other attributes) but are not selected to serve as primary keys should be classified as non-key attributes. Certain non-key attributes may be selected as access paths during database design, and are often referred to as selection attributes or secondary keys. Despite the latter term, these are generally implemented in data structures using non-unique indices (Finkelstein, 1989).

☑ Edit Rules

Each attribute should be described with one of the edit rules shown in Table 4.1. Edit rules were first documented by Clive Finkelstein, and he provides an excellent description of their use in *Information Engineering: Strategic Systems Development* (1992). An edit rule defines (1) whether a value is required for the attribute upon creation of an instance of the entity in which it appears, and (2) whether the value, once provided, can be updated for that instance of the entity. Edit rules are an essential descriptive characteristic for database and application design. For example, attributes that are 'add now' (see the table below) will need to be implemented as NOT NULL columns in an SQL CRE-

Table 4.1. Edit Rules (from Finkelstein, 1989)

Edit Rule	Definition
Add now, modify allowed	A value for the attribute must be provided at the time a new instance of the entity is created. The value of the attribute may be changed one or more times after it is created.
Add now, modify not allowed	A value for the attribute must be provided at the time a new instance of the entity is created. The value of the attribute cannot be changed once it is created.
Add later, modify allowed	A value for the attribute may or may not be inserted at the time a new instance of the entity is created. The value of the attribute may be changed one or more times after it is created.
Add later, modify not allowed	A value for the attribute may or may not be inserted at the time a new instance of the entity is created. The value of the attribute cannot be changed once it is created.

ATE TABLE statement, or the equivalent in other database definition languages.

Primary keys always have a value of "add now, modify not allowed." The edit rule for a primary key migrated to another entity as a non-primary foreign key will depend on the nature of the relationship with the parent entity. An optional relationship to the child entity would translate to "add later," while a mandatory relationship would translate to "add now."

☑ Domain

Every attribute must eventually be assigned a domain of permitted values. Domains need not be determined immediately upon identification of an attribute, but certainly will need to be established before the model can be considered completely stable.

Attribute domains consist of at least one, and possibly two elements:

A **general domain**, also known as a data type, which describes the manner in which the values are represented. Commonly used general domains include alphanumeric, real numbers, integer only,

Boolean, and other standard information processing domains. A general domain must be defined for each attribute. The selected general domain should be the one that represents values of the attribute in a meaningful manner to the user. For example, a person's name could be represented using a hexadecimal coding scheme in place of alphabetic characters, but its utility for users of the data would be severely diminished. The objectives of defining a general domain for each attribute are to select the domain with greatest utility for users, and the one that can be readily translated into data types available in potential or target database management systems. Data models increasingly contain complex data types, such as those required to support sound, digital video, or photographs. See Modeling Complex Data Types in Chapter 9 for further discussion of complex data domains.

General domains may be bounded with high and low range limits. The decision to identify a range of values within a general domain should be done in consultation with the users, and only after careful consideration of both current and future potential values.

A **specific domain**, also known as an enumerated domain, prescribes a specific set of values that are valid and permitted for the attribute. For example, the attribute *property type* in a model for a real estate firm might have the values "townhouse, single family detached, duplex, apartment, . . ." We sometimes refer to these as "static values," since the values in an enumerated domain tend to be relatively stable over time.

☑ Abbreviation(s)

If any abbreviations are used in the attribute name (often required due to limitations of CASE tool in use) or in the attribute description, then it is important to document the abbreviation and a full definition of it as part of the overall description of the attribute. Use of abbreviations should be consistent with any conventions established within the data management community of your organization.

☑ Acronym(s)

We do not recommend using acronyms as a substitute for a full attribute name, although their use may be a practical response to limitations imposed by CASE tools. Acronyms suffer from a couple of common problems—they may not be known or understood by parties outside the business area being modeled, or even by all parties within the area; and acronyms are often not unique. As with abbreviations, if you use acronyms be sure to document them as part of the description.

☑ Key Use

This rule applies only to primary keys. A primary key that is migrated to another entity will serve in one of two possible roles in the child entity: primary key or foreign (nonprimary) key. The key use depends of course on whether the attribute is required to uniquely determine an instance of the entity into which it is migrated. Note that there are specific rules governing the migration of keys, and these are spelled out in detail in this chapter.

☑ Source

This defines whether the attribute is derived or primitive. A derived attribute is one whose value is generated from one or more other attributes in the model according to a specified formula. A primitive attribute is one whose value is not derived within the scope of the model. A primitive attribute may in fact be derived outside of the scope of the model, but its derivation is not performed within the enterprise. For example, suppose Company A acquires products from Company B. Company A records a *product price* on a purchase request. It is not concerned about how that price is determined by Company B; it simply needs to know how much to pay. If we are building a data model for Company A, the attribute is defined as being primitive. However, suppose Company B actually computes the *product price* according to a tiered pricing structure based on the size of the order. If we are building the data model for Company B, the *product price* is derived (from order size, base product price, and price-quantity discount).

☑ Derivation Formula(s)*

If the attribute source is determined to be derived, then the modeling team, with participation of informed business experts, must establish the formula by which it will be derived. It is extremely important that this is documented, to ensure that eventual users have confidence in the quality of data generated. Derivation formulas can be relatively simple, such as *total sales tax* = *total price* × *sales tax rate*, or they can be

---

* Applies only to derived attributes.

more complex, with adjustments to the formula based on values or conditions associated with the attribute. The formula should explicitly identify any other attribute(s) required to generate a value for the derived attribute. We will revisit derived attributes in greater detail later in this chapter.

☑ Derivation/Attribute Dependency Links*

Derived attributes are almost always dependent on at least one other attribute in the model. This dependency has been referred to as a *derivation dependency* (McClure, 1993). You should maintain documentation of such links as an aid to understanding the derived attribute, and as input to eventual information system planning, design and development.

☑ Requirements Traceability

This is information pertaining to the cause or purpose of the enterprise's interest in the attribute. The requirement may have one of several sources, depending on the nature of the data modeling activity (e.g., reverse engineering, strategic information systems planning, etc.) Traceability may be attained through (1) reference to the source of the need (e.g., citation of a statement, clause, paragraph, or section of a regulation, policy or plan; or, reference to a physical data structure element, program variable, or human interface component in the case of current systems analysis sources); and, (2) mapping to another metadata object created and managed as part of the system lifecycle, such as a planning statement (e.g., critical success factor, goal, objective) or a physical system or system design element (e.g., file, data element, table, program element). In other words, you need to document where the entity came from, and where it is going to be used.

☑ Ownership Authority

You should maintain a record of individuals, functions, or organizations that have authority over each attribute for the following purposes:

Stewards have authority for defining and approving metadata. Individuals participating in the development of a data model are defining, and at least preliminarily, approving metadata. Attribute names,

---

* Applies only to derived attributes.

descriptions, enumerated values and other characteristics fall under the authority of stewards. Your data administration organization should have policies and procedures for metadata control.

Custodians create and use data. These are the individuals or organizations that have been granted authority within the enterprise, usually through policies and procedures, to perform business operations or processes that result in creation of data. Although access authority is granted through many different means, it will be important to understand *and plan* who within the enterprise has authority to create, read, update, and delete data. The planning of data manipulation will become increasingly important as more and more organizations move toward the distributed, shared data environments inherent to client/server architectures.

4.2   DERIVED ATTRIBUTES

Derived and calculated attributes must be represented in the data model, along with their dependencies to the base attributes used in the derivation or calculation.

Discussion

We begin the discussion of this rule with definitions of some key terms. Like many of the terms used in the information resource management discipline, these have become overloaded through years of use. We are not suggesting that our definitions become the standard; we provide them simply to clarify discussion of the rule.

A *derived attribute* is one that is created by accumulating values of multiple instances of one or more other data attributes and, optionally, performing some additional computation on those values in order to create a value for the subject derived attribute (Inmon, 1989). Thus, it represents an aggregation or summarization of existing information, and introduces a derivation dependency within the model (between the derived attribute and the other attribute(s) from which it is derived). A derivation dependency exists between a derived attribute and the base attribute(s) from which it is derived (McClure, 1993). Figure 4.1 presents an example of a derived attribute and its dependencies.

A *calculated attribute* describes some characteristic about a single instance of the entity, and is generally calculated from another single instance of a related attribute. In the simplified example in Figure 4.2, the attribute *task duration* is a calculated attribute, created by subtracting the completion date from the start date. As with derived attributes,

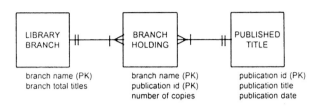

Derivation:

branch total titles = count of (BRANCH HOLDING)
where BRANCH HOLDING.branch name = LIBRARY BRANCH.branch name

Figure 4.1   A derived attribute and its derivation formula.

calculated attributes introduce a dependency between the calculated attribute and the base attribute(s) from which it is calculated.

The differences between *calculated* and *derived* are not as important as the similarities. Both involve some form of processing, and both usually involve other attributes in the model. For ease of reference, we will use the term *derived attribute* and *derivation dependency* when discussing both calculated and derived attributes in the remainder of our discussion.

This rule will spark some controversy, but it is one that the data modeling community must come to terms with. We have participated in

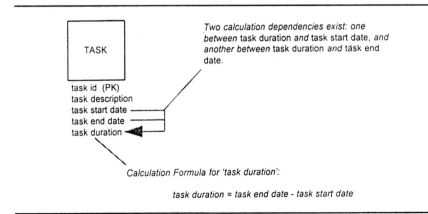

Figure 4.2   A calculated attribute and its calculation dependencies.

many lively discussions on this topic, and have heard sound arguments presented on both sides of the issue. We recommend including derived attributes, and documenting derivation dependencies, for the following reasons.

• Derived attributes represent the information that management really wants and needs. The old view of modeling only, the primitive data of an organization no longer fits either management's need for information or the reality of new decision-oriented information systems architectures. In "Managing by Wire," an article for *Harvard Business Review* (1993), Stephan H. Haeckel and Richard L. Nolan present case studies of organizations that have successfully developed data models providing strategic advantage through "manage-by-wire capability." Haeckel and Nolan report on Global Insurance (a pseudonym):

> ... data models were developed to interpret the market research, transaction history, demographic, and economic information that Global collected from the field, external databases, and internal operations ... Elaborate data models are worth fortunes to banks, airlines, food manufacturers, and large retailers like Wal-Mart, because they help these companies reorient themselves continually.
>
> At Global, a decision-support system used the patterns its data models revealed to trigger exception reports or approval requests that then appeared at managers' terminals. For instance, a manager whose product was losing ground to a new competitive offering would have the option of modifying the existing policy or creating an entirely new one.

Haeckel and Nolan refer to patterns of data, decision support, and interpretation of data. These are clearly terms associated with aggregating raw data into forms usable for meaningful analysis. The ability to perform such management-oriented activities simply cannot be accomplished using data models that record only primitive, transaction-level data requirements. Obviously, the degree to which any particular system's view of the enterprise data model includes derived data will depend on the purpose of the system. However, even the most mundane transaction processing system will contain some data that is derived or calculated. And most management information systems have a proportionally large amount of derived data. Thinking back to our definition of a high-quality data model, it should be clear that thorough modeling of derived data leads to greater completeness and ultimately—sometimes directly—to greater utility.

• Derived attributes represent data requirements of the users. They in turn drive other data requirements (e.g., the base attributes used in the derivation), perhaps through several layers of dependencies and calculations (see our example). Therefore, identifying and including derived attributes in a data model provides an opportunity to validate that all necessary base data is being captured. This is especially important when derived data is built on external data. This latter category of data is frequently overlooked by data modeling teams. However, as information exchange increases across enterprise boundaries, understanding external sources of data becomes vital to meeting user requirements. Including derived attributes provides a very important completeness check for the modeling team. By linking the derived attributes to the base attributes from which they are derived (these may be derived attributes also), the team can easily determine whether the model contains all data elements necessary to create and update the data required by the users.

• Where else would you document derived data requirements? A derivation algorithm or formula, and derivation dependencies represent data about data (metadata). These things describe data attributes. Arguments for including derived data only in process or activity models are inappropriate. A process model is inadequate for capturing the necessary relationships completely and in context. Some CASE tools now provide specific support for recording attribute derivation formulas as part of the attribute metadata.

• Users have an opportunity to specify the business rules for the derivation, and to do so in context of the data model. This is particularly important for decision support information, as these tend to be data-intensive applications and are rarely subject to thorough process modeling. Therefore, the data model serves as the only opportunity to document these requirements.

• When the model is translated into a design, the developers have a readily mapped set of requirements from which design decisions can be made, and later tested. For example, attribute derivation implies a dependency sequence among attributes that may not be readily apparent from other relationships in the model.

• Including derived attributes in a data model does not imply anything about their physical implementation. Surprisingly, we have heard even experienced analysts claim "Why are you including derived attributes in your model? You don't want to have to store those in your database." Who said anything about physical implementation? We're building a data model of *requirements*. No design or implementation decisions have been made. If anything, including derived attributes in the data model makes the design process easier. All the data is contained in one model, and the database designer can make fully informed decisions about what to store and what not to store, once access statistics, frequency of update, cost of computing the attribute, and other criteria are gathered. In the case of derived attributes that are infrequently updated but are frequently accessed, the design decision may very well be to store the attribute in the database. Certainly decision support databases will consist of a large proportion of derived data values.

Understanding derived data requirements will become increasingly important as many organizations move to client/server architectures. Much of the information needed on the client end of the architecture is derived—summarized, aggregated snapshots of the production database. Modeling these needs is vital to establishing a requirements baseline upon which distributed data architectures can be analyzed and designed. Attempting to map a data model that does not represent derived data to the users, locations, and applications of a client/server architecture leaves you with only a small—and increasingly narrow—perspective on what data is needed and how it will be used. As you move more toward a business-driven modeling perspective, the increasingly central role of derived data in the data architecture of the well-connected enterprise will become apparent.

A final note: Derived attributes should never serve as primary key attributes Derived attributes are subject to change, rendering them ineffective for use as primary keys.

Example

Our example contains both calculated and derived information. We have traced the dependencies for each. As you can see in Figure 4.3, the creation of management's decision information regarding *total product period sales* is derived by accumulating *total sales price* for individual orders whose *order date* falls within the *period start date* and *period end date* of interest to management. Note the derivation dependencies mapped in the diagram. This view of product information might be implemented in a decision support or executive information system. However, the data model clearly maps the dependency back to basic order information. The development team can devise the best update strategy for the manage-

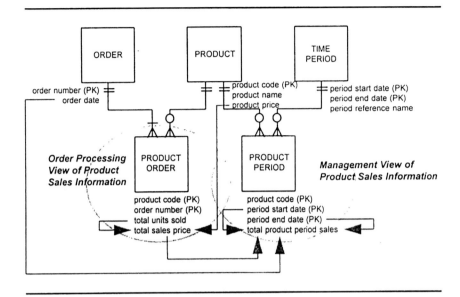

Figure 4.3   Derived and calculated data attributes and dependencies.

ment view based on managers' need for timely data, cost of updating from order data, and other parameters. If a logical-to-physical mapping is maintained, the team will also know exactly where to go to get the information needed to derive *total product period sales*.

The order processing department's view of the data is a little different from the management view. It is concerned with moving orders quickly from receipt to shipment, and with creating accurate information for billing. The *total sales price* is calculated from *product price*, which may be under the control of a product management team, and from the *total units sold*, which comes through on the order. The *total sales price*, as we have said, is used by management to derive historical summary data (*total product period sales*), and will also be used by the billing process (not shown on the data map) to create an invoice, compute a net payment discount, or determine if a customer is overextended. While this model fragment has been vastly simplified, you can readily see how including derived attributes aids in building a valuable picture of how data is interconnected across the enterprise. As connectivity increases in most organizations through client/server architectures and linked databases, the importance of gaining insights about these kinds of data dependencies will become increasingly important.

4.3 ATTRIBUTE NAMES

Every attribute should be given a unique name that represents its business meaning.

Discussion

Developing names for attributes is more difficult than it sounds, particularly if you are managing data models across a relatively large enterprise. Some organizations, particularly in the government sector, have of necessity created rigorous naming standards to enhance data standardization and sharing initiatives. If you have a data administration group, chances are you already use a set of naming standards or conventions for your data modeling efforts. If not, then you should at least ensure that attribute names adhere to the following generally accepted rules.

1. **An attribute name should be clear, concise, and self-explanatory.** It should immediately convey to the reader the logical concept embodied by the attribute. Obviously, more detail will be provided by the attribute definition and its other metadata characteristics; however, utility of a large model will diminish rapidly if attribute names are poorly constructed.
2. **Name attributes according to logical considerations, not physical characteristics.** After all, you are building a logical data model. Avoid limiting or distorting the concept with physical features.
3. **Use the minimum number of words necessary to uniquely identify the attribute and to convey its meaning.** Practice moderation in all things, and especially attribute naming. Get to the point, but don't leave anything out.
4. **Minimize the use of special characters.** There are several things to consider when using special characters. Use of ampersands and slashes may indicate that the attribute is not really atomic. If you are tempted to use them, then perhaps you should take a closer look at the attribute's domain and definition. Using hyphens between words is a common practice, but tends to look to much like "computerese" to business experts. There is another consideration—many CASE products limit the use of special characters in name fields.
5. **The length of the attribute name should comply with existing naming conventions or standards. If none exist, consideration should be given to establishing a de facto standard that is supported by the CASE tool or data dictionary**

product(s) used in the organization. Many CASE tools support attribute names with lengths of greater than 50 characters, which provides the modeling team with important flexibility in establishing meaningful names. However, some tools have limitations of 32 or 33 characters, which can cause problems in large models, and often require a workaround solution. When confronted with the latter situation, we have used abbreviations in the tool's attribute name field, supplemented with a full length name in the first line of the description (or definition) field. This leads to additional overhead in managing models, requires establishing standard abbreviations for naming, and is generally not a good situation in a dynamic modeling environment.

6. **An attribute name should specifically NOT:**
   a. Replace or contradict the definition of the attribute.
   b. Contain abbreviations or acronyms, except those established and approved by the data administrator or other authority.
   c. Contain any of the following:
      - Names of organizations, computer or information systems, directives, forms, screens or reports, such as
         FAMIS code (FAMIS is a Finance/Accounting system)
         block 61 title (refers to a specific field on a form)
         monthly status report total cost (refers to line on a report)
      - Plural words, such as
         product names
         state postal abbreviations
      - Possessive forms
         individual's birth date
         product's unit cost
      - Articles (a, an, the), such as
         the annual membership fee
         a service type
      - Conjunctions (and, but, or), such as
         batch or lot number
         next scheduled maintenance and repair date
      - Verbs, such as
         person owns property
         organization hires person
      - Prepositions (i.e., from, at, by, under, for, of, in, . . .), such as
         cost of item
         name of person
         quantity received by warehouse

Your data administration group may also establish a set of generic terms that are used repeatedly in attribute names. For example, the attributes *product assembly total cost* and *facility acquisition total cost* share the generic element "total cost." By defining a set of generic elements with established domains and general structures, you can assure that use of terms such as "total cost" will be consistent across models. Note that derivation, source or other characteristics will remain unique to each attribute.

4.4   ATTRIBUTE DESCRIPTION

Every attribute should be documented with a complete description of what it is and why it is important to the business.

Discussion

If properly written, the attribute description serves several purposes:

- During the modeling process, the act of creating a description forces the modeling team and business experts to think carefully about the nature of the data requirement they are attempting to capture. If the participants have difficulty describing the attribute, chances are additional investigation is needed.
- The attribute description provides the rationale for why the attribute is in the model. A dictionary definition alone is often not sufficient to allow those using the model to understand the requirement.
- The description also provides documentation of the attribute for later use. How many times have you attempted to review a data model created by someone else, only to become frustrated because the description of the model components was inadequate to allow you to fully comprehend the model? Modeling teams should remember that their model will be used by other analysis teams, systems designers, data administrators and database administrators. Comprehensive documentation is a necessity if models are to be effectively used across the enterprise and throughout the system lifecycle.

A good attribute description has the following characteristics:

- Builds on and is consistent with the attribute name.
- Is clearly and economically worded. In particular, be careful that the wording does not open the possibility of differing interpretations.

- Stands alone; it is not dependent on another attribute or entity definition to convey its meaning. In particular, beware of circular attribute definitions—those that rely on another attribute definition, which in turn refers back to the original.
- Avoids explaining *how*, *where*, or *when* the attribute is used. These properties are best documented elsewhere.
- Includes definitions of terms used within the description that are not generally known or that might be misinterpreted.

Some of the practices to *avoid* in an attribute description include:

- Simply restating or rephrasing the name of the attribute or its characteristics (such as length, data type, domain values).
- Depending solely on the use of examples as a basis for comprehension. However, one or two examples that have universal applicability go a long way toward explaining what an attribute is.
- Using a lot of technical jargon, unexplained acronyms or abbreviations, or arcane references.
- Limiting the description to a direct extract or quotation from a dictionary or encyclopedia. These types of references may be useful in forming part of the description, but relying solely on them does not give any insight into the enterprise's interest in the attribute (e.g., the *why* part of the description).

The worst situation that anyone attempting to use a model can possibly encounter is a missing description. The model is a communication device; missing descriptions severely diminish its ability to communicate. Similarly, poorly written descriptions, while better than none at all, also diminish the model's utility. Both missing or weak descriptions generally indicate that the team has not followed a rigorous modeling process.

Examples

These examples have been drawn from actual models, although they have been altered to avoid any reference to specific organizations. Note how easy it is to differentiate between good and bad descriptions.

Attribute Descriptions in Need of Improvement

location name—The name of a location.

line item number—Number assigned to an item that is not destroyed or consumed when used.

communications device type—The COMIS designator for UNICOR, UPSCOR and AMFOR comm elements.

directional indicator—E, W, N, S, SE, SW, NE, NW, NNE, ENE, ESE, SSE, SSW, WSW, WNW, NNW.

order line total quantity—A six-digit integer total.

Pretty Good Attribute Descriptions

operating quantity—The calculated, demand-driven quantity of a material item that must be maintained and replenished for use in day-to-day operations.

safety level quantity—The calculated minimum quantity of a product SKU (stock keeping unit) that must be on hand to reduce risk of out-of-stock conditions.

professional privileges date—The date upon which a health care professional is granted privileges to practice within a particular health care facility, establishing the provider's eligibility for patient care assignments and liability coverage.

4.5   ATOMIC ATTRIBUTES

Every attribute in the data model should be atomic.

Discussion

Date (1986) provides a series of definitions that will be important to our understanding of atomic attributes:

> The smallest unit of data in the relational model is an individual data value ... Such values are considered to be *atomic*—that is, they are non-decomposable so far as the model is concerned. Domains of atomic values are more accurately referred to as *simple* domains, to distinguish them from *composite* domains.

Interpreting from this definition, we can state some important characteristics of atomic attributes:

• An atomic attribute represents a single fact about the business, and does not contain within it any other facts that may be meaningful but are "hidden" to the users of the model. We present two very different practical situations where the data analyst is most likely to encounter attributes representing more than a single business fact.

Codes or identifiers. Most organizations have built sophisticated codes comprised of a series of concatenated pieces of information in an effort to "relate" different business facts. Information systems are riddled with data elements that contain position-dependent information, such as that shown later in our example. The job of the modeling team is to dig below the surface to discover the individual business facts contained in each component of these composite sets of information.

Text blocks or "comments" attributes. How many times have you heard a user say "Just give me a text block to record any additional information I might need" during a modeling session? How tempted were you to just put the attribute in and move on to the next task? Text fields or comment blocks should be investigated vigorously by the modeling team. The majority of the time, these attributes contain data that should be defined as separate, individual attributes. If you are looking at existing systems, peruse actual records of the text fields to see if there are any patterns in the recorded information. It is quite common to find vital data that has been put in a text field simply because the system had no data element(s) in which to record the values. We have found phone and fax numbers, parts lists, billing information, and other essential information recorded in undefined text fields. There are legitimate reasons to have an attribute to record unstructured information, such as customer comments, or maintenance action descriptions, or . journal article abstracts. Note, however, that the attribute still must serve a single business purpose, and record a single business "fact."

• An atomic attribute has a simple domain that is indivisible in its use within the enterprise, but which may be shared either partly or wholly with other attributes. In other words, the single business fact represented by the attribute must be supported by a simple domain. Composite domains indicate a requirement for access to information that renders the attribute non-atomic. Shared domains have no effect on the determination of whether an attribute is atomic or not; they do raise issues about the uniqueness of the attribute if the domain is enumerated.

• An atomic attribute represents a single value within the simple domain for each instance of the primary key. Remember, *relations do not contain repeating groups* (Dale, 1986). A model is not normalized if it contains any attributes representing a repeating set of values.

• Complex data types, such as photographs, bit-mapped graphics, even audio or video, do not necessarily violate the single fact concept of an atomic attribute. Remember, the issue is whether the attribute is *nondecomposable so far as the model is concerned* (e.g., so far as the enterprise is concerned), and whether its domain is *indivisible in its use* within the enterprise. The issue, then, is to determine whether the enterprise has a requirement to access the components of these data types—individual objects within a graphic, a frame or cell in a video, or an object in a photograph—thereby rendering them no longer *simple*. If there is a requirement to do so, then the model must be extended to account for the additional data requirements, and the single business fact must be decomposed into its constituent facts.

Failure to identify all attributes in the model at an atomic level results in the likelihood that important business rules will not be recorded, and access to information will be lost or at least hindered.

Examples

Our example illustrates the embedded logic that permeates so many information systems in operation today. In this case, a company has decided to implement a property management system to track equipment, furnishings, and other durable items it has acquired. The data analysis team has finished its initial model and presented it to the users, who have embraced it. This model is shown in Figure 4.4. The users especially like the "information rich" equipment identifier the data analysis team has built.

Looks like a lot information the user needs is available, right? Provided the users are properly trained, they will be able to glance at a property item identifier and be able to tell you a considerable amount of information about that piece of property. They can see from the property category code whether this is a piece of furniture, or computer equipment, or shop floor machinery. They can determine which organization is being charged depreciation and maintenance (*accountable organization*) and which organization in the company has physical possession of the item (*holding organization*). Finally they can determine if the number in fields 13 to 30 represents a serial number assigned by the manufacturer, or in cases where the manufacturer does not provide a serial number, the property tag number assigned by the company. Why stop now? Why not put all of the information about a PROPERTY ITEM in a single "smart" attribute? Because there are some fundamental problems with this attribute.

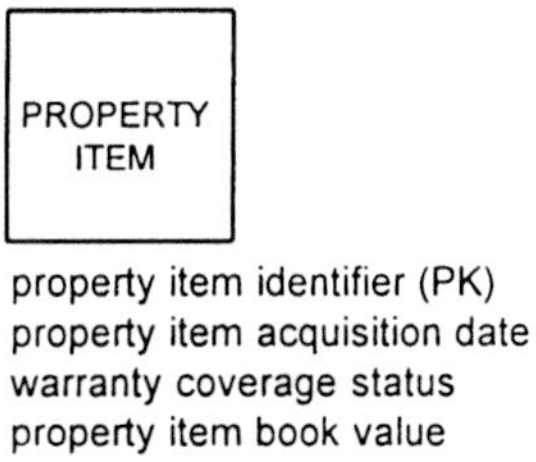

```
┌─────────────┐     ┌────────────────────────────────────────────────────┐
│ PROPERTY    │     │ Design of Property Item Identifier                 │
│  ITEM       │     │ Position 1-2    Property category code              │
│             │     │ Position 3-5    Accountable organization code       │
└─────────────┘     │ Position 6-8    Holding organization code           │
property item identifier (PK)  │ Position 9-11   Manufacturer organization code      │
property item acquisition date │ Position 12     Manufacturer serial number or company│
warranty coverage status       │                 property tag number indicator       │
property item book value       │ Position 13-30  Manufacturer serial number or company│
                    │                 property tag number                 │
                    └────────────────────────────────────────────────────┘
```

Figure 4.4   Non-atomic attribute *property item identifier.*

First, the attribute violates the generally accepted definition of an attribute. Remember that an attribute represents a single fact, single concept. Obviously, we have many facts recorded in the *property item identifier.* Second, it is inflexible. Suppose the company continues to grow, and two characters are no longer adequate for organization codes. The company moves to a three character organization code. Most likely a considerable amount of software would be built around *property item identifier* to parse and interpret its component elements. All of that would be affected, as would the data structures containing the attribute. Third, it hides or obscures characteristics of its components. It contains repeating groups, optional data, and may obscure dependencies on other elements of the model. Finally, in this particular example, *property item identifier* serves as primary key, yet its values could be subject to constant change as a piece of property moves from one *holding organization* to another. Figure 4.5 presents one of many possible resolutions. The company decided to change its property tagging policy, and began tagging all property items, maintaining the manufacturer's serial number for reference when available. Note that normalization caused the modeling team to create additional entities, and to establish a relationship with the ORGANIZATION entity. The latter was obscured by the proposed *property item identifier* in our original model.

But what of the users? Will their desire to see an encapsulated set of property item information be ignored? Not necessarily. Remember, the data model does not limit the manner in which the information is presented, and will most likely lead to physical representations that are more effective at conveying information to users. If the users still want to see their property item identifier the same as they are used to seeing it, the information is available in the model to construct a screen or report element to smash it all together.

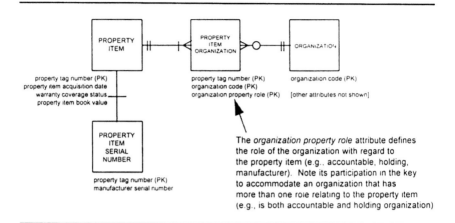

The *organization property role* attribute defines the role of the organization with regard to the property item (e.g., accountable, holding, manufacturer). Note its participation in the key to accommodate an organization that has more than one role relating to the property item (e.g., is both accountable and holding organization)

Figure 4.5   Non-atomic attribute resolved to atomic elements.

4.6   ATTRIBUTE DOMAINS

Every attribute must have a domain that consists of at least two values.

Discussion

An *attribute* is a formal relational term (Date, 1986) used to describe a business fact or concept about which the enterprise requires information, and which has a given domain of values. The attribute, therefore, is a logical representation of a set of actual data values. It describes the data requirement, and is not in and of itself the actual data required.

The issue here is whether an attribute can correctly have a domain whose set of values always (now and evermore) consists of one member. The value of that member may change over time; it does not have to be constant. However, at any point in time, there is only one valid member of its domain.

Common indications that an attribute with a single domain value has been modeled include:

- the name of the attribute referring to a specific value or values, usually those of the primary key attribute(s)
- several similar attributes in the model having variations on the name (these are the other domain values that have been incorrectly modeled)
- the attribute is in a subtype entity, yet serves as an indicator or discriminator for the supertype entity

These attributes could creep into the model for at least a couple of reasons:

* the modeling team has limited participation, resulting in a perspective that recognizes or cares about only a single value for the domain
* the attribute was defined too strictly, possibly out of context of the remainder of the model.

We have never run across a case where an attribute with a single valid value for its domain is conceptually correct. If you find one in your model, look for alternative ways of modeling the concept. As a hint, look for other attributes that appear to be very similar to the suspect attribute, and consider whether they actually represent a single business concept.

Example

In the following example, the PRODUCT entity contains several attributes that violate the single attribute domain concept. Why is this so important? Imagine what the set of attributes will include in 1999! Single domain attributes such as these introduce database maintenance problems—changes or additions that properly should be handled as INSERTs of new rows would result in changes to the database schema if this model were implemented as shown.

In a corrected model (Figure 4.7), these values have been abstracted to the *total product units shipped* attribute, and the attribute has been moved to the entity PRODUCT PERFORMANCE in recognition of the

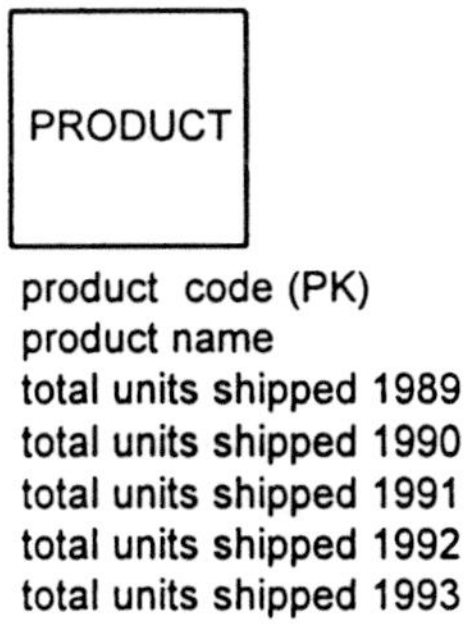

PRODUCT

product code (PK)
product name
total units shipped 1989
total units shipped 1990
total units shipped 1991
total units shipped 1992
total units shipped 1993

Figure 4.6   Single attribute domain (incorrect).

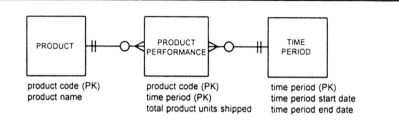

Figure 4.7   Resolution of single attribute domain.

fact that *total product units shipped* would be a repeating attribute in PRODUCT (a violation of 1NF). Note that the primary key now contains a second attribute, *time period*, to accommodate the year values (or any other defined period of time that is of interest to the business). See Chapter 9 for a further discussion of flexible modeling of time periods.

4.7   ATTRIBUTE ORIGINATION

Attributes originate in only one entity. Attributes that form the primary key of an entity may migrate (cascade) to other entities to support relationships. Non-key attributes never migrate, and exist in only one entity in the model (the one in which they are placed in accordance with the rules of normalization.)

Discussion

This rule leads us back to the many discussions we have already had about minimizing redundancy, controlling consistency, and ensuring integrity. Attribute origination rules:

• Non-key attributes originate in the entity in which they are placed through normalization. Existence of the same non-key attribute in more than one entity indicates that a problem exists either with attribute homonyms, determination of dependencies and keys (e.g., normalization), or perhaps with the integration of multiple perspectives (e.g., differences among constituent groups in the enterprise).

• Key attributes originate in one entity. Each key attribute in the model should be traceable back to a single entity, via the relationship paths along which it has cascaded.

• Each use of the key attribute in an entity other than the one it originated in must be a result of supporting a relationship (e.g., the key cascades from the "one" to the "many" side of a relationship to serve as a relationship reference).

The CASE tool you are using should help you manage origination of attributes by identifying attempts to place non-keys in more than one entity, incorrect key migrations, or attempts to reuse a key attribute without a corresponding relationship.

Examples

In our example scenario, we have a modeling team that is recording the data requirements for employee job assignments. As you can see in Figure 4.8, they have a need to relate employees to jobs, and also to retain some information about jobs and employees. The users have expressed a desire to be able to see details of the job description and the employee when they make the job assignment online. Unfortunately, the modeling team has translated the users' screen requirements into the model, ignoring the fact that the relationships between JOB AS-SIGNMENT—JOB, and JOB ASSIGNMENT—EMPLOYEE will allow a computer-human interface design team to build a screen that accommodates the users' desires without introducing redundancy into the model. Note that both *job description* and *employee* name in JOB AS-SIGNMENT also violate Second Normal Form (the attribute is partially dependent on a compound primary key).

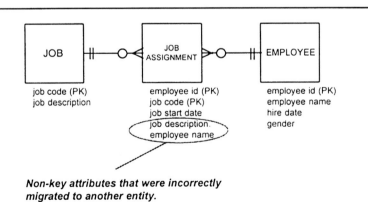

Non-key attributes that were incorrectly migrated to another entity.

Figure 4.8   Non-key attributes that incorrectly appear in two entities.

4.8 DEFAULT VALUES

Never assign default values to an attribute with the intent of using those values for insertion into a database.

Description

A default value in this context refers to one that is inserted into the data structure if no other value is provided for the attribute upon creation of a record in the table or file. It does *not* refer to the value or values displayed to the user on a screen as the first (visible) entry in a scroll window. These "screen default" values are context sensitive, and are drawn from the data values that have been recorded for the attribute in question.

Specification of default values leads to the introduction of erroneous data. It is tempting to try to find some value to insert in order to avoid creation of a null value. Regardless of what default value is selected, it will be wrong. Once entered into the database, an incorrect value takes on a legitimacy it does not deserve. Anyone accessing that information will have no way of knowing that the value is incorrect, and will use it blissfully ignorant of its true character. If enough invalid data is entered into the database, the users will eventually lose faith in the data and begin to work with other sources.

There will be infrequent cases when a default value matches a desired insertion value. A nice coincidence, but nothing more. And the value is not a default anyway—the user had a known value to insert. If you are tempted to define a default value for one or more attributes in your model, we recommend that you do not. If you do, the odds are very good that your database design team will never speak to you again. Try the following strategy instead:

- For each non-key attribute, record an edit rule that defines whether it is "add now" or "add later." The former indicates that a value must be inserted at the time a new record is created (primary keys obviously fall into this category); the latter indicates that a value may be supplied at creation of a new record, or may be added later, during an update. Note that a value is expected eventually; it is not optional or inapplicable (see Optional Attributes Rule).

- If the attribute requires a value upon creation of the record (i.e., it will be implemented using the equivalent of a NOT NULL parameter in the CREATE TABLE statement), then the requirements development team should not circumvent the requirement for a correct value by specifying an alternative value that is wrong. Of course, the eventual system users can always insert a bogus value; that's where a sound data quality engineering program, supplemented by a data management educational program, comes in to play.

* If the attribute does not require a value upon creation of a record (it has an "add later" edit rule), then unknown or unavailable attribute values should be handled using null values until the record is updated with a known value.

Example

Assume that you have been asked to review a data model and accompanying system requirements documentation. In the course of studying the model, you encounter the entities shown in Figure 4.9, annotated with a requirements statement.

At first glance this might seem reasonable. Anyone reviewing an employee's record would notice that the date is a default, and that the employee's birth date has *obviously* not been recorded. But suppose the company is considering an early retirement bonus for individuals aged 55 years and over. In order to estimate the impact of making such an

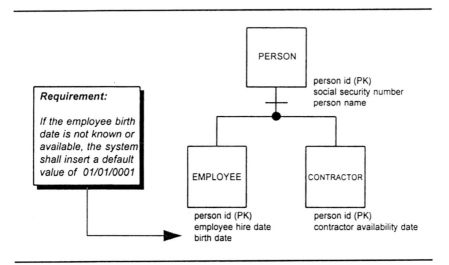

Figure 4.9   Default value identified for *birth date*.

offer, the company benefits coordinator is asked by the strategic planning committee to report the number of individuals who will be eligible (i.e., over 54 years of age) within the next year. A query of the database for "birth date" to count the number of individuals born before the specified year (say 1939) would return a result that includes the default values. Assume only 2 percent of the records have default values, and the company has 1,000 employees. The report to the planning committee will be off by a count of 20, a variance of as much as 10 to 20 percent, depending on the demographics of the company.

While this is a relatively trivial example, the reality of missing or erroneous data is very real, and has significant repercussions. In many cases, users are unaware that their data is compromised. Data modeling is a tool to improve data quality—make sure your modeling practices do not inadvertently contribute to additional problems.

4.9   SPLIT DOMAINS

Do not split single logical domains of enumerated values into multiple attributes.

Discussion

The Atomic Attribute rule established the need for an attribute to represent a single concept or single fact about the enterprise. But what if an attribute captures only part of a single concept? As a corollary to the Atomic Attribute rule, the Split Domain rule establishes the requirement for an attribute to *completely* capture a single concept. For example, you may view an individual's name as a single fact. However, it is generally accepted that a name, as defined in most European and North American nations, consists of a first name, a middle name, and a last name. These latter concepts are separate and distinguishable from an individual's full name, which is an ordered collection of three distinctly different facts (the order may be changed to fit presentation requirements, such as surname-first name-middle initial; the fact that one component of a name is the surname does not change). But you would not further subdivide a person's first name into its component parts. There is no business meaning tied to the letter 'J' in a person's name, for instance. Sure, you can sort names into alphabetized lists using the sequence of letters, but each letter still carries no *business* meaning.

It is very rare to encounter problems with overdecomposing attributes that have general domains (i.e., numeric, alphanumeric, etc.) However, you may encounter violations of this rule more frequently when dealing

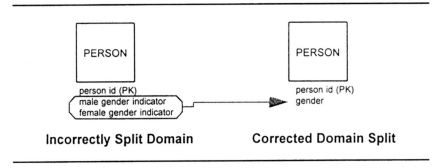

Incorrectly Split Domain   **Corrected Domain Split**

Figure 4.10   Enumerated domain split with correction.

with attributes with enumerated domains. Attempts to arbitrarily divide a logically complete domain of enumerated values into more than one attribute leads to problems in accessing and maintaining the entire domain, and results in separation of a single business concept.

Example

Figure 4.10 shows a domain that has been incorrectly split between two attributes. On the left, the single logical concept of "gender" has been split into two attributes, each with a Boolean (TRUE/FALSE) domain. The entity on the right shows the correct method for handling the concept of gender as a single attribute with an enumerated domain of "male" and "female."

4.10   MIXED AND MISREPRESENTED DOMAINS

Avoid mixing or misrepresenting domains in conflict with business rules or entity/attribute definitions.

Discussion

A mixed or misrepresented domain is one in which the specified domain of the object (entity or attribute level, we provide examples of both) is inconsistent with or in direct conflict with the stated business rule or model component definition. In the heat of data modeling, it is easy to lose track of the purpose of an entity or attribute, to essentially "forget" what the model component is supposed to represent, and to mix or misrepresent domains relative to the business rule or model component definition (our examples were drawn from actual models we reviewed). The result is a model that obscures or incorrectly represents the model component or the business rule as originally defined. The potential for doing this reinforces the need to provide sound definitions for model objects, and to maintain current and comprehensive traceability from model objects to business policies, plans, requirements statements, or other sources from which rules have been derived and which, hopefully, were used as direct input to the modeling exercise.

Examples

Our first example deals with a set of subtypes that have been defined inconsistently with some stated personnel policies for ABC company. Assume that the ABC Company has two definitive policies about its employees:

Policy 1 ABC Company hires both full-time and part-time workers.

Policy 2 ABC Company places its managers on a salary, while other employees are hourly.

After discussions with ABC's Personnel Department, the modeling team developed the model fragment shown in Figure 4.11.

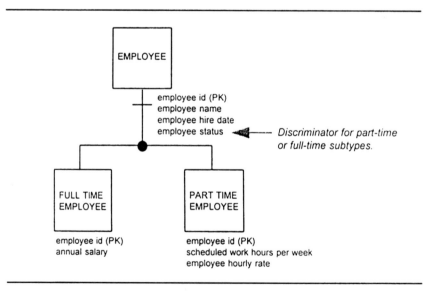

Figure 4.11   Model fragment that does not match ABC policies.

Note that the model fragment incorporates a rule that was not stated in either policy. The team incorrectly assumed that no managers (see Policy 2) would be part-time. However, there is no clear statement to that affect, and the team has mixed an employee's workweek status (e.g., full- or part-time) with pay type (e.g., salaried or hourly). This is something that should be highlighted during a conceptual review of the model, then brought before the domain experts for resolution. One potential resolution of the original model fragment is shown in Figure 4.12.

In our second example, a transportation agency for a small foreign country has installed a series of RADIO BEACONs to aid marine vessels and aircraft navigating through its coastal waters and airspace. Note the definition of values for the attribute *marine radio beacon indicator* in Figure 4.13. The domain of the indicator attribute is obscuring information, forcing anyone reading the model to interpret a value of "no" correctly as an "aviation radio beacon." Imagine if this were to be implemented in a system. Unfortunately, this kind of interpretive domain definition is all too familiar. The purpose of modeling is to be as explicit and unambiguous as possible. Be extremely careful in naming, defining, and establishing enumerated domains to ensure that these

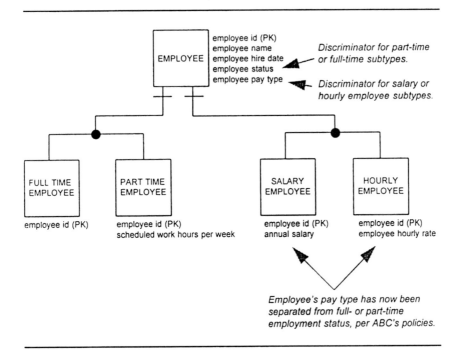

Figure 4.12   Resolution of mixed domains.

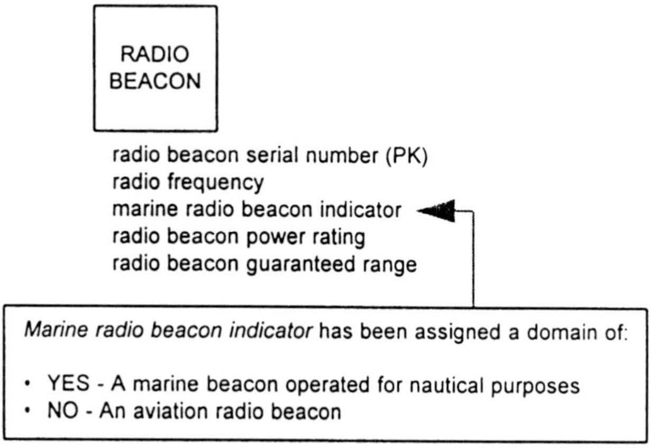

Figure 4.13   Improperly defined attribute domain.

are consistent and will be correctly interpreted by both designers and eventual users.

In our revised model, we have substituted *radio beacon type* for *marine radio beacon indicator*, and clarified the domain.

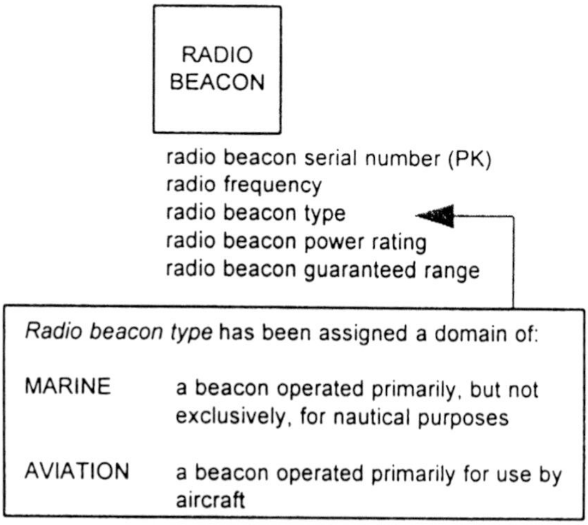

Figure 4.14   Revised attribute definition and domain enumeration.

4.11   OPTIONAL ATTRIBUTES

Move attributes from entities in which they are optional to an entity (creating one if necessary) in which the attribute is mandatory for all instances. Every instance of an entity should eventually have a value for each attribute within it.

Discussion

An optional attribute is one that is never assigned a value for one or more occurrences of the entity. In other words, the attribute simply does not apply to certain entity occurrences. This indicates that there exists some business fact differentiating those occurrences for which the attribute is a valid characteristic, and those for which it is not. For example, not every individual living in the United States has a Social Security number (SSN). Individuals who have been assigned an SSN are eligible for certain benefits under our current form of social security administration. They are subject to a different set of business rules than those individuals who do not have an SSN. If our enterprise has rules that apply only to those individuals with SSNs, then we need to ensure that we have a means of efficiently separating them from people without SSNs, so that we may apply our rules (e.g., withhold social security taxes from pay). The point is, in our simple example, we have two types of people, those with SSNs and those without, and we may elect or be required to treat them differently in accordance with the rules of our business.

Our objective in developing data models is to depict the business rules and logic as precisely as possible, and we need to differentiate groups or types or categories of things in order to obtain the level of precision necessary to build information systems that support the business rules. Optional attributes, when left unresolved, represent unclear or incomplete separation of a unique business fact. In addition, optional attributes lead to introduction of null values in implemented databases; extensive arguments relating to problems with null values have been advanced by Date and others.

In complying with this rule, be careful to distinguish between the following types of attributes:

- those attributes that, for some instances of the entity, will never have a value (other than null), and
- those attributes that may not be assigned a value upon creation of the entity instance, but that must eventually be assigned a value.

In the latter case, we simply have a difference in the timing of creation. An attribute where all entity instances will eventually have a value is *not* an optional attribute.

Clive Finkelstein describes one of his Business Normal Forms (Finkelstein, 1989) to deal with optional attributes. He refers to Fourth Business Normal Form (4BNF) entities as meeting the following test:

> . . . when an attribute has been relocated from an entity where it is optional to an entity where it is wholly dependent on the key and must exist, and so is mandatory.

The Federal Information Processing Standard for IDEF1X data modeling technique also identifies what is referred to as the No Null rule. In both cases, rules have been established to remove optional attributes to entities in which their existence is mandatory, although as we discussed before, not necessarily immediate. Both 4BNF and the FIPS No Null rule specify resolution of optional attributes in essentially the same manner:

Step 1 Create a subtype entity that is a specialization of the entity in which the optional attribute resides. The original entity becomes the supertype in a generalization-specialization hierarchy.

Step 2 Migrate the primary key of the supertype to the subtype entity.

Step 3 Move the optional attribute from the original entity (now the supertype) to the subtype, where it is functionally dependent on the primary key (remember, the primary key in a subtype entity is the same as that of the supertype) and where it is now mandatory for all instances of the subtype.

Step 4 Define a subtype discriminator, in accordance with the Subtype Discriminators rule, to define occurrences of the supertype that will have corresponding occurrences of the subtype.

Examples

Since we know that a primary key can never be optional (or at least *should* never be optional), we will look at the two scenarios in which an optional attribute may appear—a non-key attribute, and a migrated key supporting a relationship that is optional in nature at the parent entity.

Our first example deals with a non-key attribute that is entirely optional—there are instances of the entity that will *never* have a value

EQUIPMENT
ITEM

equipment item number (PK)
equipment item book value
equipment item acquisition date
equipment item warranty expiration date

Applies only to equipment items
purchased with a warranty.

Figure 4.15   Unresolved optional attribute.

for that attribute. Assume that a small company is tracking equipment it uses in its daily operations. Some of the equipment it purchased came with a warranty, while other pieces of equipment are not warranted. Figure 4.15 depicts the EQUIPMENT ITEM entity as originally modeled. The attribute *equipment item warranty expiration date* is optional—some of the EQUIPMENT ITEMs are not and never will be under warranty.

Following the resolution steps prescribed for optional attributes, the model has been refined to depict the special case of EQUIPMENT ITEMs that have warranties. Note two key aspects of the refinement. First, a subtype for non-warranty equipment was not created. All information about non-warranted items is present in the attributes of EQUIPMENT ITEM. Second, note the presence of the attribute *equipment item warranty status*. This new attribute is referred to as a subtype discriminator, and establishes whether each EQUIPMENT ITEM has a warranty (and thus requires creation of an instance of EQUIPMENT ITEM WARRANTY) or not (and thus requires no further information pertaining to warranty).

Our second example deals with an optional foreign key. The fact that an optional attribute is a foreign key has little bearing on the manner in which the model is refined. The same resolution strategy is performed. However, it does illustrate the implications that this rule has for improving representation of business rules. In this case, MATERIAL TYPE represents a standard stock item held in a company warehouse. Some of the materials held are considered hazardous (flammable,

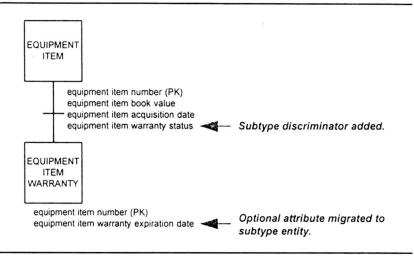

Figure 4.16 Resolution of optional attribute.

corrosive, poisonous), and the company has established a hazardous material rating and response procedure to ensure proper handling and rapid response to incidents involving the materials.

However, only certain types of material are considered hazardous (note optional nature of the association from MATERIAL TYPE to HAZ-

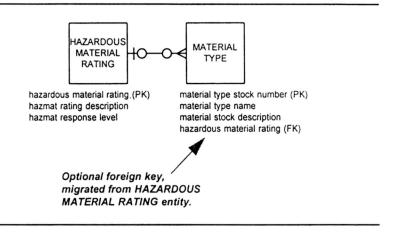

Figure 4.17 Unresolved optional foreign key attribute.

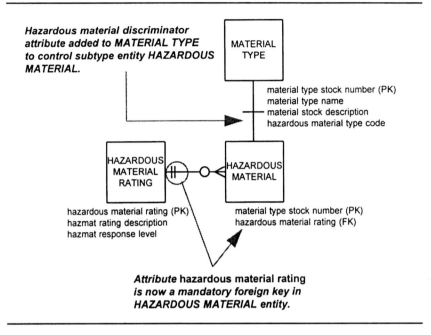

Figure 4.18   Resolved optional foreign key attribute.

ARDOUS MATERIAL RATING). Therefore, the business rules and information requirements pertaining to management of hazardous materials only apply to those types of material deemed hazardous. In order to refine the model to precisely depict the business rules, and to position the design team to develop a better database design, the HAZARDOUS MATERIAL entity has been created in Figure 4.18. Note the migration of the *hazardous material rating* foreign key to HAZARDOUS MATERIAL, and the change to the nature of the relationship to HAZARDOUS MATERIAL RATING (now from HAZARDOUS MATERIAL, rather than MATERIAL TYPE). Also note the introduction of *hazardous material type code*, a discriminator attribute serving to control population of the new subtype entity.

4.12   PRIMARY KEY ATTRIBUTES

Every entity in a data model shall have a primary key whose values uniquely identify occurrences of the entity.

Discussion

A criticism that is leveled at various data modeling representations is the insistence of data model developers to have a primary key for every entity in the model. Usually, these comments (often made by object modelers!) are followed with examples of real-world objects for which no primary key exists. How does one distinguish between the numerous quotes made on an individual stock during a trading session or the mileage an individual drives to work every day?

Entities are representations of a person, place, or thing. If we have two occurrences of an entity, then we must have a mechanism for distinguishing between them. The only reliable method for identifying an individual occurrence of an entity in a data model is the primary key. A primary key is an attribute, or combination of attributes whose values uniquely identify each entity occurrence. Each and every entity in a data model must have a clearly identified primary key (Date, 1986).

Example

In Figure 4.19, the *social security number* is the unique identifier for the PERSON entity, *organization name* is the primary key for the OR-GANIZATION entity, and PERSON ORGANIZATION is missing a primary key. It appears the data modeler has forgot to cascade the primary keys into the model or is undecided about the unique identifier for PER-SON ORGANIZATION. In either case, it is a violation of the primary key rule. All entities must have a mechanism to uniquely identify occurrences.

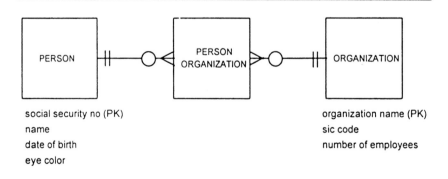

social security no (PK)   organization name (PK)

name   sic code

date of birth   number of employees

eye color

Figure 4.19   Entity missing primary key.

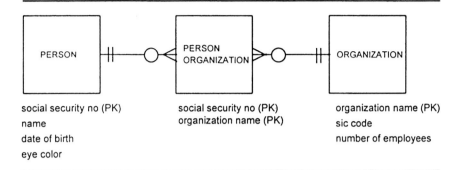

social security no (PK)
name
date of birth
eye color

social security no (PK)
organization name (PK)

organization name (PK)
sic code
number of employees

Figure 4.20   Primary key resolved.

The situation is resolved in Figure 4.20 by cascading the primary keys from the two parent or owner entities (PERSON and ORGANIZATION) into the PERSON ORGANIZATION entity. PERSON ORGANIZATION now has a compound primary key composed of *social security number* and *organization name*. All entities in the model have a primary key.

In the second example (Figure 4.21), the PERSON entity contains a number of attributes, but none have been designated as the primary key. The attributes *social security number, passport number, employee id*, and *drivers license number* are all candidates for the primary key designation.

PERSON

social security number
passport number
employee id
drivers license number
date of birth
name
eye color

Figure 4.21   Primary key not declared.

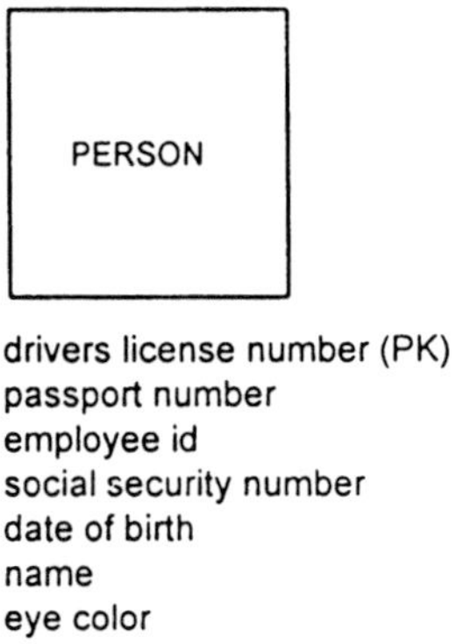

PERSON

drivers license number (PK)
passport number
employee id
social security number
date of birth
name
eye color

Figure 4.22   Primary key identified.

If the application domain is all Maryland drivers (see Figure 4.22), then the candidate key, *driver's license number* appears to be an acceptable choice for this situation. Differing application domains will influence the analyst's decision.

4.13   PRIMARY KEY CHARACTERISTICS

A primary key shall be (1) stable, (2) minimal, (3) factless, (4) definitive, and (5) accessible.

Discussion

Entities contain an attribute or combination of attributes that are used to uniquely identify an entity occurrence. These attributes are known as *candidate keys*. The selected candidate key becomes the primary key, while the remaining candidate keys become *alternate keys* or *selection attributes*. For example, a U.S. citizen may have a driver's license number, a passport number, and a social security number. Given the proper domain for the entity, each one of these attributes may be used as the primary identifier. How does the data modeler determine the best alternative ?

The first characteristic of a good primary key is *stability* (Brooks, 1992). The value of a primary key must not change or become null throughout the life of each entity occurrence. If a primary key value changes, then it is another occurrence, it is not the same object. A stable primary key (Whitener, 1989) will help the model maintain referential integrity and guarantee update rules will not produce anomalies.

The primary key must be composed of the *minimal* number of attributes that ensures entity occurrences are unique. Extremely large composite primary keys are discouraged. If a primary key is compound, each component must be examined to ensure that its participation contributes to the uniqueness of the entity. The data modeler should ask, if this attribute were not included as part of the primary key, is every occurrence uniquely identifiable? If it is, the component should be eliminated from consideration.

The primary key must be *factless*. It should not contain "intelligence"—groupings of digits or characters within a value of the key that hold additional meta-information. This violates atomicity requirements for attributes, increases the potential that the primary key value would change, and is an indicator that business rules have not been explored in the required detail.

A primary key must be *definitive* in that a value exists for every entity occurrence at creation time. The primary key acts as a constraining mechanism for the entity because an entity occurrence cannot be instantiated unless the primary key value also exists.

Finally, the primary key must be *accessible* (Whitener, 1989) to all users. If we have selected a primary key to uniquely identify an entity of some type, then we need to ensure that it is available to any and all creators and consumers of that entity.

Examples

In Figure 4.23, the entity domain is, "all of the organizations that are publicly traded on the NASDAQ, AMEX, and NYSE." An analyst working in this environment would most likely consider an organization's *stock symbol* to be the primary key.

Additional analysis, however, shows that an organization's *stock symbol* is in fact unstable. An organization may be acquired, merged, or renamed. Each of these activities may change an organization's stock symbol. Imagine trying to maintain this model during the financial turbulence of the 1980s. A more stable model is portrayed in Figure 4.26. An artificial key is used to stabilize the primary key, and an additional relationship describes the business rule, "an organization may contain more than one stock symbol." The stock symbol history is captured in the ORGANIZATION STOCK SYMBOL entity.

stock symbol (PK)
organization name

Figure 4.23   Unstable primary key.

In the second example, an employee is identified by his or her *employee id* and their *social security number*. If an employee id is unique, then there is no need for the social security number to be included. This illustrates the *fat key concept*—a component of the primary key is not required for uniqueness.

Figure 4.26 resolves the fat key. The employee id is the sole designator and social security number has been moved to non-key status.

In the third example, intelligent keys obscure business rules needed to ensure completeness of the data model. The PRODUCT entity appears to contain a good identifier for an occurrence of a PRODUCT, *product code*.

Closer inspection by the analyst reveals *product code* has three embedded components : *plant id*, *product category*, and *product identifier*. Each of the components has associated business rules that must be

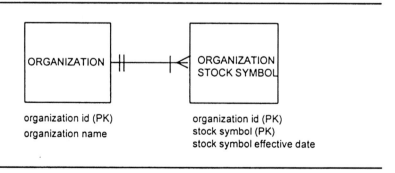

organization id (PK)   organization id (PK)
organization name   stock symbol (PK)
                                     stock symbol effective date

Figure 4.24   Stable primary key.

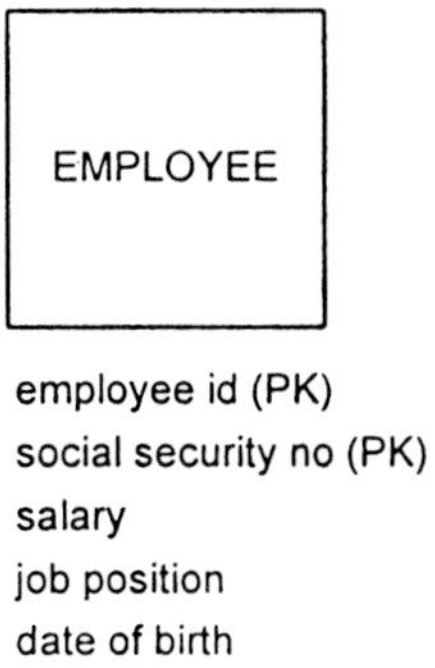

Figure 4.25   "Fat" key.

Figure 4.26   Minimal primary key.

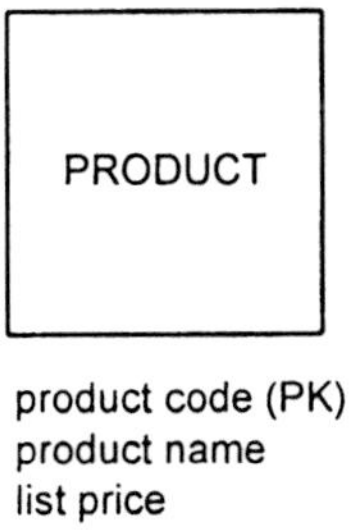

Figure 4.27   Intelligent key.

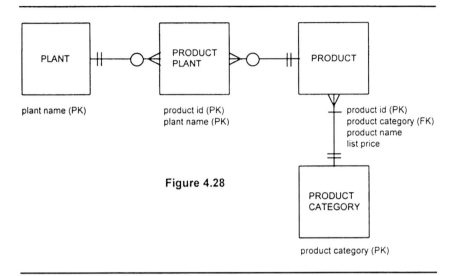

Figure 4.28

Figure 4.28   Factless primary key.

placed into the data model. The hidden intelligence is extracted to form Figure 4.28.

Fourth, primary keys, unlike other attributes, must contain a value when the entity is created. If this were not true, then there would be entity occurrences that could not be explicitly referenced, and the integrity of our models would be in doubt. Figure 4.29 shows a PERSON

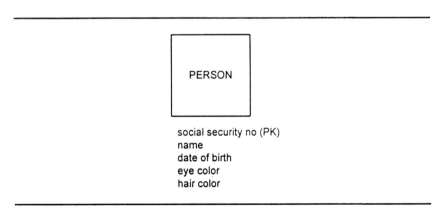

Figure 4.29   Invalid primary key (not definitive).

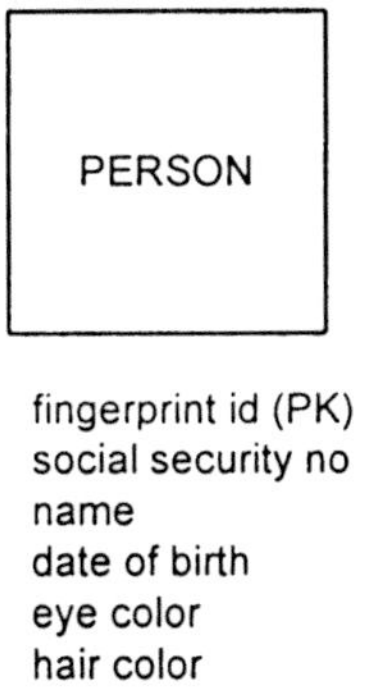

PERSON

fingerprint id (PK)
social security no
name
date of birth
eye color
hair color

Figure 4.30   Definitive primary key.

entity identified by his or her *social security number*. If the domain were, "all U.S. citizens," this would not be a definitive primary key. Children are not required to have a social security number until two years of age.

A more appropriate primary identifier may be a *fingerprint id* (see Figure 4.30). This complex data type may be used to identify all U.S. citizens and can be used at entity creation time. All U.S. citizens have their fingerprints on record.

In the last example, Figure 4.31 represents an entity that captures

AGENT

top secret clearance id (PK)
name
date of birth
social security no

Figure 4.31   Inaccessible primary key.

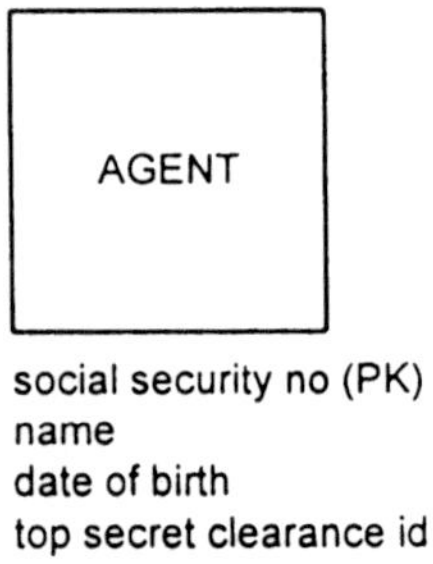

Figure 4.32 Accessible primary key.

data regarding top secret agents out in the field. Every agent has a *top secret clearance id* that uniquely identifies that agent. The problem with this representation is that not every organizational unit has access to this attribute. It can only be viewed by employees with the highest levels of security. This renders it incapable of being designated as a primary key.

Figure 4.32 updates the AGENT entity with a new primary key, *social security number*. All organizational units have read authority to this attribute and can reference other information contained in the entity. The attribute *top secret clearance id* has been moved to a non-key attribute position.

4.14 OPTIONAL PRIMARY KEYS

Primary keys shall not, in part or whole, be optional.

Discussion

Values for primary keys, by definition, cannot be optional (i.e., null), as this would render them incapable of uniquely identifying an occurrence of the entity. This rule holds for the entire primary key as well as each individual component. If a component of the primary key can be null, then it may not participate as a primary identifier. Optional components of a primary key compromise the quality of the data and obscure business rules.

Examples

The AUTOMOBILE Occurrence Table in Figure 4.33 has no vehicle identification number for the Toyota Tercel. This is a violation of the optional primary key rule. There is no way to distinguish between the two Toyota Tercels. Unique identification is the responsibility of the primary key. Without a populated value, we have no integrity in our data model. A primary key value must be created when the entity is instantiated.

The analyst has to discover why the vehicle identification number is null. Has there been a misinterpretation of a business rule? In this example, the problem is an undiscovered business rule, "An automobile

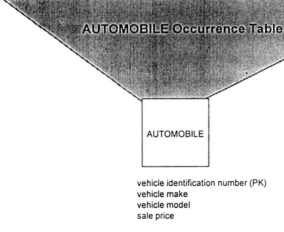

vehicle identification number (PK)	vehicle make	vehicle model	sale price
02 - 70987 - 89746 - DF	Toyota	Tercel	$11,210
19 - 33012 - 43002 - DC	Chrysler	LeBaron	$18,100
--------------------------------	Toyota	Tercel	$11,210
20 - 43987 - 38162 - MD	Volvo	850 XL	$34,130
11 - 09479 - 25093 - CA	BMW	325 i	$25,670
09 - 03432 - 34493 - AK	Saab	9000s	$38,990

AUTOMOBILE Occurrence Table

AUTOMOBILE

vehicle identification number (PK)
vehicle make
vehicle model
sale price

Figure 4.33   Optional primary key.

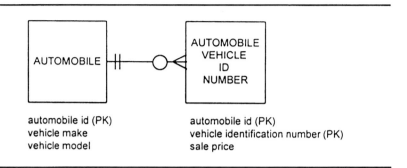

automobile id (PK)   automobile id (PK)
vehicle make   vehicle identification number (PK)
vehicle model   sale price

Figure 4.34   Optional primary key resolved.

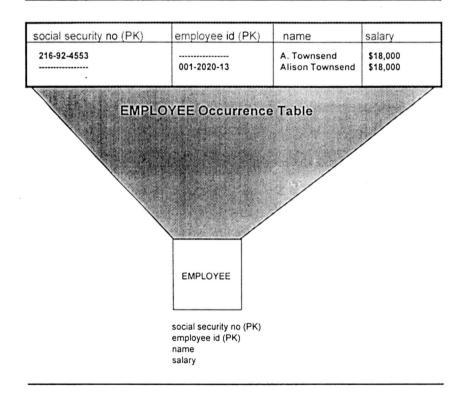

social security no (PK)
employee id (PK)
name
salary

Figure 4.35   Optional primary key component.

may have zero, one, or many vehicle identification numbers. A new one is assigned each time the vehicle is sold. This explains why the vehicle identification number is null in the occurrence table. It cannot be used as the primary key. An artificial key, *automobile id*, is assigned as the primary key and *vehicle identification number* is moved to the AUTO-MOBILE VEHICLE ID NUMBER to satisfy the business rule. The *sale price* is also moved to the new entity (see Figure 4.34).

As a second example, Figure 4.35 shows the EMPLOYEE entity, its attributes, and the Occurrence Table. The compound primary key, *social security number* and *employee id*, as a whole, maintains a value, but its constituent parts are intermittently null. This compromises the integrity of the model. In this instance, we do not know if we have two employees or one.

To resolve the situation, the analyst sought clarification on a few business rules concerning employees. The organization captures the

Applicable Business Rules

- All employees must provide their social security numbers to Human Resources for Federal income tax purposes.

- All contacts with individuals outside the organization will be logged. Minimum reporting requirements are the individuals names.

- Individuals who have accepted employment offers with our organization will be assigned internal identifiers. This will be placed on their timesheets and paychecks to uniquely identify individual employees.

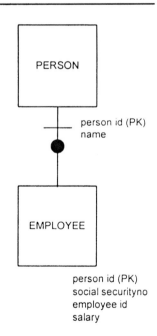

Figure 4.36 Optional Primary Key Component Resolved.

social security number and employee id only for employees. It appears A. Townsend and Alison Townsend are the same individual. The data model is updated in Figure 4.36 with this additional input. The primary key is redefined as an artificial key and the attributes, *social security number* and *employee id*, move to non-key status in EMPLOYEE.

4.15   REPEATING PRIMARY KEYS

Primary keys shall not be repeating.

Discussion

Repeating primary keys signify identical occurrences of the same entity or indicate that the primary key is repeating in relationship to some other value. In the latter case, the model is not fully normalized and bears further investigation.

Examples

As a first example, repeating primary keys are discouraged because they add redundancy to the model. Imagine the situation portrayed in Figure 4.37. The PERSON entity is identified by his or her *name*. The Occurrence Table clearly shows a problem with this structure; John Doe holds three driver's licenses and his information is repeated for every occurrence. The primary key, *name*, is repeating in relationship to the *drivers license number*.

The analyst has resolved the problem by reviewing the business rules. The assumption, "a person may hold one driver's license" is incorrect. A person may hold more than one driver's license from different locations. The analyst has introduced the PERSON LICENSE entity in Figure 4.38 to resolve the redundancy. In addition, two more information requirements were uncovered, *date of issue* and *place of issue*.

In a second example, data models provide us with a nonredundant view of an organization's information requirements. The introduction of a primary key whose values are repetitious violates the relational model. This (Figure 4.39) is exactly the problem we try to solve with these models.

A repeating primary key introduces redundancy into the model and increases the cost of maintaining quality data. This is an obvious error in the model and must be resolved before proceeding. It violates the fundamental principals of the relational model and introduces integrity problems.

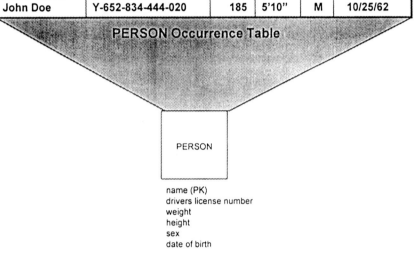

name (PK)	drivers license number	weight	height	sex	date of birth
John Doe	R-526-603-441-822	185	5'10"	M	10/25/62
James Christian	W-348-098-321-009	210	6'3"	M	08/28/60
John Doe	H-000-212-431-222	185	5'10"	M	10/25/62
Dan O'Brien	X-111-999-276-465	311	5'11"	M	02/12/38
John Doe	Y-652-834-444-020	185	5'10"	M	10/25/62

PERSON Occurrence Table

PERSON

name (PK)
drivers license number
weight
height
sex
date of birth

Figure 4.37   Repeating primary key.

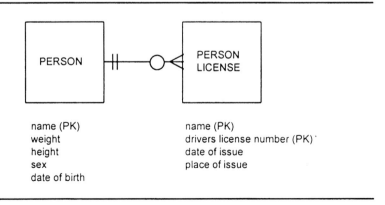

PERSON

PERSON
LICENSE

name (PK)
weight
height
sex
date of birth

name (PK)
drivers license number (PK)
date of issue
place of issue

Figure 4.38   Repeating primary key resolved.

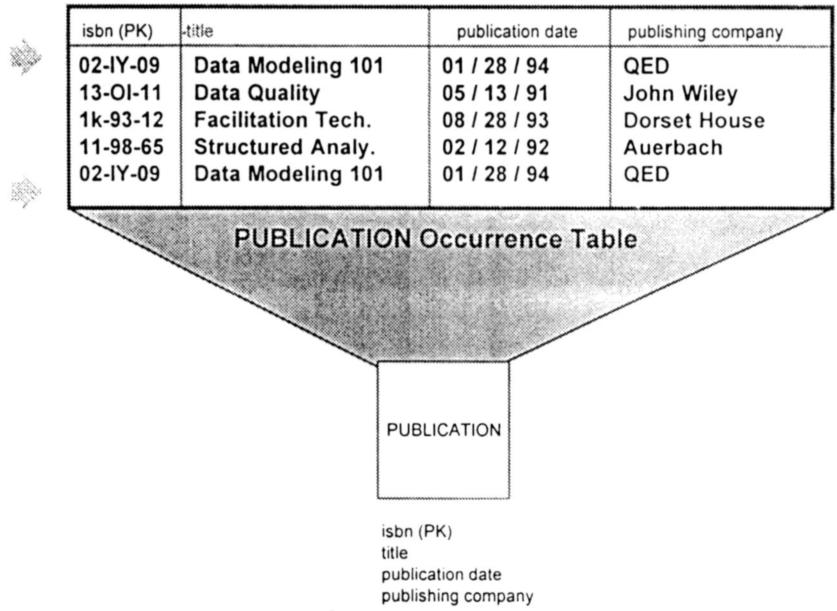

isbn (PK)	title	publication date	publishing company
02-IY-09	Data Modeling 101	01 / 28 / 94	QED
13-OI-11	Data Quality	05 / 13 / 91	John Wiley
1k-93-12	Facilitation Tech.	08 / 28 / 93	Dorset House
11-98-65	Structured Analy.	02 / 12 / 92	Auerbach
02-IY-09	Data Modeling 101	01 / 28 / 94	QED

PUBLICATION Occurrence Table

PUBLICATION

isbn (PK)
title
publication date
publishing company

Figure 4.39   Repeating primary key.

4.16   ARTIFICIAL KEYS

Artificial keys are permissible under one of the following prescribed circumstances: (1) no attribute possesses all the primary key characteristics, or 2) candidate keys are large and complex.

Discussion

An artificial key is a single key attribute whose values have no business meaning, but serve to uniquely identify an entity occurrence. There are several reasons that a data model may contain artificial keys (also known as surrogate keys, pseudo-keys or system-generated keys, although this latter term implies some assumptions about how values will be assigned): There is no natural key available, or a large and/or extremely complex key is currently utilized.

Entities are often discovered that *do not have any readily identifi-*

able primary keys. The attributes may be subject to change (update) during the life of an entity occurrence, or they may contain other characteristics (intelligence, not available during creation), which render them ineligible to be a primary key. In this situation, an artificial key is a perfectly acceptable alternative.

Another situation that suggests the use of an artificial key is when the *size and complexity* of any alternative primary key(s) would detract from the ability of subject matter experts and technical developers to effectively interpret and use the model. Models with complex relationships (compound keys cascading from entity to child entity, to child entity, and so on) usually contain instances where artificial keys can be applied to clarify the model.

It is interesting to note that the object-oriented community utilizes object identifiers (oids) in all of their modeling activities. The object identifier, which is nothing more than an artificial key, is an implicit part of every object model.

Examples

In one example, if the candidate primary key is not under the control of the enterprise, then it is more likely to change than if it was not. In this case an artificial key can be introduced. In Figure 4.40, a *passport number* is used to identify a PERSON occurrence. If we assume a domain of "all travelers requiring a passport," then this may appear to be an appropriate primary key.

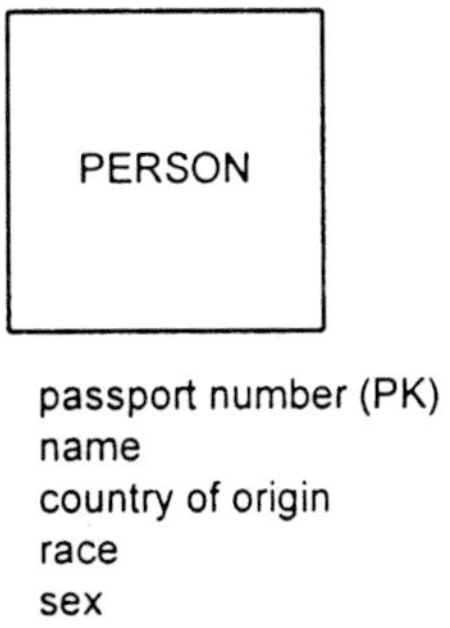

PERSON

passport number (PK)
name
country of origin
race
sex

Figure 4.40   Uncontrolled primary key.

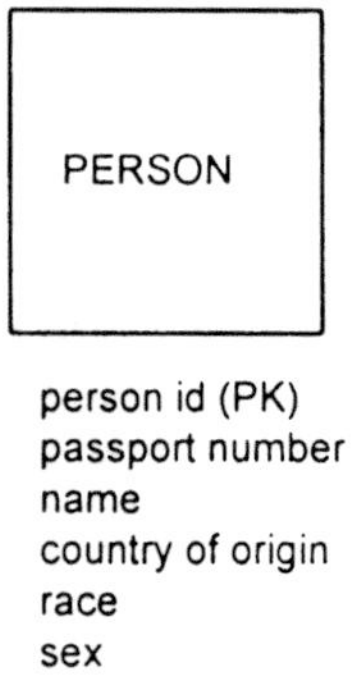

PERSON

person id (PK)
passport number
name
country of origin
race
sex

Figure 4.41   Artificial key inserted.

A *passport number*, however, is not under the control of our organization and is more likely to change, as passports have a finite lifetime and must be replaced or reissued with a new number. An artificial key, *person id*, is substituted for *passport number*. This change will make the model more stable and allow for the new passport number to replace the older one without affecting the primary key (see Figure 4.41).

In a the second example, Figure 4.42, an AIRPLANE or other carrier must be concerned with the LOAD that it takes from the origin to destination point. A LOAD can be packages, letters, people, or a variety of other transportable items. How does the analyst identify a particular LOAD? In the example below, each occurrence is identified by the *departure point, destination point, date of departure,* and the *time of departure.* As LOAD is associated with other entities, such as LOAD STRUCTURE—a recursive association—all four components of the primary key are cascaded into the other dependent entities. This can present problems to business users as they attempt to digest their data models. Does LOAD STRUCTURE easily communicate to subject matter experts?

An artificial key is introduced in Figure 4.43 to make it more understandable than the large, unruly key above. The artificial key, *load id,* allows all of the business information to be represented, reduces the overall complexity of the data model, and allows reviewers of the data model to gain a more immediate understanding of the information presented.

In the third example, an artificial key should be introduced with care. The use of artificial keys in the data modeling community is in-

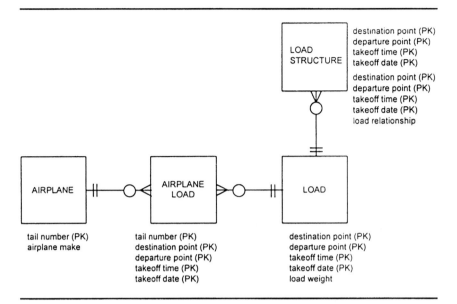

Figure 4.42   Large and complex primary keys.

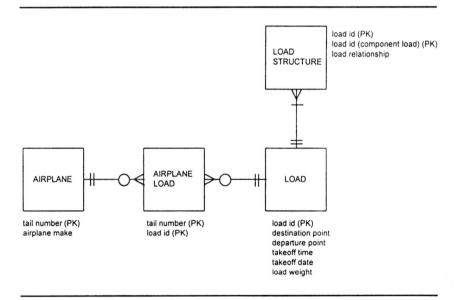

Figure 4.43   Artificial key introduction.

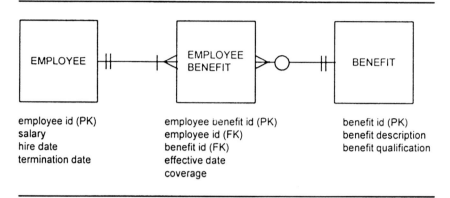

Figure 4.44   Inappropriate artificial key use.

creasing, but they are often overused. In Figure 4.44, EMPLOYEE is identified by a natural key, *employee id*, and BENEFIT is identified by *benefit id*. The problem with the model fragment is the associative entity, EMPLOYEE BENEFIT. We maintain referential integrity by cascading *benefit id* and *employee id* into EMPLOYEE BENEFIT. These two attributes are sufficient to guarantee uniqueness and should serve as the primary key. The data modeler, however, has added the artificial key, *employee benefit id*, to serve in the primary key role.

This introduces an extraneous attribute into the model and potential integrity problems. *Only independent entities may contain artificial keys as their wholly defined primary identifier.* Figure 4.45 corrects this.

In our fourth example, natural keys versus artificial keys is a dis-

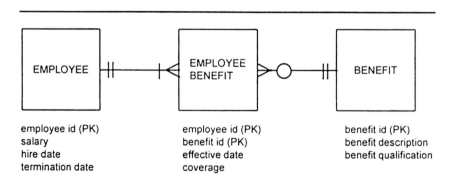

Figure 4.45   Artificial key removed.

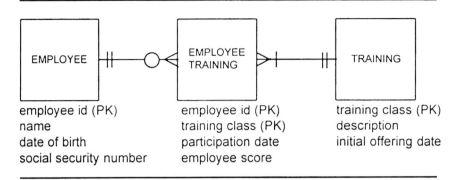

Figure 4.46 Natural keys.

cussion that occurs daily between data modelers. Natural keys, if they are present, are the preferred method for primary identification. One problem with their use is the scope of the project and the reusability of the models. For example, let's define the domain for our modeling effort as the "training we provide to our employees." We may have a model fragment as seen in figure 4.46. EMPLOYEE is defined by the natural key, *employee id*, TRAINING is defined by the natural key, *training class*. EMPLOYEE TRAINING is identified by the compound key, *employee id* and *training class*.

This is fine for this domain, but what happens when we begin to expand our data model to include other individuals, such as customers, marketing contacts, or family members? A generalization hierarchy will be constructed to accommodate other individuals and the natural key, *employee id*, no longer is valid for all individuals. An artificial key must be inserted. Figure 4.47 corrects this.

The larger the scope of the data model, the more difficult it is to continue to utilize natural keys. They are very good for specific domains, but enterprise models or those that cross multiple organizational boundaries are difficult to define in this manner.

4.17 TWO OR MORE ENTITIES WITH IDENTICAL PRIMARY KEYS

No two entities shall have a primary key comprised of the same attribute or set of attributes, with the exception of entities within a generalization hierarchy.

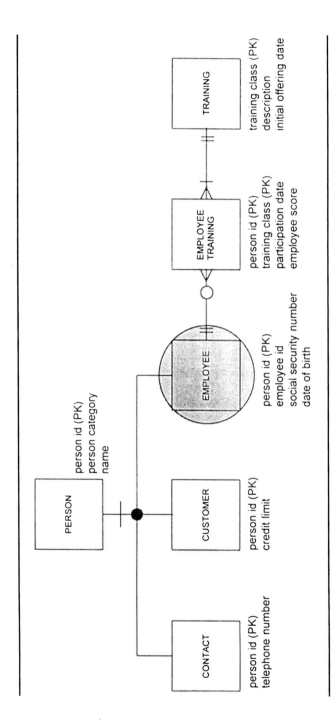

Figure 4.47 Artificial key inserted.

Discussion

The existence of two entities with the same set of attributes serving as the primary key indicates one of two circumstances:

- The entities actually represent two different "things" in the business, and the primary keys in one or both of the entities require further development and refinement; or,
- The entities actually represent the same "thing" in the business, and should be carefully re-evaluated to reconcile the differences.

Correct resolution of this problem may require careful examination—in coordination with subject matter experts—of other properties of the entities (e.g., entity definitions or entity-attribute domains), the business statements and rules linked to the entity, or the use of the entity in process models. The sequence of primary keys is irrelevant in assessing duplication—primary keys consisting of the same set of attributes are considered duplicated, regardless of sequence.

Examples

In the first example, Figure 4.48 demonstrates how entities with the same primary key may emerge during the course of modeling. Generally, these are easily identified by the modeling team. In the example, two data models have been created during concurrent modeling sessions. Workshop One participants consist of individuals who work on aircraft. They have created two entities that reflect the domain they are familiar with, AIRPLANE and PILOT. Workshop Two participants consisted of senior level managers. Their perspective includes other trans-

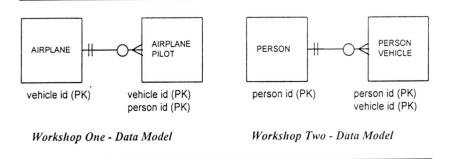

Workshop One - Data Model   *Workshop Two - Data Model*

Figure 4.48   Identical primary keys.

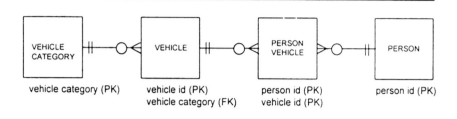

Figure 4.49   Consolidated workshop model.

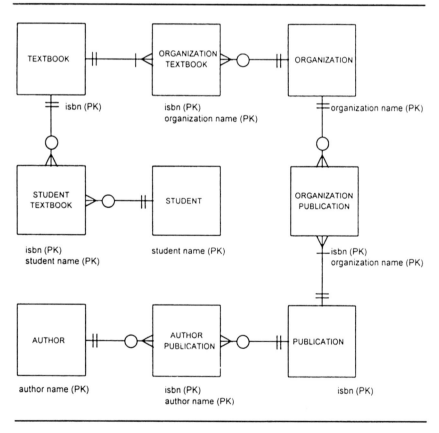

Figure 4.50   Identical primary keys.

portation mechanisms, of which an AIRPLANE is one type. Their model is more general to include the other types.

Both workshop facilitators recognize the importance of one data model. At the end of their weekly sessions, they get together and begin to resolve inconsistencies between the data models. The primary keys in AIRPLANE PILOT and PERSON VEHICLE are identical, even though their sequence is reversed. These are resolved in Figure 4.49. Note that the analysts chose to portray the model at the level of abstraction in line with the senior management group. This will provide the group with more stability than the model developed by the participants in Workshop One.

In Figure 4.50, the analysts are developing a data model that contains two entities with an *isbn* as the primary key. The two entities should have their definitions examined to determine if they are the same object, or perhaps a part of the same generalization structure. Without non-key attributes it is difficult to make this decision. Note the presence of AUTHOR and STUDENT in the model: These should be reviewed to determine if a more appropriate structure can be applied to this domain.

One possible resolution of this problem is portrayed in Figure 4.51.

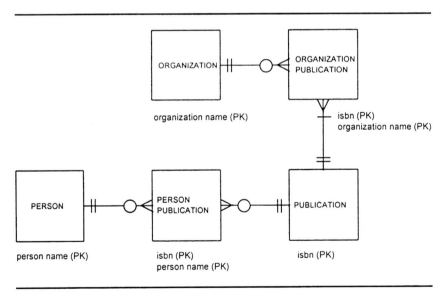

Figure 4.51   Identical primary keys resolved.

TEXTBOOK is assumed to be another type of PUBLICATION. There are no additional attributes in either entity, so they are collapsed into the PUBLICATION object. The STUDENT and AUTHOR entities are contained in the PERSON entity below. The attributes *student name* and *author name* are abstracted into *person name*. All of the information contained in the model above is still represented below.

4.18   INDEPENDENT ENTITY PRIMARY KEY ORIGINATION

At least one new primary key shall originate in each independent entity.

Discussion

An independent entity is one that does not participate as a child in identification-dependent relationships with other entities in the model. In other words, it does not require the primary key of another entity to help establish unique identification for occurrences. Therefore, its identifier (primary key) must originate in the entity—migration of all or part of its primary key from a parent would create an identification dependence.

This is an important concept for the Quality Assurance effort because it impacts the referential integrity of the model. In order to ensure proper navigation through all parts of the model, the analyst must look and see that the primary keys are created in the proper places, and then cascaded through the rest of the model. In addition, many data modeling notations employ distinct graphical notations for describing independent entities versus dependent entities. This syntax is seldom enforced by the supporting CASE product, and therefore must be captured during the review process.

Examples

In the first example, Figure 4.52, PERSON CLASSIFICATION, PERSON, and ORGANIZATION entities are independent entities; they do not require another primary key to uniquely identify entity occurrences. The associative entity, ORGANIZATION PERSON, requires the primary key from PERSON and ORGANIZATION for unique identification and is, therefore, a dependent entity. The independent entities, PERSON CLASSIFICATION, PERSON, and ORGANIZATION must introduce a new primary key into the model. They do!

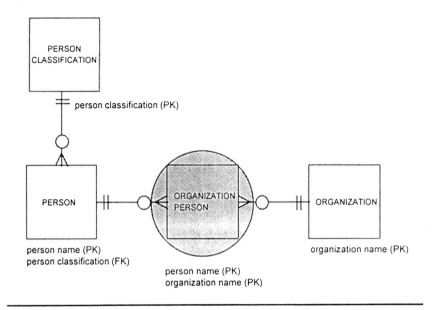

Figure 4.52   Dependent entity.

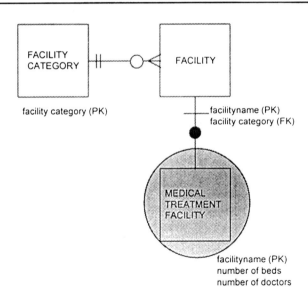

Figure 4.53   Dependent entity.

In our second example, generalization hierarchies can have both independent and dependent entities in the same structure. The supertype is usually an independent entity, while the subtype is always dependent. The subtype is required to be dependent because it cannot exist without its parent object, the supertype. In Figure 4.53, FACILITY CATEGORY and FACILITY do not require any other primary keys for unique identification. MEDICAL TREATMENT FACILITY is a subtype of FACILITY and inherits its primary key, *facility name*. It is therefore dependent upon the existence of a FACILITY. FACILITY CATEGORY and FACILITY must introduce new primary keys into the data model. MEDICAL TREATMENT FACILITY is not responsible for the generation of a new primary key.

4.19   PRIMARY KEY MIGRATION

Primary keys shall migrate in their entirety from the parent entity to the related child entity.

Discussion

All attributes comprising the primary key of a parent entity must migrate to each and every child entity as either primary keys or foreign keys. This ensures the model maintains its required referential integrity (Martin, 1983). There are groups of data modelers who believe that it is entirely proper to use some, but not all, of the cascaded keys as primary keys. These are split into foreign and primary key components. Although this is technically feasible, it is not considered to be good practice. A split key is generally indicative of a need for further refinement of the model. Primary keys migrate through the model to become primary or foreign key components in other entities, not to become non-key attributes.

Examples

In Figure 4.54, PRODUCT has a relationship with four entities: PERSON PRODUCT, SUPPLIER PRODUCT, PRODUCT PART, and PRODUCT REGULATION. Each is described below.

* The first relationship is an invalid migration. The primary key of PRODUCT, *upc code* and *product id*, is not cascaded into the PERSON PRODUCT entity. Without this migration, the organization is not able to identify who bought or sold a product. The relationship

should be removed if this is not important information, or PERSON PRODUCT should be supplemented with the primary key from PRODUCT.

- The second relationship with SUPPLIER PRODUCT is invalid, but for a different reason. In this case, only one primary key from PRODUCT has migrated to SUPPLIER PRODUCT. To uniquely identify a PRODUCT, we must have the *upc code* and the *product id*, one alone does not guarantee unique identification. The organization will not be able to answer questions relating to the SUPPLIER of a PRODUCT.
- The relationships with PRODUCT PART and PRODUCT REGULATION are an example of correct migration from parent to child. The entire primary key has cascaded to become a foreign key in PRODUCT PART and primary key components in PRODUCT REGULATION.

In the second example, Figure 4.55 depicts a split key occurrence. A ROUTE is uniquely identified by the *origin point* and *destination point*; however, to uniquely describe an AIRCRAFT ROUTE, the analyst has only provided the *origin point* and the *aircraft tail number*. The *destination point* has become a foreign key component. The decision to split the key has a number of impacts on the model. The first impact is that it limits the occurrences in AIRCRAFT ROUTE. If aircraft E-9311 flew the Baltimore to San Antonio route and the Baltimore to Las Vegas route, only one occurrence could be represented because the primary keys for AIRCRAFT ROUTE are *origin point* and *aircraft tail number*. The *destination point* has been split and is a foreign key. It does not contribute to uniqueness. This limits occurrences to a first-come, first-served scenario. This arbitrary population mechanism is not a preferred method for our models or our information systems.

Though technically feasible, this situation indicates that perhaps some additional analysis needs to occur. Arbitrarily restricting the domain does not reflect reality. A more pleasing solution is offered in Figure 4.56. The destination point is now a part of the composite key. Now if aircraft E-9311 flew the Baltimore to San Antonio route and the Baltimore to Las Vegas route, both occurrences could be represented. A split key situation should signal to the analyst to re-examine the model area.

Figure 4.57 offers one more potential solution. The split key situation is resolved by eliminating the relationship between AIRCRAFT and ROUTE, and establishing a new relationship between ORIGIN and AIRCRAFT. This contains the identical primary keys, but is represented with different relationships. The destination point of the AIRCRAFT ROUTE is lost.

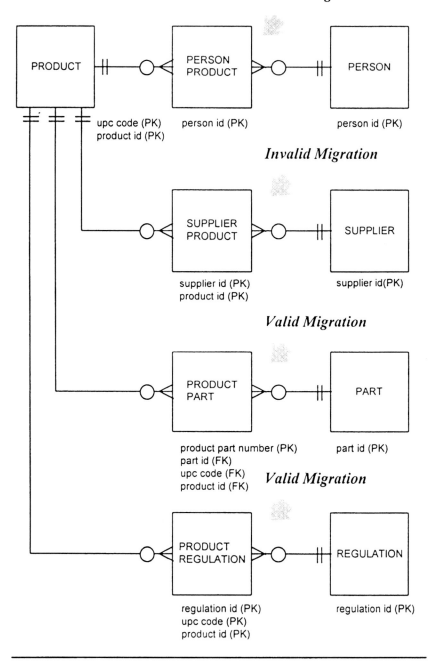

Figure 4.54   Primary key migration.

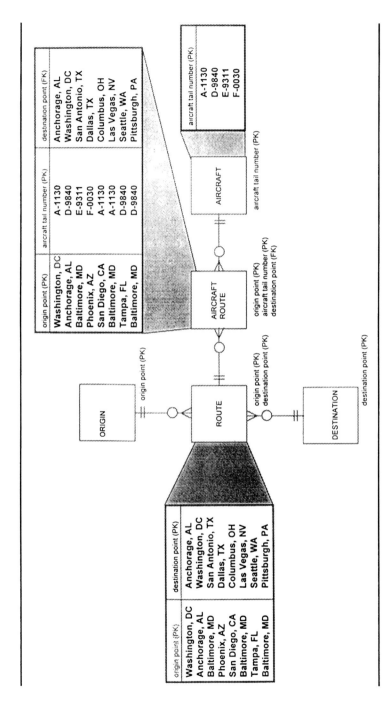

Figure 4.55 Split key.

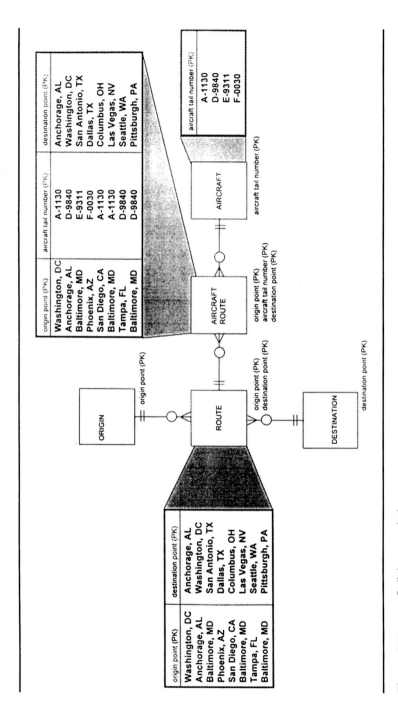

Figure 4.56 Split key resolution.

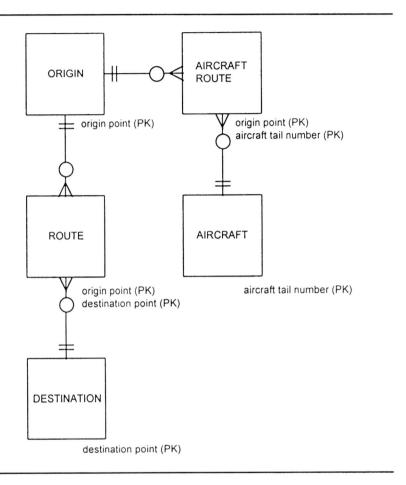

origin point (PK)

origin point (PK)
aircraft tail number (PK)

origin point (PK)
destination point (PK)

aircraft tail number (PK)

destination point (PK)

Figure 4.57   Split key potential resolution.

A final note about the split key example. It was not easy for the authors to create an example. Every time we attempted to put one together, it caused heartache because we knew how horrendous this modeling practice is. However, we hope the point has been made that this is not a practice condoned by more experienced practitioners.

4.20   ARTIFICIAL KEY ACCESS PATH

If an artificial key is used to uniquely identify an entity, sufficient attribution must be present to access the data.

Discussion

One problem with employing artificial keys is that they may not be intuitive or even available for use as an access path. In these instances, it is important that the data modeler provide sufficient attribution to access a specific entity occurrence. This additional attribution may be *alternate keys* or *selection attributes*. Alternate keys or selection attributes possess many of the same characteristics as primary keys, but usually fail to meet one of the four criteria. They can serve the data modeler by providing a path to the information, though not unique, in an entity occurrence.

There are a number of data modeling notations, notably IDEF1X, that progress in phases. An initial model is constructed that consists of only entities and relationships, the next phase introduces keys and resolves indeterminate relationships, and in the last phase, non-key attributes are introduced. In these notations, the lack of an access path occurs with greater frequency. Adherence to this rule is only expected at the completion of the fully attributed or similar phase.

Example

In Figure 4.58, two artificial keys, *person id* and *skill id*, have been introduced to uniquely identify a PERSON and a SKILL. This is a reasonable approach, until the organization needs to extract information about an occurrence of PERSON and its associated skill level. The artificial keys are meaningless, and do not provide an access path to the PERSON SKILL entity.

The access path problem is resolved in Figure 4.59 with the introduction of the PERSON NAME entity and the *person name* attribute. Now we have access to the information piece, skill level in this data model fragment. We can select an individual's name with *person name*, and then use *person id* to access the *skill level*. The SKILL entity has an additional attribute, *skill name*, to allow us to identify the skill in lay terms.

4.21 ALIAS NAMES

Aliases shall only be permitted when a single attribute is inherited more than once. All other situations are discouraged.

Discussion

Once an attribute, entity, or any other model object has been named, it must keep the same name in all domains. This means that all foreign

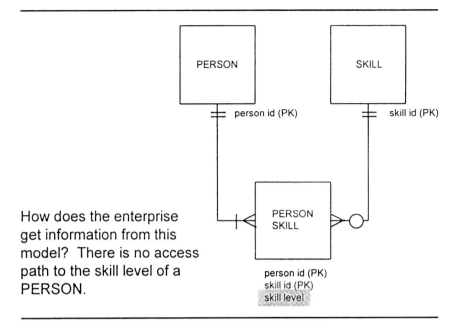

How does the enterprise get information from this model? There is no access path to the skill level of a PERSON.

Figure 4.58   No access path to skill level.

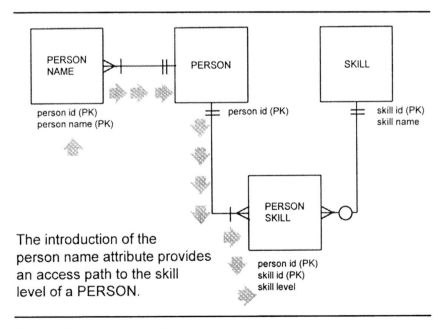

The introduction of the person name attribute provides an access path to the skill level of a PERSON.

Figure 4.59   Access path resolved.

157

key attributes must retain the same name they held in their originating entity. Since the attribute refers to the same business concept, whether it is a primary key or foreign key, it should maintain the same label. This will increase the level of understanding across multiple domains or functional areas. In addition, it is helpful to identify the foreign keys (and therefore the relationships) in the data model.

The only exception occurs when a single attribute is inherited more than once. This may be the result of a recursive relationship between an entity, or when there are multiple relationships between two entities, resulting in multiple foreign keys. Because each attribute in an entity must be unique, the foreign key name is aliased to distinguish between the inherited attributes.

Examples

In the first example, the only allowable situation to alias an attribute is when there are two or more occurrences of the same attribute. In Figure 4.60, we are exchanging one currency for another. In the CURRENCY EXCHANGE entity, we have no mechanism for accessing the currency to be exchanged versus the currency it will be exchanged into. Are we exchanging dollars into yen or yen into dollars?

This is resolved in Figure 4.61 by aliasing the second occurrence of *currency name* with *exchange currency*. Now, both occurrences are unique and independently accessible. The analyst can now identify the currency being exchanged versus the exchanged currency.

As a second example, in reviewing data models, we have seen aliases improperly overused. The most frequent violation occurs when a pri-

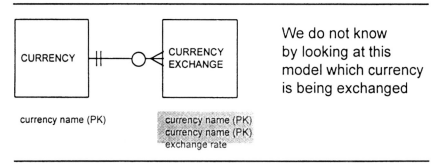

Figure 4.60 Aliases unresolved.

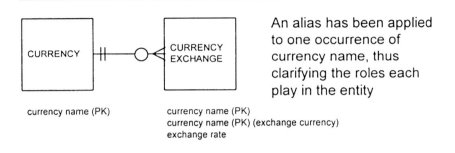

An alias has been applied to one occurrence of currency name, thus clarifying the roles each play in the entity

currency name (PK)

currency name (PK)
currency name (PK) (exchange currency)
exchange rate

Figure 4.61   Aliases resolved.

mary key is migrated in an associative relationship. The key is now in a different context and the data modeler assigns an alias to the key. This is not technically incorrect, but it may indicate a model in need of further refinement. In Figure 4.62, the use of the alias *bill payer* may indicate a requirement to classify CUSTOMER into bill payers and non-bill payers or another refinement. It is an unnecessary alias.

The model above will contribute to miscommunication among functional areas of the enterprise. One area will refer to the attribute as the *bill payer*, while other areas in the enterprise will refer to the attribute as *customer name*. This homonym will inhibit the development of a shared data environment. One resolution is displayed in Figure 4.63. The analyst has introduced a new entity into the data model. CUSTOMER CATEGORY will be used to categorize customer into bill payers and non-bill payers.

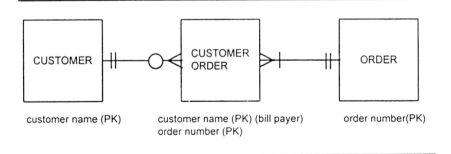

customer name (PK)

customer name (PK) (bill payer)
order number (PK)

order number(PK)

Figure 4.62   Unnecessary alias.

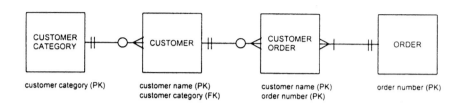

customer category (PK)   customer name (PK)   customer name (PK)   order number (PK)
                                      customer category (FK)   order number (PK)

Figure 4.63   Possible resolution of alias.

4.22 GENERALIZATION HIERARCHY PRIMARY KEY INHERITANCE

Each and every entity within a generalization hierarchy, regardless of level, shall inherit the primary key of the root generic parent entity, and shall have exactly the same primary key structure as the parent.

Discussion

Entities within a generalization hierarchy (often called subtypes, secondaries, or category entities) inherit the characteristics and primary keys of their parent. When creating or reviewing generalization hierarchies, it is important to remember that while a supertype entity and a subtype entity within the same hierarchy are represented as different entities, they are logically the same thing. An occurrence of a subtype entity must be accompanied by an occurrence of the parent(s).

This rule imposes additional constraints on entities within a generalization hierarchy.

- A subtype entity cannot be a child entity in another identifying relationship, since such a relationship would result in migration of a primary key set from the other parent.
- A subtype entity can have only one generic parent.
- A subtype entity in one relationship may be a generic parent entity in another relationship, since this does not violate the key structure rule.
- An entity may have any number of sets of independent subtypes in which it is the generic parent entity, since this does not violate the key structure rule and is often required to correctly reflect business requirements.

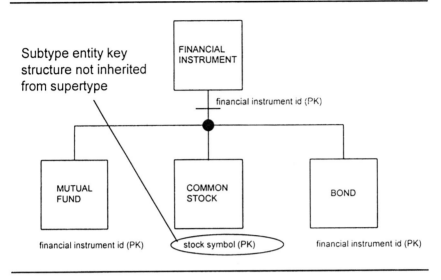

Subtype entity key
structure not inherited
from supertype

Figure 4.64   Incorrect subtype entity key structure.

Example

In Figure 4.64, a FINANCIAL INSTRUMENT is used as a supertype to
manage the diverse set of equity and debt products traded on the ex-
changes. FINANCIAL INSTRUMENT is identified with the artificial
key, *financial instrument id*. COMMON STOCK, a subtype, is identified with *stock symbol*. This is an illegal construct. The relationship
between COMMON STOCK and FINANCIAL INSTRUMENT is known
as an *is a* relationship. COMMON STOCK is a FINANCIAL INSTRU-
MENT and therefore must have the same primary identifier, *financial
instrument id*.

This problem is resolved in Figure 4.65 by moving *stock symbol* to
non-key status in COMMON STOCK. Primary keys, at all levels of a
generalization hierarchy, must be identical to that of the supertype.

4.23   FOREIGN KEY ATTRIBUTES

*Every dependent entity shall have at least one foreign key at-
tribute—singular or composite—that adheres to the following
rules:*

1. *Each relationship between two entities shall be supported by a
   set of foreign keys that correspond to the parent entity key*

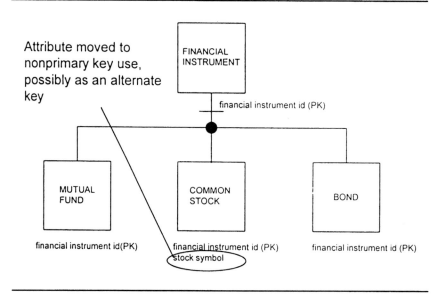

Attribute moved to nonprimary key use, possibly as an alternate key

Figure 4.65 Revised subtype entity key structure.

structure. In other words, key migration from parent (or supertype) entities to child (or subtype) entities is mandatory.
2. *The entire primary key of the parent entity shall be migrated to the child entity.*
3. *Composite keys migrated from the parent shall not be split between primary key and non-key use in the child.*
4. *Foreign keys shall not be unified in a child entity.*

Description

Foreign keys provide a method for maintaining integrity in the data model and for navigating between differing entities occurrences. Primary and foreign keys are the most basic components of relational theory, upon which data models are constructed. There are four basic rules that we need to observe.

• Each relationship in a model must be supported by a foreign key. A relationship indicates a connection between two entities. In order to understand the connection, we must have a method for understanding how a value in one entity relates to a value in another. A foreign key is the mechanism for relating the two entity occurrences.

- Primary keys are migrated from the parent entity to the child entity to maintain integrity. The entire primary key, if it is a composite key, must be migrated to the dependent entity. Partial migration will compromise integrity.
- Splitting migrated composite keys between primary and foreign key or non-key use in the dependent child entity is not permitted. It is generally indicative of a need for further normalization or additional analysis.
- Every child entity must contain a foreign key to support each relationship it participates in. Some authors believe that this does not impose a requirement that each relationship have a separate foreign key, but allows a foreign key to support multiple relationships. This concept of unification or overlapping keys is indicative of a modeling problem that should be resolved. We strongly discourage this practice.

Examples

In order to navigate around the data model, foreign key attributes are established. The primary keys of the parent must be migrated to all child entities to support the relationship. In Figure 4.66, we have no method for discovering what occurrences of the parent entity (EMPLOYEE) relate to which occurrences of the child (PAYCHECK). What employee received paycheck number 112? It is impossible to discover without a foreign key attribute.

The example is resolved in Figure 4.67 by migrating the *employee id* to PAYCHECK. Now we can answer the question posed earlier. Dave McMath has received paychecks number 112 and 113.

In order to fully identify a relationship between two entities, the entire primary key of the parent entity must be migrated. In the second example, an EMPLOYEE is identified by *person id* and *organization id*. An EMPLOYEE has many PERFORMANCE REVIEWS. This relationship should be supported by the entire primary key of EMPLOYEE. Only *person id* has migrated, which will cause integrity problems in the model. In this case, if an EMPLOYEE has worked for more than one organization, we do not know which organization performed the review.

This problem is resolved in Figure 4.69. The primary keys of EMPLOYEE, *person id* and *organization id*, have been cascaded into PERFORMANCE REVIEW. The model now contains the integrity required to identify the organization that performed the review.

Unified keys consist of merging two or more contributed foreign key attributes into a single foreign key attribute. It usually occurs in mod-

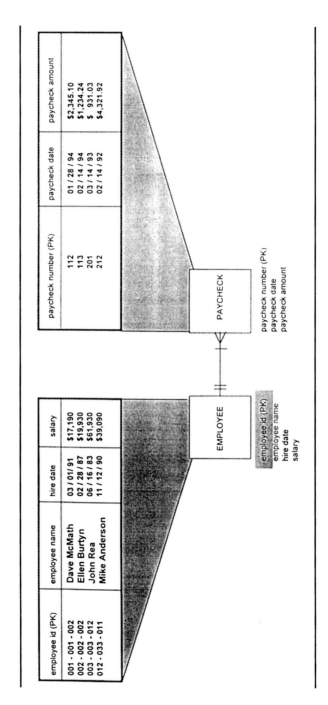

employee id (PK)	employee name	hire date	salary
001 - 001 - 002	Dave McMath	03 / 01/ 91	$17,190
002 - 002 - 002	Ellen Burtyn	02 / 28/ 87	$19,930
003 - 003 - 012	John Rea	06 / 16 / 83	$61,930
012 - 033 - 011	Mike Anderson	11 / 12 / 90	$39,090

EMPLOYEE

employee id (PK)
employee name
hire date
salary

paycheck number (PK)	paycheck date	paycheck amount
112	01 / 28 / 94	$2,345.10
113	02 / 14 / 94	$1,234.24
201	03 / 14 / 93	$ 931.03
212	02 / 14 / 92	$4,321.92

PAYCHECK

paycheck number (PK)
paycheck date
paycheck amount

Figure 4.66 No foreign key support.

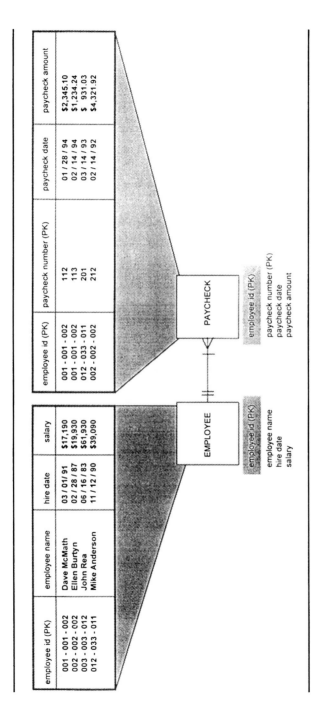

employee id (PK)	employee name	hire date	salary
001 - 001 - 002	Dave McMath	03 / 01 / 91	$17,190
002 - 002 - 002	Ellen Burtyn	02 / 28 / 87	$19,930
003 - 003 - 012	John Rea	06 / 16 / 83	$61,930
012 - 033 - 011	Mike Anderson	11 / 12 / 90	$39,090

employee id (PK)	paycheck number (PK)	paycheck date	paycheck amount
001 - 001 - 002	112	01 / 28 / 94	$2,345.10
001 - 001 - 002	113	02 / 14 / 94	$1,234.24
012 - 033 - 011	201	03 / 14 / 93	$ 931.03
002 - 002 - 002	212	02 / 14 / 92	$4,321.92

EMPLOYEE

employee id (PK)

employee name
hire date
salary

PAYCHECK

employee id (PK)

paycheck number (PK)
paycheck date
paycheck amount

Figure 4.67   Foreign key migration resolved.

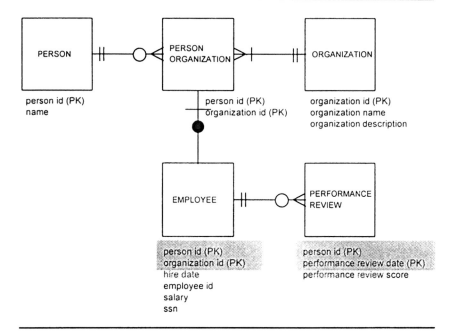

Figure 4.68   Invalid migration.

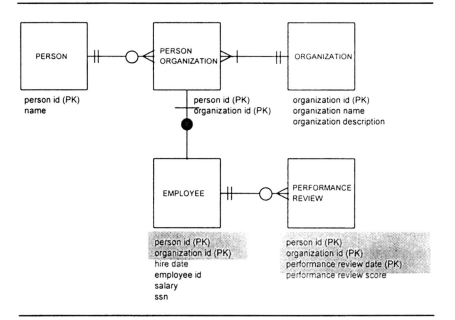

Figure 4.69   Key migration resolved.

els where the contributed keys both maintain identical values. To reduce redundancy, the data modeler removes one occurrence. This is a discouraged practice for a number of reasons. The first point is that it does not reflect reality. If we have a non-key attribute that is functionally dependent on two identical occurrences of a primary key, then we need to reflect that in our model with two occurrences of the primary key. The second point to be made is that, if we are eliminating a primary key, then we can create the same entity with differing relationships. In Figure 4.70, *primary key b* should be inherited twice. The concept of unification allows the one instance to serve both roles.

This approach leads the reviewer to believe that *non-key attribute #1* is functionally dependent on *primary key a, primary key b,* and *primary key c*. This is not true in the unified key example: *Non-key attribute #1* is functionally dependent on *primary key a, two* occurrences

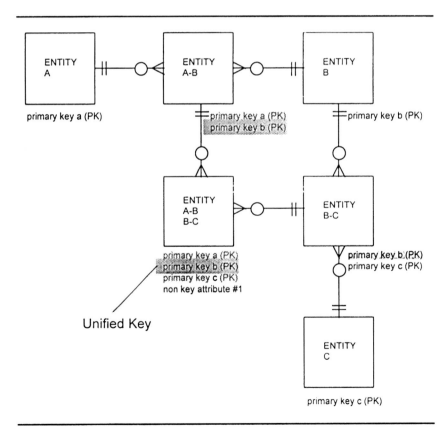

Figure 4.70   Unified key.

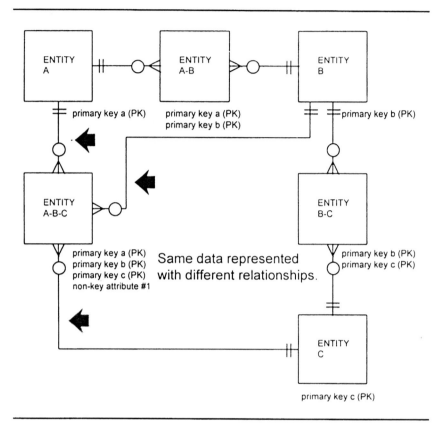

Figure 4.71   Unified key resolved.

of *primary key b,* and *primary key c.* A unified key does not precisely represent reality. If *non-key attribute #1* were functionally dependent on *primary key a, primary key b,* and *primary key c,* we could represent the model with the relationships shown in below.

We strongly discourage unified keys because the same relationship, after unification, can be represented in a manner more communicative to the subject matter experts. In the example above, if we can represent the data with *primary key a#, b#,* and *c#* (see Figure 4.71), let's do that with different relationships, and not permit a hidden migration.

4.24   DANGLING FOREIGN KEYS

Each and every foreign key in an entity shall support a relationship(s) to that entity. Any remaining foreign keys (those that do not map) shall be removed from the entity, or have a

*correct relationship established and linked to the key. Resolu-
tion shall be conceptually correct, based on business plans, rules,
and requirements.*

Discussion

A foreign key is an attribute or set of attributes whose values in one
entity are required to match those of the primary key in another entity.
The converse is not required—every primary key value does not need to
match a foreign key value in another entity. The problem of ensuring
that the data model does not include any invalid foreign key values is
known as the *referential integrity problem*. A symptom of this problem
is the dangling foreign key.

During the course of modeling, it is common to add and remove
relationships as business rules are discovered and refined. Foreign keys
may be migrated to support a relationship between entities, only to be
"left behind" when the relationship is removed during model refinement. A foreign key left without a relationship is called a *dangling
foreign key*. The resolution of a dangling foreign key must be based on
the business plans, policies, or rules that the model represents. The
resolution must be conceptually correct. Dangling foreign keys are resolved either through removal from the entity, or introduction of a relationship that the key was intended to support.

Example

Figure 4.72 depicts a model fragment that for one reason or another has
been left with a dangling foreign key. The *vehicle class code* in VE-
HICLE is unsupported by any association.

Figure 4.73 depicts one possible resolution. Note that the resolution of a dangling foreign key will depend on the business requirements. These kinds of QA findings should be presented to the subject
matter experts for resolution or confirmation. Here the work group
has realized the foreign key remains in the model from an entity
needed to classify vehicles. VEHICLE CATEGORY is reintroduced
into the model.

In the next resolution scenario, Figure 4.74, the work group real-
izes that the foreign key has been left over from a deleted model object,
and removes the attribute from the model.

4.25   OPTIONAL FOREIGN KEYS

Optional foreign keys shall be resolved.

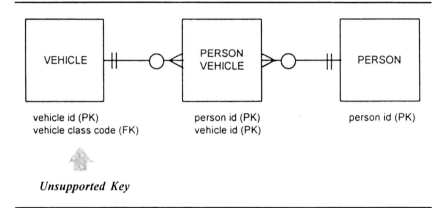

Unsupported Key

Figure 4.72 Dangling foreign key.

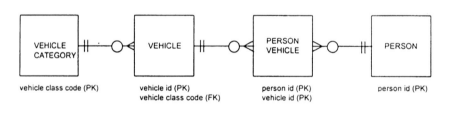

Figure 4.73 Dangling foreign key—A possible resolution.

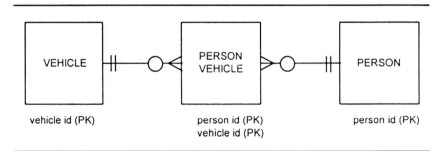

Figure 4.74 Dangling foreign key—Another resolution.

Description

An optional foreign key is a situation that occurs when a child entity has an optional parent. In some situations, the parent is required and in other situations the parent is not. This is a signal to the data model reviewer that the business rules for this area have not been satisfied.

The data analyst must discover the rules and the distinctions that apply to both situations—what circumstances require a value for the key and what circumstances do not. This condition can normally be resolved by subtyping the entity into a required condition. Remember that optional foreign keys violate the No Null rule.

Example

An INDIVIDUAL in the optional relationship in Figure 4.75 is not required to participate in the relationship with the BENEFIT PLAN entity. This is a sign that a business rule is not precise. To resolve this optional relationship, additional analysis needs to occur to uncover those

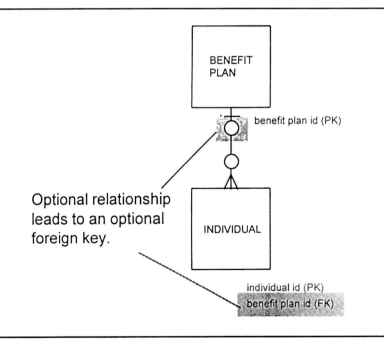

Figure 4.75   Optional foreign key.

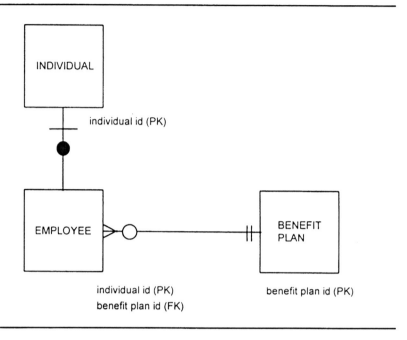

individual id (PK)

individual id (PK)
benefit plan id (FK)

benefit plan id (PK)

Figure 4.76   Optional foreign key—Resolved.

instances where a benefit plan *always* applies and where it does not apply.

In this case, Figure 4.76, the business rule states that *an employee is required to select one and only one benefit package*. This requires the introduction of an EMPLOYEE subtype and a relationship established with BENEFIT. The optional foreign key is now resolved.

REFERENCES

Brooks, Deborah L. "How and When to Use Surrogate Keys," *Database Programming and Design* 5 (2):55-57, March, 1992.

Date, C.J. *An Introduction to Database Systems, Volume I*. Reading, MA: Addison-Wesley, 1986.

Date, C.J. *Relational Database—Selected Writings*. Reading, MA: Addison-Wesley, 1986.

Finkelstein, Clive. *An Introduction to Information Engineering: From Strategic Planning to Information Systems*. Sydney: Addison-Wesley, 1989.

Finkelstein, Clive. *Information Engineering: Strategic Systems Development.* Sydney: Addison-Wesley, 1992.

Haeckel, Stephen H. and Richard L. Nolan. "Managing by Wire," *Harvard Business Review*, September–October 1993 (pp. 122–132).

Inmon, W.H. *Data Architecture: The Information Paradigm.* Wellesley, MA: QED Information Sciences, 1989.

Martin, James. *Managing the DataBase Environment.* Englewood Cliffs, NJ: Prentice Hall, 1983.

McClure, Stephen F. "Information Engineering for Client/Server Architectures," *Data Base Newsletter* 21, No. 4 (July/August 1993).

Whitener, T. "Primary Identifiers: The Basics of Database Stability," *Database Programming and Design* 2 (1):42-49, January, 1989.

Relationship Rules

5.1   RELATIONSHIP CHECKLIST

The Relationship Checklist presents the set of characteristics a data modeling team should gather and record about relationships to ensure that a complete set of requirements is represented in the data model. Our checklist directly supports the completeness aspect of data model quality.

As with the entity and attribute checklists, the list presented here has been made without regard to the limitations or capabilities of any single CASE tool.

☑   **Name***

This is the name of the relationship that meets naming conventions or standards. Some modeling techniques ordain the use of two relationship names, supposedly enabling the reader to understand the interaction of two entities much better than if only one name is used. Relationship names are actually verbs, not nouns, and therefore imply that one of the entities takes action or maintains a certain state relative to the other (and vice versa, of course).

Do not waste your time or risk the wrath of your business expert participants laboring through the creation of relationship names. Rela-

---

* Optional

tionship names generally add very little, if any, clarity to the model (even when done "properly"), tend to be repetitious, are tedious to define and maintain, and do not aid database design in any way. There is nothing more painful than watching a data modeler facilitate a group of users through a relationship naming exercise. And most analysts and business experts, judging by the models we have seen, do not do a very good job of relationship naming. The old stand-bys "has" and "owns" and "has an interest in" show up everywhere. Once you reach several hundred entities in your model, the prospect of naming relationships becomes rather dreadful. Our recommendation is that you spend your valuable time on some of the truly important aspects of the modeling process. CASE tool vendors have gotten the message, and most either no longer require relationship names or allow the modeler the option to not depict them on the data model diagrams. Unfortunately, several widely used CASE products still impose a requirement that you provide a name before adding the relationship to the model, even though you choose not to display them.

☑   Description*

The description presents the analyst an opportunity to record additional details about a relationship. This information does not duplicate other elements of the relationship; it is simply intended to add additional documentary detail to the model. In most cases, information provided in the relationship description will be available through other objects in the meta-model.

☑   Key(s)

Every relationship must be supported by the migration of a primary key (whether single attribute or multiple attributes). This is the basic precept of referential integrity, and is one of the foundations of relational data modeling. It is extremely important that the relationship be supported by the migration of the entire primary key to the child entity, and that the entire migrated key serve as either a component of the primary key or as a foreign key reference. Migrating composite keys should never be split between primary and nonprimary foreign key use in the child entity. We have outlined rules to this effect in our discussion of primary keys.

---

* Optional

☑   **Type [Required by some methodologies]**

Certain methodologies categorize relationships according to the role that the migrating keys will play in the child entity. For example, the IDEF1X modeling notation designates relationships as either identifying, non-identifying, or category. In an identifying relationship, the primary key(s) of the parent is migrated to serve as part of a compound primary key in the child. A nonidentifying relationship results in the migration of the parent entity's primary key as a nonprimary foreign key in the child. Finally, category relationships exist between supertypes and subtypes, with the primary key of the supertype 'migrating' intact to each subtype.

This property actually provides redundant information, since we know the role that the migrated keys are playing (primary or nonprimary) in the "downstream" or child entity. We have found the designation of relationship type to add very little value. In the case of IDEF1X, which we discussed above, we suspect that it emerged as part of that technique's phased approach to modeling, where key structures are not defined until the second phase. If you use a CASE tool such as Texas Instruments' IEF™ or LogicWorks' ERwin™, you may be required to designate a relationship type. Consult your CASE tool requirements.

☑   **Cardinality/Optionality**

This is also referred to as Degree/Nature or simply Cardinality. The degrees and natures of a relationship are the soul of business modeling. They allow for the precise depiction of business rules. By examining alternative degrees and natures at each end of a relationship, the modeling team can examine alternative business strategies and policies using the model as a visualization technique. We strongly urge you to read Chapter 4 of *An Introduction to Information Engineering* by Clive Finkelstein (1989) for a description of the role relationship degrees and natures can play in examining business rules and strategies.

The rules surrounding allowable combinations and depiction of relationship degrees and natures will vary, in some cases substantially, depending on the modeling notation you have selected. We suggest that you explore several methods before deciding which you are most comfortable with. Your data management policies may dictate use of a specific notation, but continue to look around. While we have chosen to use the most popular notation for this book, there are some interesting alternatives out there. Of particular interest are Clive Finkelstein's use of "optional-tending-toward-mandatory" and the IDEF1X standard's use of degrees with specific values (i.e., instead of "mandatory many," you might specify "mandatory 3 to 5," depending on your business rules) (Finkelstein, 1989; FIPS, 1992).

☑ Deletion Integrity Rules

There are three fundamental types of relational integrity—add, update, and delete. Add and update integrity rules are explicitly defined through the relationship cardinality. However, delete rules must be defined separately. There are three alternatives for establishing delete integrity—cascade, disassociate, or disallow. You will find our rule pertaining to delete integrity in Chapter 9.

☑ Relationship Quantity Statistics

Prior to moving to data structure design, you will want to gather some statistics to understand the quantitative aspects of relationships. While other statistics may be gathered, the most critical information for database design, specifically for transaction access path analysis, is the entity ratio for each relationship (min, max, and average). Figure 5.1 illustrates this concept. Current systems analysis should assist you in determining ratios, but participation of business experts will be necessary to confirm the numbers, and to assess any new requirements not found in current systems (whether automated or nonautomated).

☑ Discriminator

An attribute should be established as the discriminator for each supertype-subtype relationship. The discriminator attribute is used to record which

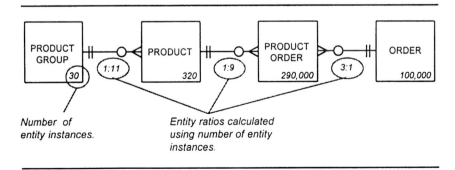

Figure 5.1   Average entity ratios for a set of relationships.

subtype(s) are applicable for a particular instance of the supertype. See Chapter 6 for further discussion of discriminators.

5.2   BALANCED ONE-T0-ONE RELATIONSHIPS

Eliminate balanced one-to-one relationships from the model.

Discussion

A balanced one-to-one relationship has the same cardinality/optionality combination at both ends of the relationship.

The introduction of balanced one-to-one relationships introduces some problems to a data model.

•   A mandatory one-to-one relationship indicates that the two entities are so closely related that one cannot exist without the presence of the other. This type of close tie generally indicates that the two things represented by the separate entities are actually character-istics of the same thing. Let's assume for a moment that we have two entities as depicted in Figure 5.3.

Recall the definition of functional dependence from Date (1986):

Given a relation R, attribute Y of R is *functionally depen-dent* on attribute X of R if and only if each X-value in R has

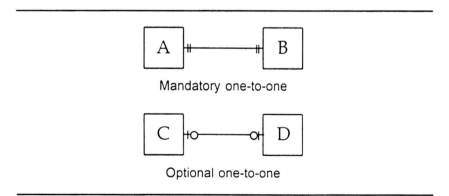

Mandatory one-to-one

Optional one-to-one

Figure 5.2   Balanced one-to-one relationships.

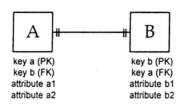

Figure 5.3   Mandatory one-to-one.

associated with it precisely one Y-value in R (at any one time). Attributes X and Y may be composite.

Now back to our model. Attribute *key a* is functionally dependent on *key b* (in entity B, each attribute *key b* value has associated with it precisely one *key a* value at any one time). Likewise, attribute *key b* is functionally dependent on *key a* (in entity A, each attribute *key a* value has associated with it precisely one *key b* value at any one time). That's interesting. We have introduced a case where the non-key attributes of both entity A and entity B are functionally dependent on both the primary key of A and the primary key of B. For each *key a* value in A, *attribute b1* and *attribute b2* in entity B have associated with it precisely one value. Likewise, for each *key b* value in entity B, *attribute a1* and *attribute a2* in entity A have associated with it precisely one value. The decomposition of A and B into two entities is therefore arbitrary. All four attributes are functionally dependent on *key a* or *key b* (both are candidate keys), and should be placed in a single entity. Selection of a candidate key as primary key for the new entity should be worked out with the business experts. The same logic holds for balanced optional one-to-one relationships. In the case of an optional relationship, the resolution may include the creation of subtype entities to manage optional attributes in the new entity (created through resolution of the balanced relationship).

We have demonstrated this situation assuming that the entities had different primary key attributes, the migration of keys was performed in order to maintain referential integrity, and the keys were migrated as nonprimary foreign keys. Suppose now that they were migrated as primary keys. Well, we would have two entities with the same primary key attributes, which violates one of our fundamental rules about primary keys (see Chapter 4 for further discussion of primary key rules).

- Balanced one-to-one relationships prevent the modeling team from establishing the data dependency path.
- Balanced one-to-one relationships introduce unnecessary redundancy into the model, and therefore raise the risk of introducing inconsistency.
- They may mask the actual logic that the modeling team was striving for, or lead to confusion over relationships and business rules.

The definition of the separate entities may come about during the course of modeling for some very understandable reasons:

- They were created by separate modeling teams, followed by an attempt to integrate the results.
- In the case of the optional one-to-one relationships, it is possible the modeling team was attempting to show that certain attributes are optional at the time of creation of an instance of the entity.
- By using the optional one-to-one relationship, the team may have been trying to indicate that the entities are mutually exclusive subsets of the same logical concept (a situation best handled with a subtype structure).
- The entities were identified in conjunction with functional or process analysis, and have been artificially separated because they are used to perform different functions or are involved in different processes.
- The attributes in the separate entities are owned by or controlled by different organizations.

These are just a few of the motivations that a modeling team may use to argue the case for employing one-to-one relationships. However, in all cases the separation of attributes is arbitrary, and therefore not repeatable consistently across the model. Remember that in order to maintain a model that can be used across an enterprise, the model must be built using techniques that lead to repeatable results. With balanced one-to-one relationships, there is no basis for dividing the attributes between the entities in a consistent fashion.

If you run across balanced one-to-one relationships, attempt to merge the participating entities into a single entity, or into a supertype/subtype structure in the case of the optional one-to-optional one relationship. The examples provided in the next section illustrate resolution scenarios.

Example

For our example, assume we have a small business that is modeling the management of its sales force. The company has defined a series of territories, and *currently* has a sales representative assigned to each. The company wants to track its sales by territory, since it has spent a great deal of time studying regional demographics and wishes to track buying habits accordingly. The sales manager, however, needs to track individual performance of each of her sales representatives. The model fragment shown in Figure 5.4 emerged from the modeling sessions (we have shown key attributes only).

It is clear that the modeling team has captured the *current* business climate from an organizational and functional perspective. In addition to the technical problems that the one-to-one relationship introduces, it also represents an artificially constrained business environment as well. The near-term solution to the modeling problem posed by the relationship might be to create a single SALESPERSON entity. However, the team should also look forward to the future sales strategies and policies of the company. How will sales territory be defined in the future? Will territories always be defined in terms of salespeople, or will they take on demographic or geographic connotations? Is it possible that a SALESPERSON could cover more than one territory? Could we have two salespersons covering a sales territory? Do we want to track different salespersons' performance in the same territory as they are reassigned? These are conceptual questions that the presence of a one-to-one relationship should prompt.

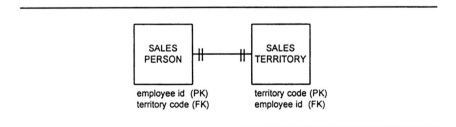

Figure 5.4   Invalid one-to-one relationship.

5.3 MANDATORY-ONE-TO-OPTIONAL-ONE RELATIONSHIPS

Carefully examine mandatory-one-to-optional-one relationships in the model.

Discussion

Technically, a mandatory-one-to-optional-one relationship is beset with the same problems that plague relationships discussed in the Balanced One-to-One Relationships rule.

The difference between the cardinality set shown here and those shown in our other rule is that we can define the data dependency chain between entities F and E as pictured above. An instance of entity F must clearly be created at the same time or earlier than an instance of entity E. In other words, we can have F without E, but not E without F. As a result, we have found that this cardinality set is a warning flag for conceptual quality problems, and have chosen to address it separately.

Guidelines for Resolving Optional-One-to-Mandatory-One Relationships

- Consider whether entity E represents a subtype of F. Does entity E actually represent one of many categories of F, but is the only one with additional attribute requirements? Many methodologies discourage the depiction of subtype entities that have no attributes other than the inherited primary key, since these may be more effectively handled by defining, and *documenting as part of the model*, a domain of values for the discriminator attribute. There is a danger in using the mandatory-one-to-optional-many cardinality to accommodate such a situation, since the domain of other subtypes may be lost if not correctly documented. Is there an attribute in F whose value triggers a requirement for populating E? If so, this

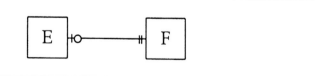

Figure 5.5   Unbalanced one-to-one relationship.

attribute serves as a discriminator, and indicates that a generalization hierarchy structure is appropriate. See Chapter 6 for further discussion of generalization hierarchies.
- Determine if E has been modeled to accommodate a time delay between the creation of F, with its primary key and non-key attribute set, and the creation of instances of the attributes in E. This situation does *not* require the identification of a separate entity to handle what might be referred to as "add later" attributes.
- Determine if E has been modeled to accommodate an expected difficulty in actually obtaining the information represented by the attributes of E. If the users expect to gather values for only a small percentage of some of F's attributes, they may have been tempted to move them to E. The logical model should not reflect such considerations, although recording such expectations will certainly aid the database design team.
- Has the cardinality for one or both of the entities been improperly defined? Check the key structure to see if only one of the two entities has a migrated attribute; that might indicate that the cardinality was incorrectly recorded.
- Review any applicable business rules to ensure that the model is conceptually correct.

Examples

The example we have selected (Figure 5.6) comes from a human resources department model, and is perhaps one of the most extreme examples of a timing difference influencing model development. The objective of the model was to separate current and former employees, since these are obviously subject to different sets of rules and different information needs. Unfortunately, the model fragment that resulted is incorrect. The modeling team has separated FORMER EMPLOYEE from EMPLOYEE based on the assumption that employee termination date is optional. However, it is not optional. Every employee will eventually be terminated for one reason or another (retirement, death, resignation, involuntary termination). The issue is one of timing. Therefore, the attribute *employee termination date* is not optional in EMPLOYEE—it will eventually apply to all employees. The modeling team has been overly influenced by the often substantial difference in the time an instance of EMPLOYEE is created and the time a value for *employee termination date* will be added. That timing difference does *not* make *employee termination date* an optional attribute. Remember that we are building a logical data model. Decisions about how best to implement this will have to be made, just not now.

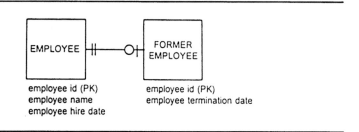

Figure 5.6 Unresolved relationship.

Our resolution is depicted in Figure 5.7. Note that *employee termination date* is now originating in EMPLOYEE.

A second resolution is depicted in Figure 5.8. This resolution increases the flexibility of the model. We have added an *employee status* discriminator to identify employees who are currently employed, have retired, have been fired, or have some other status with the company. Note that *employee hire date* and *employee termination date* become "hire" and "terminated" status values in *employee status*, combined with corresponding *employee status effective date* values. There are obviously many alternative solutions, and the correct one for your organization lies in your business policies and the needs of your business experts.

Our second example involves information that the users expect will be difficult to obtain. The users maintain data on airports around the country for a regional airline. They gather information from a wide variety of sources, but have had considerable difficulty in the past obtaining data on runway surfaces at small airports. The airline's pilots need access to this information in occasional emergencies, when they must land at unfamiliar airports. As a result, they have modeled RUNWAY SURFACE information separate from RUNWAY information.

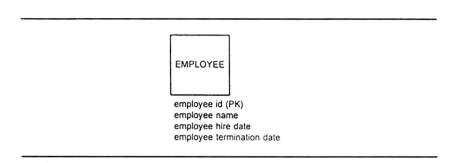

Figure 5.7 Resolved optional relationship problem.

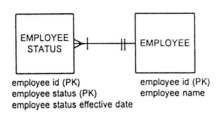

Figure 5.8   A second resolution strategy.

Unfortunately, this suggests that some runways do not have surfaces. It would be logical to assume that *every* runway has a surface of some kind. Once this kind of arbitrary division is introduced, it tends to cause additional problems. Notice *runway surface condition* has crept out to RUNWAY SURFACE, although this information is not necessarily dependent on knowing the exact type of surface. The model has been corrected in Figure 5.10.

5.4   OPTIONAL-ONE-TO-MANY RELATIONSHIPS

Resolve relationships where the parent entity is optionally related to the child entity as depicted in Figure 5.11.

Discussion

The existence of relationships of the type shown in Figure 5.11 are generally indicative of incomplete modeling. They present some interesting technical problems, which we will discuss momentarily, and they tend to

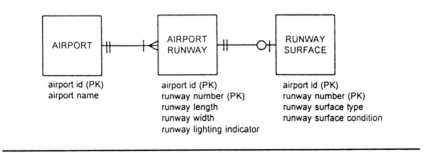

Figure 5.9   Unresolved relationship.

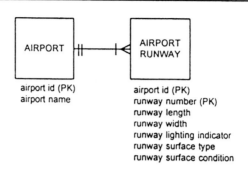

airport id (PK)
airport name

airport id (PK)
runway number (PK)
runway length
runway width
runway lighting indicator
runway surface type
runway surface condition

Figure 5.10   One possible resolution to Figure 5.9.

obscure important business logic. Resolve these by whatever means is appropriate to ensure that the relationship from the child entity (in this case both B and D) to the parent entity (A and C) is mandatory. This will improve the depiction of business logic, increase the stability of the model, and aid in the creation of sound data structures.

One might argue that there is nothing wrong with the relationships you see in Figure 5.11. Were we to add keys, we would migrate the primary keys of entities A and C (the parents) to entities B and D (the children), respectively, as *nonprimary foreign keys*. There would be a problem if we attempted to migrate those keys as primary keys in B and D, however. Recall that one rule of primary keys is that they are never optional. Since our relationships indicate that B and D are optionally

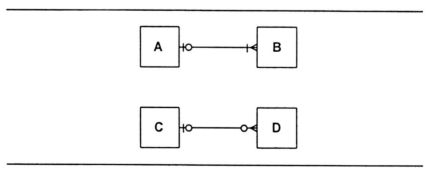

Figure 5.11   Optional-one-to-many.

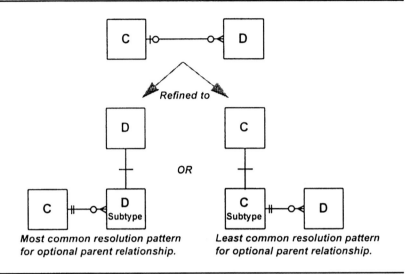

Figure 5.12   Optional parent resolution strategies.

related to A and C, respectively, migration as primary keys is out of the question. The keys for A and C could be migrated as foreign keys. However, remember that our optional attribute rule stipulates that we want to ensure that any attribute, including foreign keys, placed in an entity should be mandatory for all instances of that entity. Ignoring the possibility that the relationship was misrepresented and was meant to be a many-to-many, there are two resolution strategies that are used to resolve this type of relationship (Figure 5.12).

The selected resolution strategy will depend, of course, on the business rules applicable to the individual situation. Note that the resolution strategy on the left is by far the most common, but both are possible results. In either case, we recognize a distinguishing characteristic about C or D that reflects the business rule for a mandatory relationship.

Example

For our example, we will revisit an example we used earlier to describe optional attributes. MATERIAL TYPE represents a standard stock item held in a company warehouse. Some of the materials held are considered

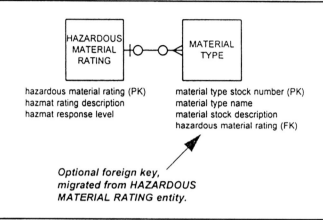

Figure 5.13 Unresolved optional relationship to parent entity.

hazardous (flammable, corrosive, poisonous), and the company has established a hazardous material rating and response procedure to ensure proper handling and rapid response to incidents involving the materials.

Only certain types of material are considered hazardous, with the result that an optional relationship nature exists to the parent entity HAZARDOUS MATERIAL RATING. The business rules and information requirements pertaining to management of hazardous waste only apply to those types of material deemed hazardous. In order to refine the model to precisely depict the business rules, and to position the design team to develop a better database design, the HAZARDOUS MATERIAL entity has been created in Figure 5.14. This resolution strategy follows the general pattern discussed above.

5.5 MANY-TO-MANY (NONSPECIFIC) RELATIONSHIPS

Resolve many-to-many relationships early in the modeling cycle.

Discussion

A many-to-many association, also known as a nonspecific relationship, cannot be implemented in any practical manner in a data structure. While this should be reason enough to resolve it, there is an added incentive to do so early in the data modeling effort. In fact, we recom-

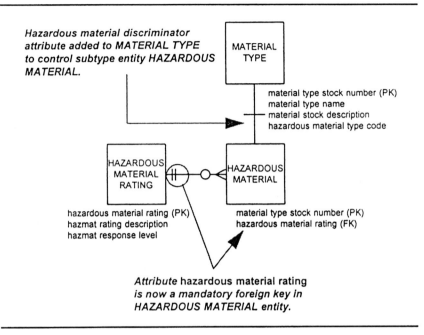

Hazardous material discriminator attribute added to MATERIAL TYPE to control subtype entity HAZARDOUS MATERIAL.

MATERIAL TYPE

material type stock number (PK)
material type name
material stock description
hazardous material type code

HAZARDOUS MATERIAL RATING

HAZARDOUS MATERIAL

hazardous material rating (PK)
hazmat rating description
hazmat response level

material type stock number (PK)
hazardous material rating (FK)

Attribute hazardous material rating is now a mandatory foreign key in HAZARDOUS MATERIAL entity.

Figure 5.14   Resolved optional relationship to parent entity.

mend that you resolve a many-to-many relationship into an associative entity as soon as the relationship degree and nature have been determined. Why the rush? For several reasons:

• The associative entity may imply additional rules or business logic that would have been overlooked if the many-to-many had not been resolved. In particular, we have found that subtype hierarchies tend to emerge from associative entities as business rules are precisely defined, and that these are overlooked in models where many-to-many relationships are not resolved early in the analysis. If you want to build models that fully capture the business rules of the enterprise, then resolve nonspecific relationships early. Also, we have found that a large portion of management control data requirements, usually in the form of derived data attributes, occur in associative entities. Refer to our discussion on derived attributes in Chapter 4. These might be overlooked, or at least underanalyzed, if nonspecific relationships are not resolved.

- Many-to-many relationships make the determination of data dependencies difficult, limiting your ability to identify logically complete subsets of the model. Recall our discussion on data dependency analysis in Chapter 2, and how it serves as an efficient, reliable, and repeatable method for dividing large data models into cohesive subsets. If you have many-to-many relationships in your model, you will have difficulty determining data dependency paths (associative entities form a large proportion of the end-points necessary to begin data dependency analysis).
- Your model will remain unstable until the many-to-many relationship is resolved. It will not be normalized, and your documentation of the model will not be complete.

The sole exception to the early resolution strategy is if you are working with executives or senior staff members, and you neither want or need to include detail in your model. However, be aware of the fact that if you are modeling management level information, many of the derived data attributes of interest to that group reside in associative entities.

Resolve many-to-many relationships by creating an associative entity that maintains the degrees and natures of the original relationship as shown in Figure 5.15.

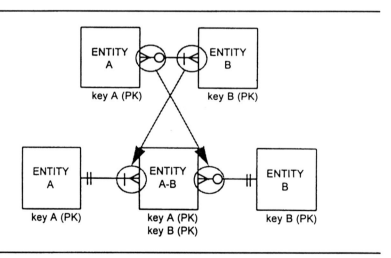

Figure 5.15   Strategy for resolving many-to-many relationships.

The associative entity formed as a result of this action (ENTITY A-B) will have as its primary key the combined migrated primary keys of the original two entities (ENTITY A and ENTITY B). Note that the relationship degrees and natures from the associative to the other two entities are *always* mandatory-one. Like any other modeling construct, there are occasions when the key structure for an associative entity can become more complex. However, this strategy will serve as a good starting point for further modeling around the associative entity.

Example

Assume we are modeling a university registrar's function. Our model has been developed to the point shown in Figure 5.16. The business experts express some concern when they view the model. "How will I be able to tell which student has enrolled in which course, and what the roster of students is for each course? The model doesn't allow me to do that, does it?" And now a new data requirement emerges as well. The business experts in the registrar's office are concerned about transcripts (grades) as well as enrollment. "Where does the attribute for a student's grade in the course belong in our model?" Well, the model fragment in Figure 5.16 simply doesn't do the job any more.

We resolve the many-to-many relationship using an associative entity (see Figure 5.17).

Now the modeling team sees the relationship more clearly, and guess what? That's right, they begin to form additional questions about the business rules, ones that were not apparent before. For example,

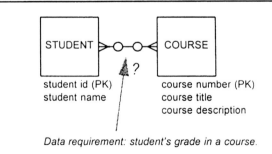

Data requirement: student's grade in a course.

Figure 5.16   Unresolved many-to-many relationship.

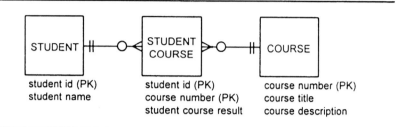

Figure 5.17   Resolved many-to-many relationship.

one member of the team raises the issue about students who take a course more than once, in order to improve their grade in a required prerequisite. The current key structure does not support this requirement. And what about students who enroll but withdraw without a grade penalty, but who are still required to pay part or all of the tuition? And does the registrar need to be able to determine a student's status in relation to the course (i.e., enrolled, completed, withdrew, etc.)? Are dates important to the student course relationship? As you can see, the modeling team can now focus on the student-course relationship, and extend the model by continuing to ask about business rules. We probably would have overlooked some or maybe all of the questions if we had not resolved the many-to-many relationship. Most modeling teams focus on entities and attributes, not relationships, when trying to define new data requirements. Therefore, resolve nonspecific relationships early in your modeling cycle, and use the associative entity as a springboard for further analysis.

5.6   CIRCULAR REFERENCES

Circular references are not permitted.

Description

A circular reference introduces a cyclical relationship into the data model, and should be avoided at all costs. Circular relationships cause problems in the migration of keys, and they prevent the modeler from establishing proper data dependency sequences (Finkelstein, 1989).

Existence of a cyclical relationship indicates that one or more of the following conditions has occurred.

- The modeling team has not clearly or correctly captured the business logic. The team should reevaluate this portion of the model, examining related business rules and policies to determine the correct requirements.
- The cardinality of one or more of the relationships has been accidentally reversed either during the modeling session or during entry to the CASE tool.
- The cardinality for one end of a relationship has been incorrectly recorded. For instance, a many-to-many relationship was recorded as a one-to-many.

Example

Our example comes from a strategic data model created for XYZ Manufacturing Corporation, and addresses the first causal condition described above. Note that we have elected to show only key attributes in this example. XYZ (an ORGANIZATION) offers each of its products and services (OFFERING) in many MARKETs around the world. In each market, it competes against many other ORGANIZATIONs, each of which has many OFFERINGs of its own. The model seems to support the logic of these statements, but there is clearly something amiss. The circular nature of our logic leads to additional questions.

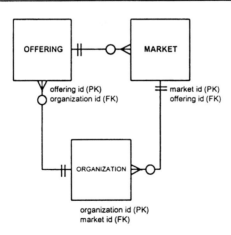

Figure 5.18   Unresolved circular reference.

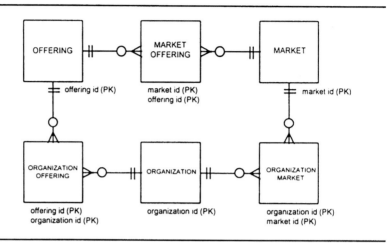

Figure 5.19   Resolution of circular reference.

Now let's examine some refinements to the model. First, we'll reverse our logical progression through the model. Each ORGANIZATION operates in many MARKETs (by virtue of having many OFFERINGs in many MARKETs, as we discussed earlier). And each MARKET has many OFFERINGS (e.g., competing products and services). Finally, depending on how we have defined OFFERING, the same OFFERING may be marketed by many ORGANIZATIONs. The result is a refined model that completes the logic that was captured in the first attempt.

5.7   TRIADS

Eliminate triads from the data model.

Description

A triad is a redundant relationship consisting of two dependency paths between the same two entities (FIPS, 1992). One of the paths consists of a direct relationship between the entities, while the other involves relationships to entities other than our two subject entities (see Figure 5.20). Triads emerge during the normal course of modeling, as teams attempt to precisely represent business policies that overlap or are contradictory.

Triads should be eliminated from the data model because they introduce redundant information, which may eventually lead to problems with database consistency.

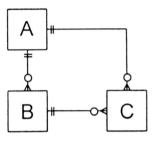

Figure 5.20   General structure of a triad.

If a triad has been created by the team, then simply resolving it in the data model may not be adequate. The existence of a triad may indicate that contradictory policies exist. Before correcting the model, examine the business statements that were used as a basis for that portion of the model, and review session notes to determine the rationale for constructing both dependency paths.

Example

In our example, we have a model fragment that records data requirements and rules pertaining to the monitoring of security alarms. The security firm has established a set of alarm classes (perhaps according to the nature of the installation under surveillance), and has a policy regarding response time for each class. A set of alarm codes exist within each class that provide instructions on how to respond. Finally, individual alarms are monitored, and the firm's performance against each alarm is measured. The firm has established a performance objective relating to beating the response time maximum. The latter objective may have caused the modeling team to create a relationship between ALARM CLASS and ALARM, to ensure that each alarm can be traced to the alarm class to which it belongs. However, the classification policy led to the construction of the ALARM CLASS-ALARM CODE-ALARM dependency path. The model fragment is a triad construct.

According to one of Armstrong's axioms (Date, 1986) on functional dependencies:

If $A \rightarrow B$ and $B \rightarrow C$, then $A \rightarrow C$.

You may recognize this as the "transitivity rule." In the case of our example, we have the following dependencies:

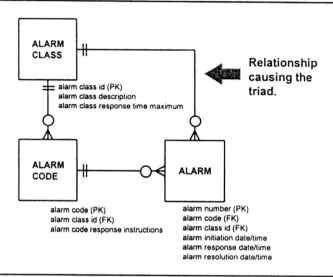

Figure 5.21 Model fragment containing a triad.

alarm number → alarm code
alarm code → alarm class

Therefore, the dependency alarm number → alarm class is "logically implied" (Korth and Silberschartz, 1986), and need not be designated with a separate relationship.

Based on this analysis, the resolution of our example triad is relatively straightforward. Note that there is a transitive dependency between ALARM CLASS and ALARM through ALARM CODE. Therefore,

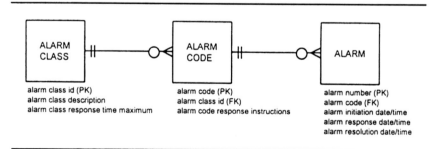

Figure 5.22 Model fragment corrected to eliminate triad.

ALARM can be readily traced to its ALARM CLASS according to the
ALARM CODE to which it is assigned. If ALARM CLASS to ALARM
CODE were many-to-many, we would have a very different situation.
You can confirm this by examining the key structures in the model. The
corrected model fragment is shown below. Note the change in the key
structure for ALARM.

5.8   MORE THAN ONE RELATIONSHIP BETWEEN TWO ENTITIES

*No two entities should have more than one relationship between
them.*

Discussion

We have encountered several experienced modelers who insist that multiple relationships add important and necessary information to the model.
Fortunately, most data modelers have already arrived at the conclusion
that multiple relationships between the same two entities actually introduce confusion into a model, rather than adding clarity. In fact, many, if
not most, CASE tools prevent the user from making this kind of mistake.

In case there are still some diehards out there, we present some
arguments in favor of this rule.

- Use of multiple relationships introduces the potential for conflicting
  cardinalities. A requirement for differing cardinalities suggests that
  there are logical subsets of the two entities (subtypes) that are governed by distinct sets of rules. The model needs to be refined and the
  hidden logic flushed out. Our first example addresses this condition.
- Multiple relationships tend to represent process logic, rather than
  data requirements and actual relationship rules. Our second example illustrates this case.
- Use of multiple relationships can also obscure or confuse other aspects of the data logic, since their use gives the appearance of comprehensive analysis. The opposite is true, as we can see by both
  examples.
- Modeling teams may attempt to document the different *reasons*
  that two entities may be related. Use of multiple relationships to
  accomplish this is a case of using the wrong tool for the job. We
  suggest documenting such information in the Relationship Description, or through use of a Reason Entity if an associative entity is
  involved. Our third example illustrates this type of situation.

Examples

Conflicting Cardinalities In this example we see how easy it is for conflicting cardinalities to invade a data model if multiple relationships are permitted. In our hypothetical organization, two separate data modeling exercises have been underway. The first involves the division level staff, who created a strategic model for their enterprise. This effort was followed up by a priority project in the Personnel Management Subject Area (identified and scoped during the strategic project). The division staff has clear strategies in mind with regard to personnel, productivity, and workforce management. These are driven by their business objectives. The modeling team for the Personnel Management area has a different set of strategies, as we can see in the model. Their reality differs from the perspective of the division staff, resulting in conflicting business rules.

If we let this conflict continue without resolution, the organization ends up with two problems. First, the requirements for information systems development will be unclear. Even if these entities are used in separate systems, an EIS for the division staff and a personnel management system, there is every likelihood that they will draw data from shared databases. But we will have introduced contradictory rules into the enterprise data architecture, and at some point will encounter problems summarizing or sharing information. Second, and perhaps more important, the model indicates a potentially serious gap in communication between division management and one of their key operational areas. Remember, the model is a representation of the actual enterprise. Our example model indicates contradictory strategies and policies exist. The business is going in separate directions.

While our example may be somewhat trivial, the reader should be able to gain a sense of the serious problems that can arise for an organization due to the cumulative effects of many contradictory rules or policies. The modeling team has a tremendous opportunity to help bring the enterprise into alignment by bringing the two groups together to discuss the different views, and to come to a mutual understanding on the business rules and strategies.

Our resolved model, shown in Figure 5.24, reflects the kinds of changes that modeling teams often encounter when attempting to resolve cardinality conflicts for multiple relationships (either before they get into the model, or after). In this case, the model manager brought the two groups together, with the result that the division staff reiterated its desire to have at least one person assigned to each job at all times. Since the personnel department could not ensure that an employee would be available to step into the job, a new strategy was devel-

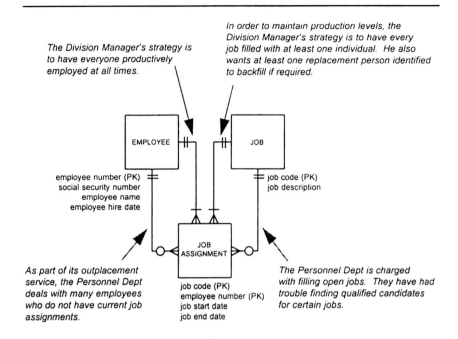

The Division Manager's strategy is to have everyone productively employed at all times.

In order to maintain production levels, the Division Manager's strategy is to have every job filled with at least one individual. He also wants at least one replacement person identified to backfill if required.

employee number (PK)
social security number
employee name
employee hire date

job code (PK)
job description

As part of its outplacement service, the Personnel Dept deals with many employees who do not have current job assignments.

job code (PK)
employee number (PK)
job start date
job end date

The Personnel Dept is charged with filling open jobs. They have had trouble finding qualified candidates for certain jobs.

Figure 5.23   Multiple conflicting relationships.

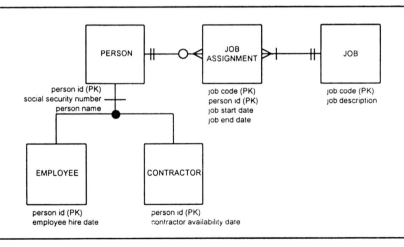

person id (PK)
social security number
person name

job code (PK)
person id (PK)
job start date
job end date

job code (PK)
job description

person id (PK)
employee hire date

person id (PK)
contractor availability date

Figure 5.24   One possible resolution of cardinality conflict.

oped to identify and retain contractors who could remain on call to fulfill the assignment. Thus, every job had at least one person assigned to cover it. The personnel department also convinced the division staff that having every employee assigned to a job was not practical. This was especially true since one of their plants was closing down, and they had several employees going through their outplacement program.

Again, this is only one potential solution, and it is highly dependent on the definition of JOB, EMPLOYEE, and other components of the model. The key message here is that violating good practices of data modeling leads not only to information systems problems, but to missed opportunities to resolve underlying business conflicts.

Process Logic in the Data Model In this example, a fuel supply firm maintains supplies of different FUEL GRADEs at several small AIRPORTs in a large metropolitan area. The modeling team charged with helping the firm build a fuel management system has created the model depicted below. Based on input from the firm's managers, the team determined that several things occur with fuel at an airport—it is received, stored, and eventually dispensed. The model, they believe, accurately portrays this situation. They have added three relationships between AIRPORT and FUEL GRADE to portray the dynamics between airports and fuel. The key word here is "dynamics." A data model is a static view of the enterprise. The modeling team has done a very effective job of identifying the events that occur during the maintenance cycle at an airport. Thus, the model portrayed below includes information that should be recorded in the dynamic model of the fuel management system. From a data modeling perspective, it is important to understand that there exists a relationship between FUEL GRADE and AIRPORT. One characteristic of that relationship is that several events and processes occur involving both an airport and fuel. Further exploration of this model should lead you to question other aspects of its construction as well.

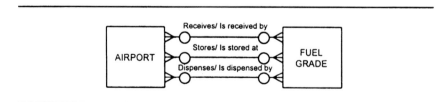

Figure 5.25   Multiple relationships representing process logic.

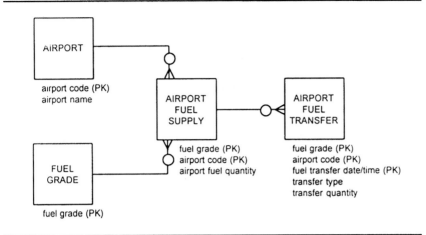

Figure 5.26   One possible resolution of multiple relationships.

In our hypothetical resolution, we have removed the process logic from the model, and returned it to its static state. This is, of course, only one possible solution.

Documenting Roles and Reasons   Our final example examines the popular use of multiple relationships to document reasons or roles that entities play in relation to each other. Figure 5.26 documents a model fragment created by an airport management team. The team wanted to capture the business rules surrounding ownership, operation, and inspection of the airport by various interested business parties.

Look closely at the model in Figure 5.27. What does it really say about the relationship between AIRPORT and BUSINESS PARTY? It says that there must be at least one BUSINESS PARTY identified as an

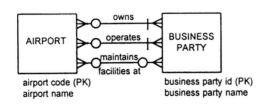

Figure 5.27   Multiple relationships for multiple reasons.

owner, and at least one identified as an operator for each AIRPORT. This set of relationships is further complicated by the fact that each is a many-to-many cardinality. In order to resolve this complex mix in an elegant fashion, the modeling team developed the solution shown in Figure 5.28. The team created AIRPORT BUSINESS PARTY to resolve the many-to-many cardinality between AIRPORT and BUSINESS PARTY (see Many-to-Many Relationships rule). In order to accommodate the multiple roles that a BUSINESS PARTY could have in relation to an AIRPORT, which were represented by the three relationships in our original example, the team created the entity AIRPORT BUSINESS PARTY ROLE, which defines a set of values pertaining to an AIRPORT BUSINESS PARTY, and whether that role is required or not required for an AIRPORT. The primary key of AIRPORT BUSINESS PARTY ROLE migrates to AIRPORT BUSINESS PARTY and is used as a primary key in that entity in combination with *airport code* and *business party id*. This key structure (in AIRPORT BUSINESS PARTY ROLE) allows an individual BUSI-

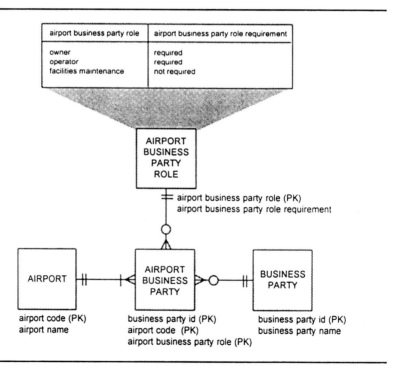

Figure 5.28   One possible resolution of multiple role problem.

NESS PARTY to perform more than one role in relation to an AIRPORT. The team included an attribute *airport business party role requirement* in AIRPORT BUSINESS PARTY ROLE in order to establish a business rule that an AIRPORT *must be* associated with a BUSINESS PARTY that assumes the role of "owner," and one that assumes the role of "operator." Therefore, when a new AIRPORT instance is created, we would expect at least one (although maybe more than one) instance of AIRPORT BUSINESS PARTY to be created with an *airport business party role* value equal to "owner" and one equal to "operator." The roles of "owner" and "operator" are required (as indicated in Figure 5.27 and the relationship cardinalities in Figure 5.28) for each AIRPORT.

5.9   PARALLEL ASSOCIATIVE ENTITIES

Parallel associative entities should not be permitted.

Description

As we discussed in the last rule, multiple relationships between two entities introduce some problems into the model. The same problems exist when "parallel" associative entities are introduced. Recall that an associative entity is created to resolve a many-to-many relationship between two entities. Parallel associative entities may creep into a model when more than one modeling team is working in the same subject area of the model, particularly when the teams have little or no intercommunication. The easiest way to identify this situation is from the identical key structures that exist. Parallel associative entities introduce the following problems into a data model:

* **Redundancy.** Each of the associative entities will carry the same set of inherited primary keys, and have the tendency to duplicate non-key information as well.
* Potential for **introducing contradictory business rules**, or for hiding conflicts in business rules that may exist in different parts of an enterprise. Remember that the data model is a key tool for identifying and resolving those conflicts to ensure consistent access to standard data products.
* Potential for **introducing consistency problems** into a database designed from the model.

The resolution of parallel associative entities is relatively straightforward—consolidate the associatives into a single associative entity. Follow the consolidation with a thorough examination of attribute edit rules and ownership authorities, to ensure that adequate requirements information is recorded to manage data integrity and security.

Example

The example depicts a series of relationships existing for a firm that sells a host of products in its line of clothing outlets. The model shown below resulted from three separate data modeling efforts—a marketing team that decides which products will be sold at each outlet according to local demographics (OUTLET PRODUCT MIX), an inventory team that must plan product orders and order inventory accordingly (OUTLET PRODUCT INVENTORY), and a financial management team that needs to track the sales and cost performance of various products at different outlets (OUTLET PRODUCT COST). When the models were consolidated, the model management team recognized three parallel associative entities.

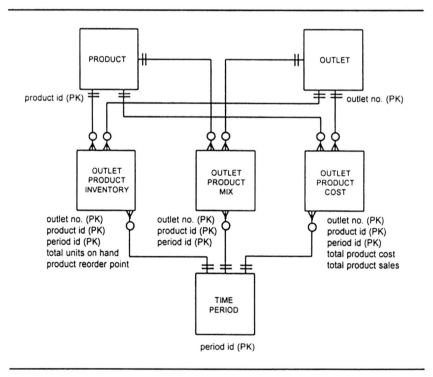

Figure 5.29   Unresolved parallel associative entities.

Note the potential for problems in this version of the model. First, the marketing team's decision to sell products at an outlet determines whether there will be any inventory or costs associated with the product at that outlet. Creation of instances of either OUTLET PRODUCT INVENTORY or OUTLET PRODUCT COST without a corresponding instance of OUTLET PRODUCT MIX is possible in the current model, but would be incorrect. Second, all three associative entities have the same key structure. This indicates, of course, that the non-key attributes of any of the three associative entities are actually functionally dependent on the primary key of all three associative entities. The model carries a clear normalization problem as a result. Finally, looking ahead to design and implementation, the creation of tables or other data structures to accommodate three entities with identical key structures in this case introduces unnecessary overhead into the system.

A recommended resolution to the multiple associative entity problem is depicted in Figure 5.30.

It is important to recognize that none of the departments has lost any information needed to perform its functions. The model is now correctly normalized (according to our assumptions), and can be implemented in one or more information systems.

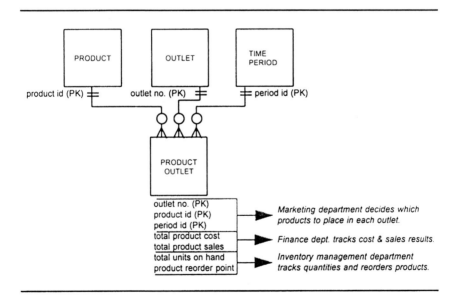

Figure 5.30   Resolved parallel associative entities.

5.10   RECURSIVE RELATIONSHIPS

Rule Resolve recursive relationships.

Discussion

A recursive relationship is one in which an occurrence of an entity is related to one or more other occurrences of the same entity. These are usually depicted with a relationship like that shown in Figure 5.31 in our example.

Example

Figure 5.31 depicts a recursive relationship from one instance of PERSON to another. A recursive relationship is often modeled this way initially.

Alternatively, we may first recognize recursive associations as relationships that exist among subtypes of the same supertype entity, as illustrated in Figure 5.32. The relationship between SUPERVISOR and EMPLOYEE implies a relationship between two occurrences of the PERSON entity, since each occurrence of EMPLOYEE and SUPERVISOR requires the existence of a corresponding occurrence of PERSON. From a business perspective, supervisors and employees have a personal relationship (or in some cases, an impersonal relationship!). Note in particular the key structure of EMPLOYEE. We have migrated the *person id* primary key from SUPERVISOR as a nonprimary foreign key in EMPLOYEE. That does not violate our rule that a subtype must have the same primary key as its parent, so we could leave the model as it currently stands, and probably not encounter any major problems.

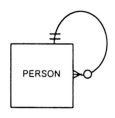

Figure 5.31   A typical recursive relationship notation.

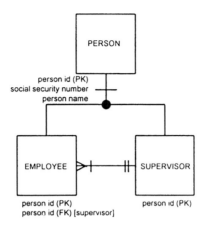

Figure 5.32   Relationships among subtypes of the same supertype.

But what if we have numerous subtypes of PERSON, each with relationships to the other? Our keys could be become increasingly difficult to handle. Or what if we have a matrix organization, where an employee could have several supervisors, or we wish to track an employee's supervisory history? Figure 5.33 shows our example modified to depict an associative entity between EMPLOYEE and SUPERVISOR.

This works if subtypes have been identified, and there are not too many of them. Recursive relationships come in all shapes and sizes, and the attempts to resolve them are often inconsistent even within the same model.

In order to deal with both simple and complex variations of recursive relationships quickly and consistently, we need a general scheme for resolving them. We have found Finkelstein's method to be very effective, and actually quite elegant (1989). Finkelstein establishes one of his business normal forms—fifth business normal form (5BNF) to be exact—to deal with recursive relationships. He defines 5BNF as:

An entity is in fifth business normal form if its dependencies on occurrences of the same entity or entity type have been moved into a STRUCTURE entity.

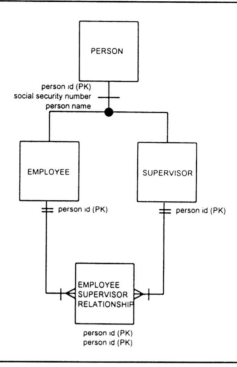

Figure 5.33   Associative entity between two subtypes.

A structure entity is a special type of attributive entity wherein two instances of the parent primary key are migrated to the child, rather than one. Additional keys are added if necessary to distinguish between multiple relationships between the same two occurrences. Figure 5.34 illustrates the general form of a structure entity primary key. Note that the presence of two instances of the *person id* primary key in PERSON STRUCTURE allows us to establish a relationship between two occurrences of PERSON. In fact, every occurrence in PERSON can be related to every other occurrence of PERSON through the PERSON STRUCTURE entity.

The structure entity is generally only used at the supertype level of a generalization-specialization hierarchy. There are several variations of the structure entity that can be used to handle special circumstances. We strongly recommend you read Finkelstein's discussions on structure entities (1989, 1992).

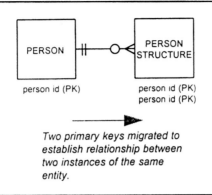

Two primary keys migrated to
establish relationship between
two instances of the same
entity.

Figure 5.34   Migration of structure entity primary keys.

REFERENCES

Date, C. J. *An Introduction to Database Systems, Volume I.* Reading, MA: Addison-Wesley, 1986.

Finkelstein, Clive. *An Introduction to Information Engineering: From Strategic Planning to Information Systems.* Sydney: Addison-Wesley, 1989.

Finkelstein, Clive. *Information Engineering: Strategic Systems Development.* Sydney: Addison-Wesley, 1992.

FIPS PUB XXX, *Integration Definition for Information Modeling IDEF1X,* September 1992.

Korth, Henry F. and Silberschatz, Abraham. *Database System Concepts.* New York: McGraw-Hill, 1986.

6

Generalization Hierarchy Rules

Human beings generally use three methods to describe entities in the world around them (Coad and Yourdon, 1990). The first method is by describing an object and its characteristics, based on the person's familiarity with a specific problem domain. We characterize an employee by his employee id, skill set, and salary. The rule sets addressed so far deal primarily with models that have been developed in this manner.

The second technique is by differentiating between a whole object and its component parts. To describe an organization, we could break down into divisions, and then break the divisions down into departments and so forth. These objects are then aggregated to provide an understanding of an organization. It is far easier to discuss each of these subjects as they relate to the whole, rather than discussing them independently.

The last method is to develop a taxonomy and use this structure to identify the differences and similarities between objects. If we are discussing the types of people we may find at an organization, we first recognize that they are all human beings. Next we distinguish between employees at the organization, and, perhaps the people who purchase products or services from the organization. This process is known as generalization and it is the focus of the next set of rules.

A generalization hierarchy is a structured grouping of entities that share common characteristics. It is a powerful tool for the data modeler because of its associated inheritance capability and the ability to represent the commonality of entities and preserve their differences. It is the

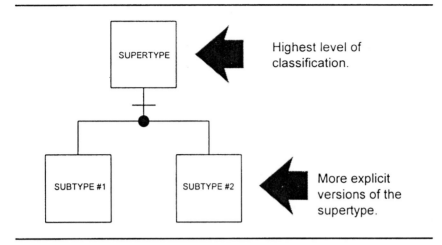

Figure 6.1 Generalization hierarchy.

relationship between an entity and one or more refined versions. The entity being refined is called the *supertype* and each refined version is known as a *subtype*.

Most data models tend to use entities associated with specific domains. Generalization allows us to construct data models that are far more stable by focusing on the similarities between entities and allowing changes to only impact entities germane to the change. Generalization can also help by reducing the number of specific entities in the data model, rendering it less complex and easier to understand.

6.1 SUBTYPE JUSTIFICATION

Each subtype entity must possess one or more of the following characteristics: (1) at least one non-key attribute, or (2) a relationship with another entity that is logically correct only for it and none other.

Discussion

Each subtype that is placed into a generalization hierarchy must be evaluated to ensure that it is a *good* subtype. It is extremely important to make sure subtypes are not based on functional differences, but rather on quantifiable characteristics or properties. A subtype that is based on functional differences will lead to the development, implementation, and maintenance of redundant data.

In order to avoid these situations, the analyst should look for generalization opportunities that possess one of the characteristics mentioned in the rule. A good subtype must be required to *specify at least one attribute, other than the primary key*. If the subtype does not possess any additional attributes, then its role in the organization is not distinct from the supertype. Modeling from a process or functional perspective leads to the introduction of VENDOR, CUSTOMER, SUPPLIER, or another role type entity that is not distinct (Palmer, 1993).

Subtypes are allowed to participate in relationships. This is an opportunity for the data analyst to describe business rules precisely. Rather than abstracting a mandatory relationship to the supertype and changing the cardinality to optional, subtypes allow explicit communication of business policies. Mandatory relationships are permitted between the subtype and other entities in the data model.

Examples

The subtypes in the first example appear to have been created by focusing on the functions of an organization rather than its characteristics. The model does not provide us with any indication of how a SUPPLIER, VENDOR, CUSTOMER, STRATEGIC PARTNER is different from an ORGANIZATION. They all maintain the same attributes. If this data model was taken into a development environment, the four subtypes would likely be allocated to their own files, thus introducing redundancy and maintenance headaches. If the characteristics of the model identify no difference in the structure, then the model should be structured as such.

The data model has been revised to capture the identical information as the previous model, sans subtypes. Here, ORGANIZATION CATEGORY contains information on the classification of the ORGANIZATION.

The second model contains both valid and invalid subtypes. The entity EARTH MOVING EQUIPMENT is a valid subtype, even though it does not possess non-key attributes. It is valid because it possesses a relationship with another entity, SIC CATEGORY. This relationship describes an important distinction between EQUIPMENT and EARTH MOVING EQUIPMENT. Only EARTH MOVING EQUIPMENT is identified by a Standard Industry Code. HOME EQUIPMENT is an invalid subtype. It adds no value to the data model, other than classification (Figure 6.5).

The same model has been revised to remove the invalid subtype. No information has been lost; the model is more stable. The entity HOME EQUIPMENT is a value in EQUIPMENT CATEGORY.

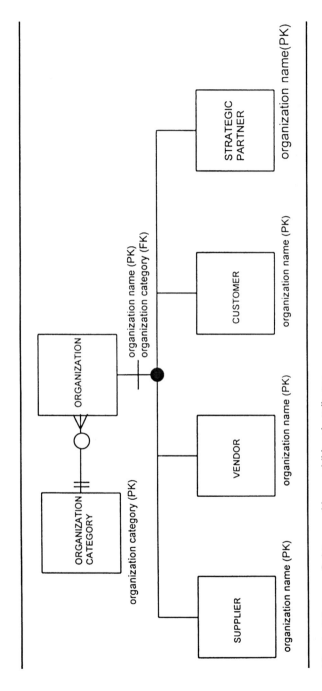

Figure 6.2   Subtypes with no additional attributes.

213

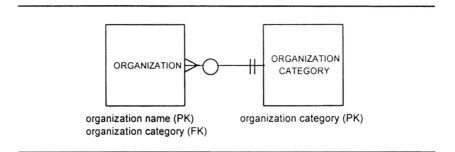

organization name (PK)   organization category (PK)
organization category (FK)

Figure 6.3   Revised model with no subtypes.

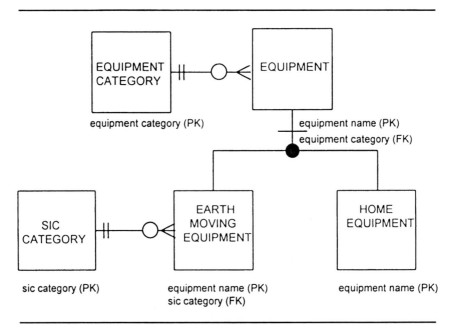

sic category (PK)   equipment name (PK)   equipment name (PK)
                            sic category (FK)

Figure 6.4   Subtype with mandatory relationship.

6.2   SUPERTYPE JUSTIFICATION

A supertype entity or generalization hierarchy should be constructed under the following conditions: (1) a large number of entities appear to be of the same type, (2) attributes are repeated for multiple entities, or (3) the model is continually evolving.

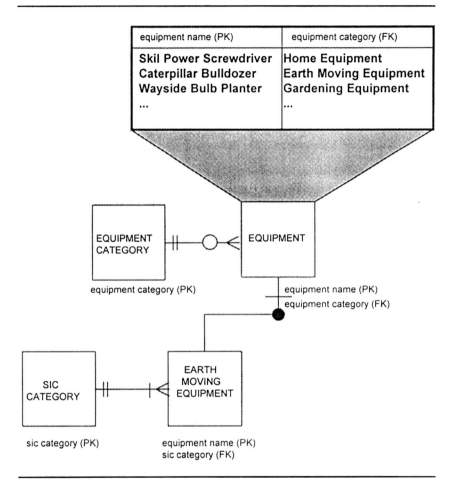

equipment name (PK)	equipment category (FK)
Skil Power Screwdriver	Home Equipment
Caterpillar Bulldozer	Earth Moving Equipment
Wayside Bulb Planter	Gardening Equipment
...	...

Figure 6.5   Revised subtype structure.

Discussion

Just as we have rules for the creation of subtypes, we need rules that allow us to identify in what situations we create a supertype. There are a number of reasons, but the three we have outlined are symptoms of models where generalization should be applied.

The first symptom is a data model not easily understood by subject matter experts. The lack of understanding is sometimes introduced by *a large number of entities that appear to have some common ancestor.*

We should strive to keep our models simple and avoid needless complication. The modeler should always keep in mind what parts of the model already exist, and prior to introducing a new piece, review any similarities with existing pieces. This will help eliminate a model that contains many subtypes of a PERSON or ORGANIZATION or VEHICLE without generalization.

Attributes that appear to exist for multiple entities is another sign the model could benefit from the introduction of a generalization hierarchy. If attributes like *person name, patient name, delivery person name, contact person name,* and *manager name* are being introduced, they should be reviewed and a generalization hierarchy potentially created. All of them appear to be names of people.

Finally, we should look for *business models that are changing at an ever-increasing rate.* This may be dictated by our industry or other environmental factors that face our business. What is the value of spending several months building a business model, if it is outdated before it is

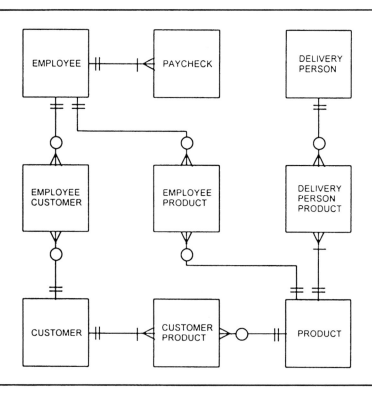

Figure 6.6   Model lacking generalization.

complete? Generalization can minimize the impact of changes to our models.

Examples

The first model, Figure 6.6, is sorely in need of generalization. At first glance, the model appears to have three types of human beings in the model. There is an EMPLOYEE, DELIVERY PERSON, and a CUSTOMER. Though the attributes are not shown, it is a safe assumption that the information among these three data model objects is quite similar and the potential to share attributes is high. Aren't an EMPLOYEE, a CUSTOMER, and a DELIVERY PERSON all going to have names, telephone numbers, and perhaps addresses?

The same model is reintroduced below with generalization. No information is missing and the relationships are easier to understand and read. DELIVERY PERSON, CUSTOMER, and EMPLOYEE are all generalized under the PERSON supertype.

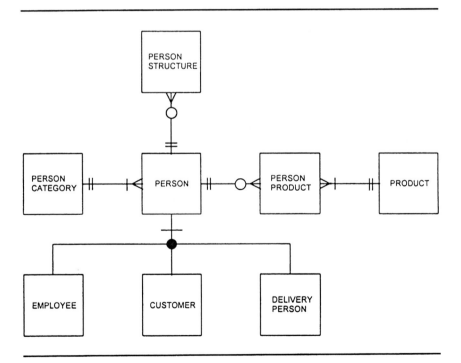

Figure 6.7   Same model with generalization hierarchy.

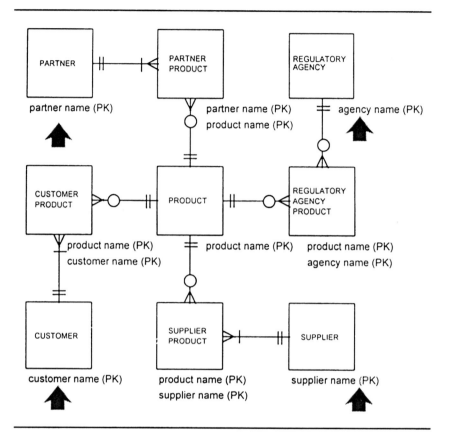

Figure 6.8   Repetitious attributes.

In our second example, entities that are similar in nature will often lead a modeler to construct a generalization hierarchy. If the entities do not provide an indication, the attributes sometimes will. As the analyst is examining entities in the model, he or she may uncover attributes that appear to be used over and over again. This is a good indication that generalization can, and probably should, occur on the model. In the model fragment in Figure 6.8, we continually see the attribute *name*. It never exists independently, it is always qualified by *partner*, *customer*, *agency*, or *supplier*. This should alert the analyst to reexamine these entities and their current structure.

The analyst has consolidated the repetitious attributes in Figure 6.9. Now *agency name*, *partner name*, *customer name*, and *supplier name* are referred by *organization name*.

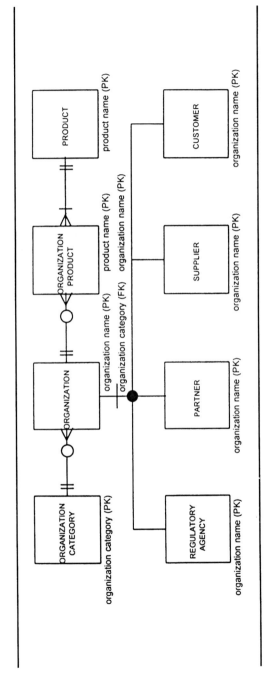

Figure 6.9   Repetitious attributes—Resolved with generalization hierarchy.

6.3 SUBTYPE DISCRIMINATORS

Every supertype must be associated with or contain a subtype discriminator.

Discussion

A subtype discriminator is an attribute that allows the supertype to be classified into an occurrence of a subtype. Every entity that participates in a supertype role must maintain this attribute. This attribute is sometimes known as a category discriminator.

The discriminator exists either in the supertype, as a foreign key or a non-key attribute, or in a mandatory away relationship from the supertype. The placement of the discriminator is an essential part of the generalization hierarchy: If we are going to distinguish between subtypes, the discriminator must be located in close proximity to the supertype.

In a generalization hierarchy, or *is a* structure, the subtype discriminator describes what kind of subtype the supertype will be refined into. It is important for the reviewer to ensure there is a mechanism in place to sort like entities among subtypes.

Examples

Figure 6.10 demonstrates a very subtle point about discriminators. OFFERING is a supertype of PRODUCT and SERVICE and OFFERING have a relationship with OFFERING CATEGORY, the entity that contains the categories of OFFERINGs. The problem with this model fragment is the optional relationship between OFFERING and OFFERING ROLE. A supertype must either contain the discriminator or have access to it in a mandatory relationship. The model fragment below suggests that only certain OFFERINGs have OFFERING CATEGORYs. This is an invalid generalization structure.

The optional relationship has been modified in Figure 6.11 to mandatory and the subtype discriminator now participates in all supertype relationships. This is now a legal generalization hierarchy.

Figure 6.12 shows an additional method for placing a subtype discriminator into a data model. Here it participates as a non-key attribute in the supertype. This situation appears frequently; the reviewer needs to ensure that the discriminator is not violating the rules of normalization and would not better exist as an explicit or domain entity.

The third data model, Figure 6.13, shows a subtype discriminator

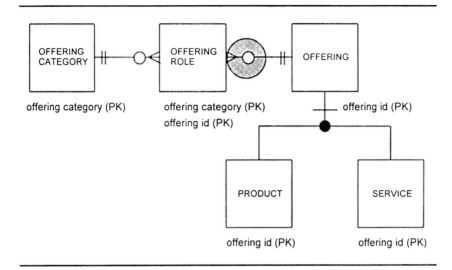

Figure 6.10   Subtype discriminator—Unresolved.

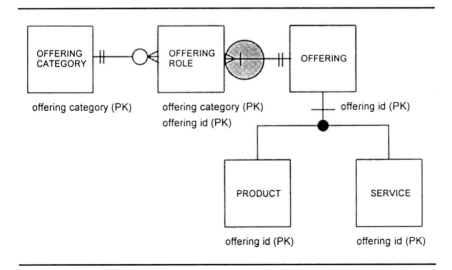

Figure 6.11   Subtype discriminator—Resolved.

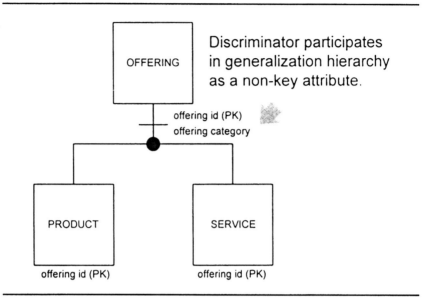

Figure 6.12   Subtype discriminator—Non-key.

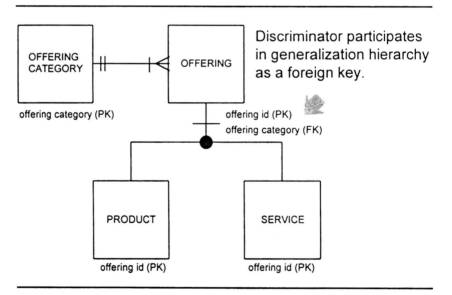

Figure 6.13   Subtype discriminator—Foreign key.

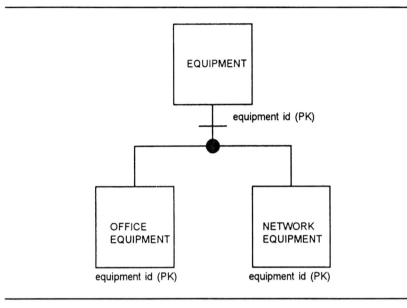

Figure 6.14   Illegal generalization hierarchy.

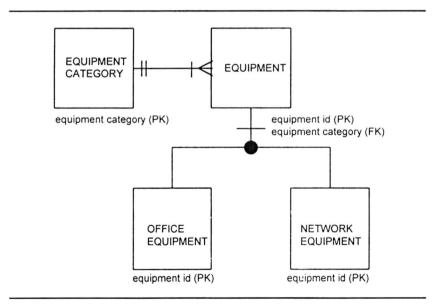

Figure 6.15   Resolved generalization hierarchy.

participating in the relationship as a foreign key. OFFERING CATEGORY is an explicit entity that contains all values of OFFERING CATEGORY.

One final example on this topic, Figure 6.14, is a supertype that does not contain a category discriminator. In this situation, the analyst has no method for distinguishing one occurrence of the supertype from another. How does the analyst determine what occurrences go into the NETWORK EQUIPMENT subtype and what occurrences are placed into the OFFICE EQUIPMENT subtype?

The generalization hierarchy is refined in Figure 6.15. An EQUIPMENT CATEGORY is added to the structure to discriminate between the two subtypes.

6.4   CATEGORY DISCRIMINATOR CONTROL

A category discriminator can provide the domain for only one generalization structure.

Discussion

Subtype discriminators exist in a variety of settings. They can become a Type or Domain entity and maintain a mandatory relationship with the supertype, or they may become a non-key attribute in the supertype. The question arises, can this same domain of values apply to multiple generalization structures? The answer is a resounding no.

Type entities control subtype entities that are part of a specific domain. Since the No Null rule causes the Type entity control, it is a part of the same domain of values represented by the supertype entity. Although there is a set of entities created to capture the data about a principal entity, the data is still part of the domain of data relevant to the principal entity business information requirement. Using a Type entity to control subtype entities of two different supertype entities would indicate a mixed domain represented by the Type entity, and therefore a need to separate the domain into two Type entities and controlling the domain secondaries of the appropriate principal entity.

Example

In Figure 6.16, we have a type entity, MILITARY - CIVILIAN, that is being used to classify the OCCUPATION, PERSON, and POSITION supertypes. At first glance, this appears to be a reasonable approach. After all, we have Military and Civilian Occupations, Military and Civilian Persons, and Military and Civilian Positions. The same domain

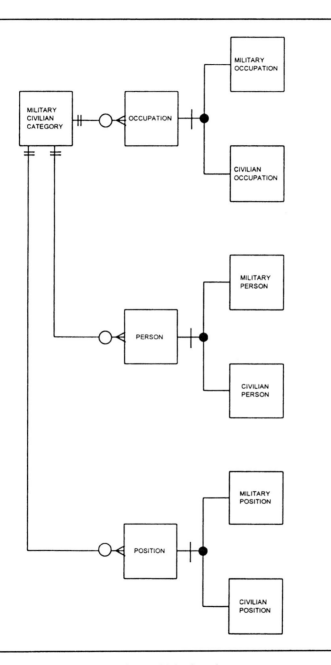

Figure 6.16   Type entity crossing multiple domains.

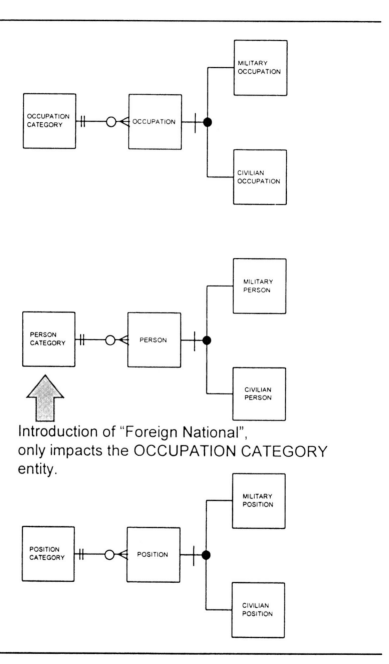

Introduction of "Foreign National", only impacts the OCCUPATION CATEGORY entity.

Figure 6.17   Type entity crossing multiple domains—Resolved.

can be applied to multiple generalizations, so the complexity of the model can be reduced by reducing the number of entities—we will not require a MILITARY CIVILIAN OCCUPATION TYPE or a MILITARY CIVILIAN PERSON TYPE or a MILITARY CIVILIAN POSITION TYPE. This is flawed reasoning. If we add another OCCUPATION subtype, say FOREIGN NATIONAL, this value would have to reside in the type entity, even though, it will never apply to POSITION or PERSON. This is a mixed domain.

Note that the introduction of a new value in Figure 6.17, FOREIGN NATIONAL, will have no impact on the model except where appropriate.

6.5   MULTIPLE INHERITANCE

A subtype entity can only be a member of the set of subtypes for one generalization relationship.

Discussion

Multiple inheritance permits an entity to have more than one parent and to inherit features from both. It is used quite extensively in object-oriented applications to gain greater flexibility in specifying classes for reuse. The disadvantage is a loss of conceptual and implementation simplicity. There is no longer a clear definition of the object that inherits characteristics from two ancestors. In data modeling applications, this is an illegal construct.

A subtype entity can belong to only one supertype. A subtype that maintains membership in more than one hierarchy violates the concept that it *is a* class of the parent, and also would cause conflict for the primary key, which must be the same as the parent. The multiple inheritance relationship described above can be represented with the mechanisms available to the data modeler.

Example

Multiple inheritance violates many of the rules we have described thus far. The first problem is how to identify the object. In Figure 6.18, is an AUTOMATON a PERSON or an INFORMATION SYSTEM? The obvious answer is, it is both.

Though an object model provides us with additional constructs to develop our models from, there is nothing that we cannot represent with the data modeling tools we have. This is also true of network and

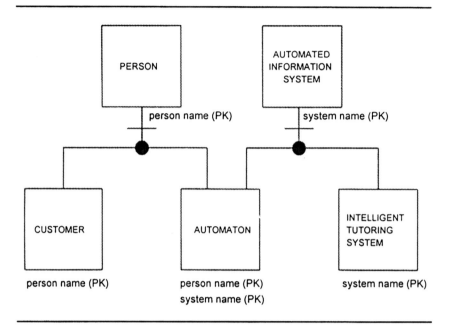

Figure 6.18   Subtype with two supertypes.

hierarchical models. Nothing is unrepresentable using the data modeling notations available.

In Figure 6.19, we have eliminated AUTOMATON from the model and created a relationship between PERSON and SYSTEM. The SYSTEM PERSON entity is described in the same manner as AUTOMATON was in the previous model. This structure also provides the organization with a bit more flexibility. Not only can we represent an AUTOMATON, but we could also represent other SYSTEM PERSONs such as an OPERATOR, DEVELOPER, MANAGER, or END USER.

6.6   NESTED GENERALIZATION HIERARCHY

A subtype entity may become a supertype in another generalization hierarchy.

Discussion

Nested generalization hierarchies are a required tool for the modeler who wishes to show extremely precise business rules, while allowing

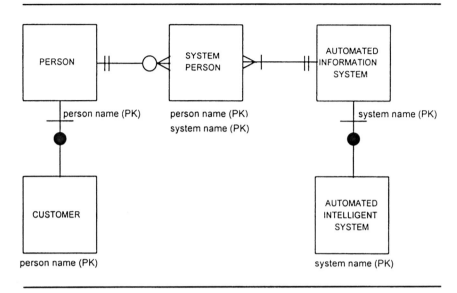

Figure 6.19   Multiple inheritance—Possible resolution.

the subject matter experts to maintain the overall context. The hierarchies tend to get deeper as we begin to uncover more operational level business rules.

The entities that play two roles in a nested hierarchy, subtype and supertype, must adhere to the guidelines laid out for both. This means that in its role as a subtype the entity must have a mandatory relationship with another entity, and in its role as a supertype, it must possess a discriminator. In this situation, the mandatory relationship is usually to the entity that contains the discriminator.

There is no right or wrong when it comes to the depth of a generalization hierarchy, however, care should be exercised in construction. A hierarchy so abstract that it results in miscommunication among business experts is not helpful, nor is a hierarchy that is extremely deep. As a rule of thumb, re-examine all hierarchies greater than four levels deep (Rumbaugh, 1991).

Examples

EMPLOYEE has two roles in Figure 6.20. It is a subtype to the PERSON entity, and it is a supertype of FULL TIME EMPLOYEE and

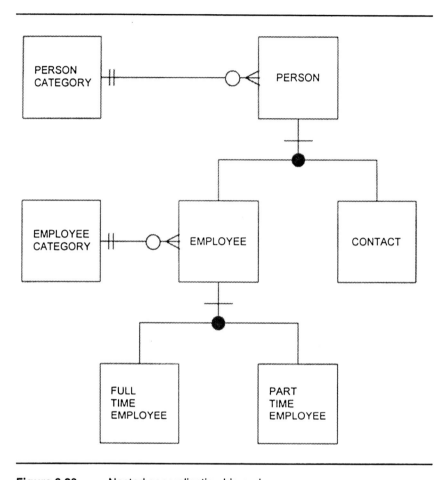

Figure 6.20   Nested generalization hierarchy.

PART TIME EMPLOYEE. This a perfectly acceptable scenario. It is extremely easy to follow the logic behind this structure; it is very communicative.

In the second example, Figure 6.21 abstracts to the OBJECT level. Is this too deep? It certainly needs to be reviewed; however, the generalization structure is determined by many factors. Do we want to record all the detail or only the general rules? Are the ANIMAL KINGDOM and PLANT KINGDOM entities necessary? Generalization structures are more resilient to changes, but abstraction to this level may be overkill.

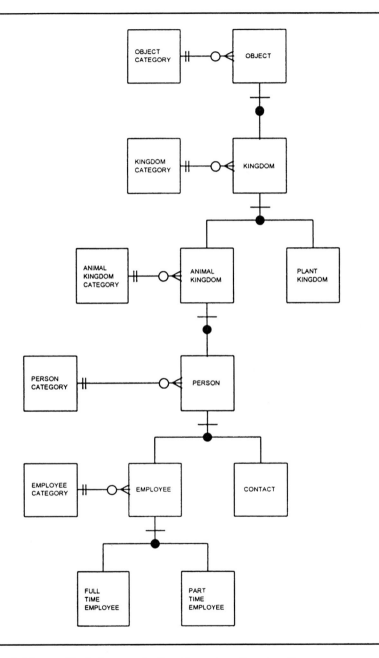

Figure 6.21   Nested generalization hierarchy—Too deep?

6.7 RELAXATION OF MUTUAL EXCLUSIVITY REQUIREMENT

All subtype entities governed by the same discriminator shall NOT be required to be mutually exclusive. A role entity shall be used to record mutually inclusive instances of a single discriminator.

Discussion

Some data modeling notations have a rule stating that subtypes governed by the same subtype discriminator must be mutually exclusive. This reflects a fundamental weakness of the current notation, in that it requires an arbitrary splitting of a single logical domain. It is anticipated that future releases of these standards will recognize the problem inherent in the mutual exclusivity requirement, and will acknowledge the use of a role entity. The Role entity is created due to normalization requirements (the discriminator becomes a repeating attribute in the parent entity if the mutual exclusivity rule is relaxed).

Examples

Figure 6.22 illustrates a very simple case in which a Role entity reduces duplication in the model and results in a more meaningful representation of the enterprise requirements. In this example, a university wishes to manage information about its people. Students are often employed by the university, and its administrative staff often takes evening courses. Furthermore, it retains visiting professors, who are often taking post-graduate or post-doctoral courses. The first diagram depicts the model according to the mutual exclusivity requirement. An observer can readily see its tendency to introduce a series of Boolean attributes to accommodate mutually inclusive types of persons. The logical concept of a person's role is lost in a potentially lengthy series of "indicator" attributes used to accommodate the syntax required by notation. The same semantic idea can be more precisely depicted through the use of a Role entity, as shown in the second diagram.

Figure 6.23 depicts a Role entity used to record a mutually inclusive discriminator. Note that the generic role relationship resolves a First Normal Form problem of repeating "person type id" in the generic parent.

Figure 6.24 demonstrates the use of a Role entity as an associative between the generic parent and a Type entity. This is the most common use of a Role entity.

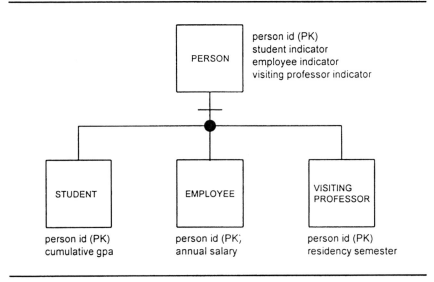

Figure 6.22   Inclusive subtypes modeled as mutually exclusive subtypes.

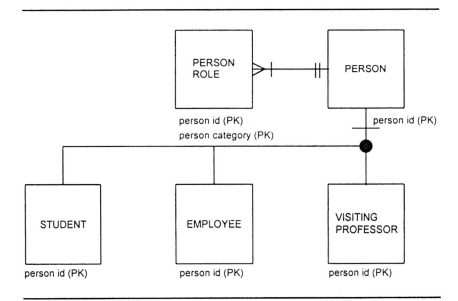

Figure 6.23   Use of a Role entity without Type entity

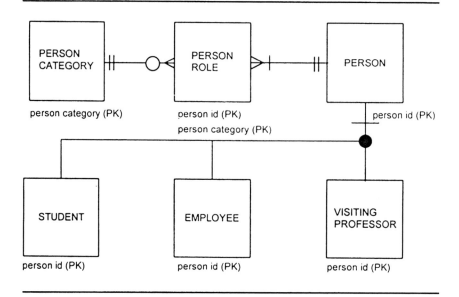

Figure 6.24 Use of a Role entity with Type entity.

6.8 SUBTYPE RELATIONSHIP DEPENDENCY

A subtype entity shall not be a child entity in any other identifying relationship in the data model.

Discussion

Subtype entities, by definition, must have the same primary key as the generic parent. If they are involved in an identifying relationship with an entity other than the parent, the subtype entity will inherit the parent's key, resulting in a primary key that is not identical to its generic parent.

Example

The following example, Figure 6.25, illustrates an unresolved identifying relationship, and one scenario for its resolution. Note that when subtype entities are involved in an identifying relationship (other than with the parent), the modeler is attempting to get the proper key structure, but does not recognize that in fact it is a many-to-many relationship that is required.

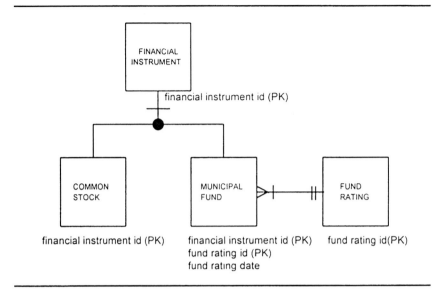

Figure 6.25   Illegal subtype dependency.

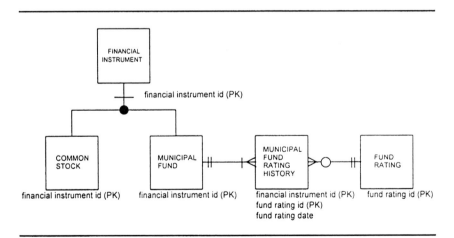

Figure 6.26   Subtype relationship resolved.

The subtype relationship is resolved in Figure 6.26, by recognizing that the MUNICIPAL FUND to FUND RATING relationship is a many-to-many. This removes the additional primary key from MUNICIPAL FUND.

6.9 GENERALIZATION HIERARCHIES OF DEPENDENT ENTITIES

Generalization hierarchies may exist for both associative and structure entities, provided they comply with all rules established for generalization hierarchies. They should be used to depict optional information in multipurpose associations.

Discussion

Generalization hierarchies exist to ensure that subsets of an entity—the supertype—that share common attributes or relationships distinct from other subsets are separately defined, in accordance with the No Null rule. The supertype may be either an identifier-independent entity or an identifier-dependent entity. This rule applies to the latter, and recognizes the frequent need to capture different subsets of information about associative and structure entities based on differing reasons for the association.

Examples

In Figure 6.27, we have a requirement to capture total hours that a provider spends in a health care encounter, perhaps for gathering patient care metrics to be used in cost estimating or resource planning. Since our requirement applies only to those individuals who are playing the provider role in an encounter, we need to differentiate the PROVIDER category entity from other individuals involved in the encounter.

Note that not all attributes are depicted in this diagram. Furthermore, although not pictured here, there may be relationships or information unique to PATIENT that would be supported by the hierarchical structure. Finally, by illustrating the nature of the business as precisely as we have here, the data modeler may define opportunities for new business strategies (part of the contribution that high-quality data modeling makes to the overall quality of the functional process improvement activity). In this case, we may question the business experts about whether capturing total hours for both providers and patients is advantageous, in order to measure both provider performance (remember we

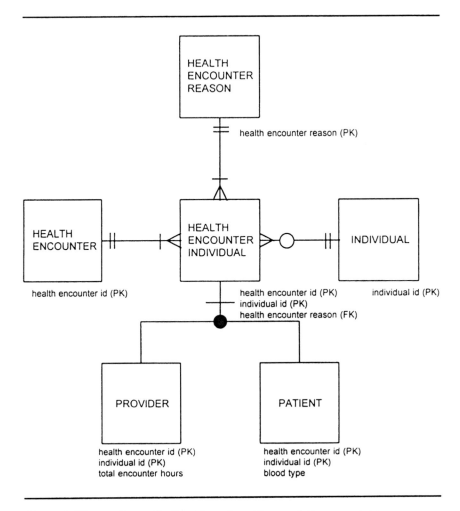

Figure 6.27   Generalization hierarchy with associative supertype.

may have many providers involved in an encounter) and to measure how quickly service is provided to customers. The customer service measure provides information that may lead to new customer service strategies (if service times are too lengthy) and may lead to requirements to capture new information (e.g., encounter start and finish times).

In Figure 6.28, structure entities, those entities that resolve recursive relationships, are also permitted to be a supertype in a generalization hierarchy. In the world of telecommunications, a CIRCUIT is an extremely important component. We capture information about its

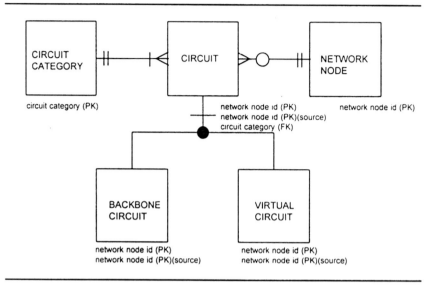

Figure 6.28   Generalization hierarchy with structure supertype.

response time, availability, mean time between failure and other pertinent data. A CIRCUIT, in company Y, is defined as, *a relationship between two nodes*. The data modeler has created the CIRCUIT entity by resolving the recursive relationship between NODE.

6.10   SUPERTYPE LIMITS

An entity may have any number of relationships in which it is the supertype, since this does not violate the key structure rule and is often required to correctly reflect business requirements.

Discussion

Generalization hierarchies are powerful mechanisms for displaying business rules. There are times, quite often, when the data modeler needs to represent two distinct hierarchies with the same supertype. This will result in a more understandable data model.

Example

In Figure 6.29, EMPLOYEE is subtyped a number of different ways. There is a FULL TIME EMPLOYEE, PART TIME EMPLOYEE, MALE

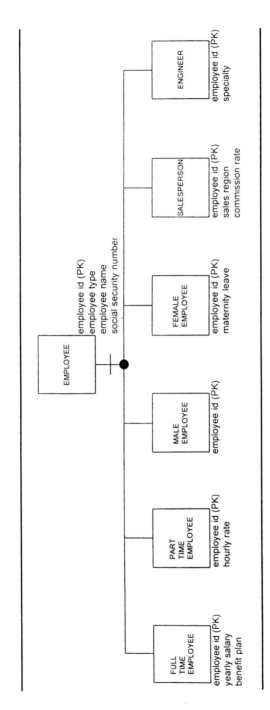

Figure 6.29   Confusing generalization structure.

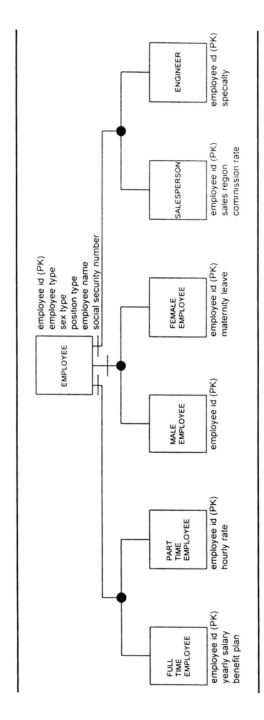

Figure 6.30   Revised generalization structure.

EMPLOYEE, FEMALE EMPLOYEE, SALESPERSON, and ENGI-NEER. The number of subtypes is confusing to the reviewer because they are not classified by any method. The subtype discriminator identifies all of them as *employee types*.

A more readable structure is displayed in Figure 6.30. EMPLOYEE is subtyped into the same entities, but this represents a more precise description for the organization. FULL TIME EMPLOYEE and PART TIME EMPLOYEE are classified by the *employee type* discriminator. They represent the way our organization classifies employees for compensation purposes. MALE EMPLOYEE and FEMALE EMPLOYEE are classified by the *sex type* discriminator. It is an important consideration for our organization because of Equal Employment Opportunity laws. SALESPERSON and ENGINEER represent the two employee positions. They are classified by the *position type* discriminator in EMPLOYEE.

This generalization structure is more understandable. A reviewer of the model can see that there appear to be three distinct classifications of employees, all important to the business. Business rules can be validated against each classification subtree as opposed to having to search the entire structure.

REFERENCES

Coad, Peter and E. Yourdon. *Object Oriented Analysis*. Englewood Cliffs, NJ: Yourdon Press, 1990.

Palmer, John, "The Problems with Inheritance, Part I," *Object Magazine* 3(4): 82–83, (November–December 1993).

Rumbaugh, James et al. *Object Oriented Modeling and Design*. Englewood Cliffs, NJ: Prentice Hall, 1991.

7

Data Model View Rules

To promote data sharing and increase control over our information resources, we need a mechanism for communicating across diverse business areas. A data model provides that ability. As each business area develops its information requirements, they are unified or merged into an enterprise model (this is a bottom-up technique for the development of an enterprise model, a more robust method is top-down). Conflicts that arise during the merge—business rules in disagreement, homonym and synonym problems—are resolved through the data administration or information resource management function. The end result is **ONE** model that represents the information requirements and business rules of the enterprise (see Figure 7.1).

Now each business area is not interested in the entire model of the enterprise. Human Resources is not interested in the price of equipment, overall customer satisfaction index, or how many times the organization's name has appeared in print. They would like to see the data and information components germane to applicants, employees, and benefits. A Human Resources view, or any other business area view is constructed from the enterprise model (see Figure 7.2).

Views are merely subsets of the enterprise data model. They can be constructed for a variety of reasons, but are usually developed for existing organizational units and projects in progress. As each view is extracted from the enterprise model, it inherits all of the constraints dictated by the top level model. This ensures that "stovepipe" data models are not constructed, and each subset is supportive of organizational

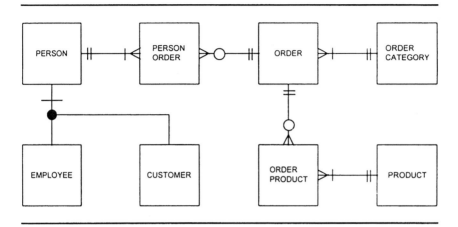

Figure 7.1   One data model of the enterprise.

goals and objectives. Views provide the data modeler with an opportunity to reuse components from an existing model, then expand and refine the model as required by the project.

Thus far, the term "data model" has been used to refer to (1) models that are contained in separate encyclopedias, either as independently developed models or as extracts of another (parent) model, or (2) model views that have been created in a single encyclopedia and that represent distinct, logical groupings of data objects. Since both separate models and model views actually represent logical subsets of the enterprise data requirements, all rules described apply equally to both. Therefore, model views will have names, definitions, and all other features, in accordance with the rules outlined in this section.

7.1   MODEL AND MODEL VIEW NAME

Every data model and data model view shall be given a name.

Discussion

Every data model or data model view must have a name that uniquely describes the business area objects it contains. A data model is not a static object—it represents the business and therefore, is dynamic. If an enterprise is to maintain a data model and the unique views of the organization, it must have a mechanism for its identification. The name

244

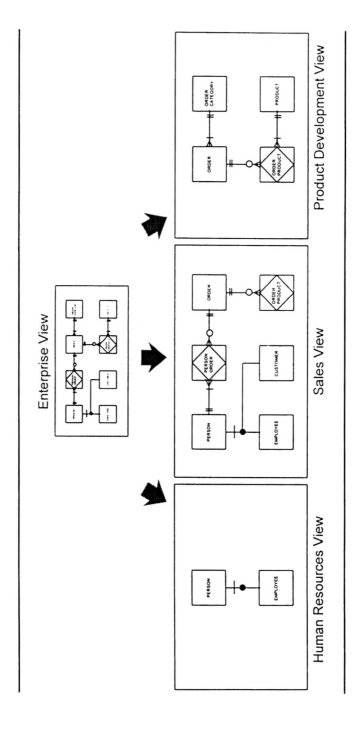

Figure 7.2 Model views.

provides the basis for identification and care should be provided during its selection.

The name of the data model provides the reviewer with some context to review the model. The data model name provides the first glimpse of what is maintained in the data model or data model view.

Examples

Figure 7.3 contains an unacceptable model name, Enterprise Model. How do we distinguish this data model from any other organization's data model? An analyst should have better expectations after hearing the name of the model. The analyst is unsure what information requirements are contained in the model.

The name of the model must provide a qualification of the objects contained in the data model or data model view. The Quality Assurance reviewer should be able to provide a cursory conceptual review, based on the name alone. The Enterprise Model has been revised with a qualifier (Figure 7.4) to make the model name more explicit. Now as a review is in progress, we can draw on our knowledge of the Perma-Door corporation. Just the name alone implies information that we may want to keep. We would be surprised to find a firm that does not capture information on its

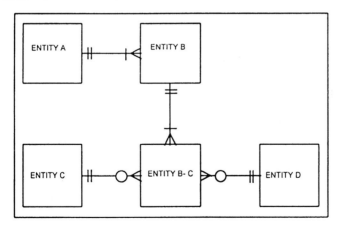

Enterprise Model

Figure 7.3   Unacceptable model name.

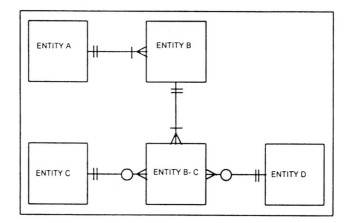

Perma-Door Inc. Enterprise Model

Figure 7.4   Revised model name.

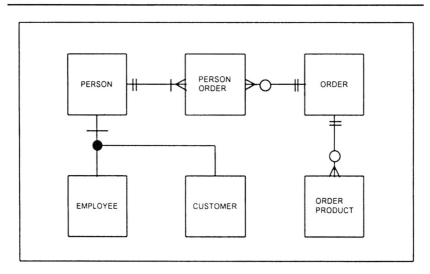

MCI Business Area Model

Figure 7.5   Unacceptable model view name.

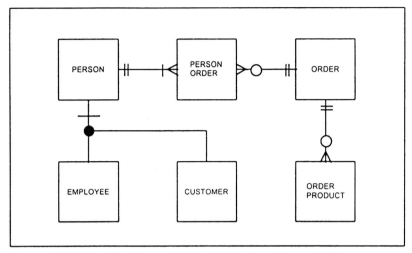

MCI - Sales Administration View

Figure 7.6   Model view name—Revised.

employees, customers, and the like. Also this particular firm, Perma-Door, probably manufactures or distributes doors or door parts.

The second example, the MCI Business Area Model is displayed in Figure 7.5. This is certainly an improvement over the previous generic model name, but it does not identify the business area. Is this Human Resources, Order Processing, or some other functional area?

The model view name has been revised to include the functional area being modeled: the Sales Administration area (Figure 7.6).

7.2   MODEL AND MODEL VIEW PURPOSE

Every data model and data model view shall include a statement of purpose. The purpose should describe, in technology independent terms, the reason for the data model's or data model view's existence and the goals or objectives it supports.

Discussion

The data model or model view purpose provides the Quality Assurance reviewer with additional insight with which to review the data model. The data model purpose should be completed and agreed upon before moving forward with the development of the model. The purpose statement provides critical context to begin an in-depth examination.

The model purpose should describe the reason(s) for the data model's *existence*. Models are created with a purpose in mind. They may be used for the development of an application system, to show potential shared database applications, or as the foundation for a business reengineering effort. This must be communicated to the reviewer of the model.

A model purpose should describe how it interacts with its environment to achieve some planned objective. Each piece of data in an organization is used to satisfy either internal or external stakeholders. Identification of the stakeholders will help to identify data model objects and during the subsequent review, validate such pieces.

Finally, a data model purpose should be *technology independent*. Technology is simply an enabler and it should not be used to camouflage the reason for an application systems development.

Examples

In Figure 7.7, the model purpose includes too many technical details. It does not describe the reason we are building this application. A good rule of thumb is that a model purpose should not change if the underlying technical details change. This is clearly not the case in this example.

The model purpose has been revised in Figure 7.8. The technical details were removed, the business reason for the development of the

The employee skills application will operate on a UNIX platform. It will show an end user a screen to enter an employee id into. The system will take the employee id, look at the skills he or she require for his or her job, and print our available training classes.

Figure 7.7   Model view purpose.

The employee skills application will provide senior management of the organization with a means of identifying employees for skills training and then recommend appropriate training programs and classes for the employees' growth. This is an important application because we strive to provide our employees with lifetime growth opportunities.

Figure 7.8   Revised model view purpose.

The Land System will provide chart of account information concerning our organization's land transactions.

Figure 7.9   Model purpose.

The Land System will provide financial management information about our organization's Real Estate business in the most efficient and cost-effective manner. The information contained in the Land System will provide performance measures to senior management and provide Public Relations with a consistent source to respond to requests from External Stakeholders.

Figure 7.10   Revised model view purpose.

system has been added, and the corporate strategy that this system will support has been identified.

In Figure 7.9, the model purpose describes the type of information contained in the view. This is a good start, but needs to be expanded to incorporate other aspects of the model. Why is this system important to the organization?

The model view has been revised in Figure 7.10. It provides insight into the type of information we would find in the view, the importance of the system, and it describes performance measures that will be returned from this system.

7.3   MODEL AND MODEL VIEW CATEGORY

Every data model and data model view shall be classified into a category that describes the type of model view.

Discussion

As previous mentioned, a data model can be built for a variety of reasons. Each model view should be categorized to provide the reviewer more concrete material on which to base the review. Though not exhaustive, the following list should provide an overview of the differing types of views that can be constructed.

- **For Exposition Only (FEO)** A model view that is constructed for display purposes alone. These models usually violate some or all of the syntax for a specific notation. They are used to communicate critical aspects of the data model.
- **Process View** A model view used to show the data consumed during the execution of a process. The process model can be used to validate the objects in data model. This is sometimes referred to as a data view diagram.
- **Functional Area View** The most common type of model view. It shows the data requirements of a particular subset of the organization. Human Resources, Finance, Marketing, Sales, Distribution are all examples of functional areas.
- **Planning Level View** Separates a variety of information classes from each other. Multiple planning views exist, including strategic, tactical, and operational. Strategic and tactical planning views hold derived information or that data used in executive information or decision support environments. Operational planning views hold the transactional data needed to carry out the day-to-day activities of the business.
- **Application System View** Most data modeling efforts begin with an automated information system in mind. This view takes a part of the enterprise data model, defines an automation boundary, and moves these pieces forward for implementation in a specific technology.
- **Time Dependent View** Business process improvement projects have two prerequisites. The first is that a current, AS-IS, model is used to represent the current business rules, policies, assumptions and constraints. The second is the construction of a future, TO-BE, model that represents the business rules, policies, strategies, and constraints that reflect the way in which the organization intends to or needs to conduct business in the future. It should be based on business improvements, changes to policies, revised strategies, and new/revised objectives captured in the business plan.

The value of the categorization is that it provides the Quality Assurance reviewer with additional criteria to examine the data model. If the analyst knows the data model objects are maintained in a For Exposition Only (FEO) view, then there is no need to examine it for syntax and other quality characteristics. It would fail. A review may be required to ensure it is getting the basic point across to the audience.

The communication of the model view category is vital to correct interpretation and use by all parties. This can be accomplished through report headers/footers, report titles, identification/data stamps on diagrams, or means that comply with organizational document control requirements.

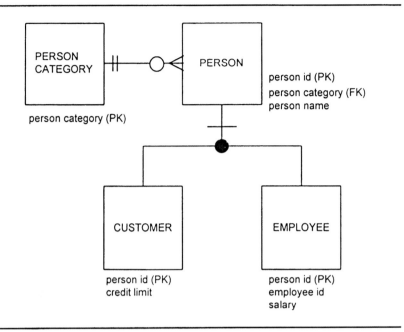

Figure 7.11   Enterprise Data Model.

Examples

The first example depicts how the Enterprise Data Model is used to construct a For Exposition Only diagram. The data modeler is presenting to an audience only concerned with EMPLOYEE information.

The author has violated syntax in order to make the model more understandable. There is no primary key, person name has been transformed into employee name and mandatory relationships are not shown.

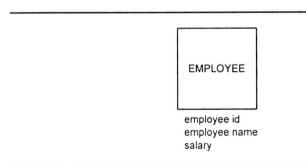

Figure 7.12   FEO model view.

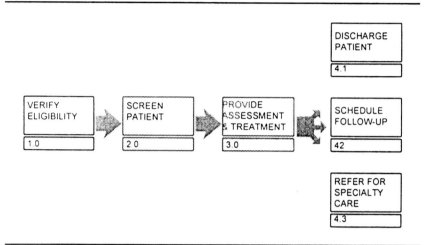

Figure 7.13   Health care encounter process model.

In the second example, Figure 7.13 illustrates a process model for a health care encounter. It describes a set of sequential activities that need to occur when a patient visits a medical treatment facility. The process model requires data to function, which is not displayed in this diagram.

A model view that displays the data required by the process is constructed in Figure 7.14 by the analyst. The reviewer may use matrices or other mechanisms to verify the accuracy of the model. The process model can also be used to check the completeness of the data model.

7.4   MODEL COMPONENT CONTROL

Every data model component in a view shall be marked with a control classification.

Discussion

Metadata control is a difficult concept to understand, but critical to the successful development and maintenance of the model. Let's begin by discussing what it is not. We often see data models that have model view authorities associated with them—create, read, update, and delete. For example, the Human Resources functional area may *create*, *update*, and *delete* EMPLOYEE occurrences. This is an important concept, but it is not metadata control, it is data control.

One benefit of data modeling is a common understanding of the

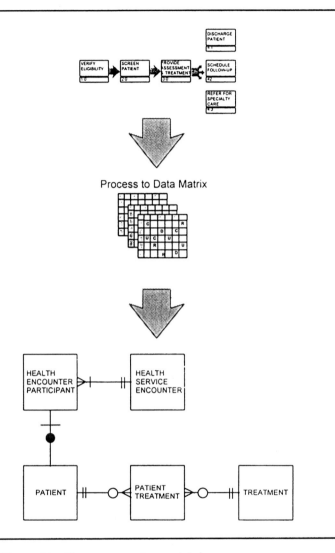

Figure 7.14   Health care encounter model view.

information components of an organization. If this is true, then it should not matter what business function creates, updates, or deletes an occurrence. They are all using the same structure for their operations (the entity template) and will be abiding by the same business rules. The only concern should be that the data is created once and reused many times. The issue of consequence is the control of the metadata.

Metadata control identifies what area of the organization, or what individual in the organization, has the authority to create, update, or delete the entity templates. To go back to our example, it may indeed make sense for the Human Resource area to assert metadata control over the EMPLOYEE template. It is the most likely area of the organization to be informed of changes to the Equal Employment Opportunity Act or other policies that will impact the structure of this template.

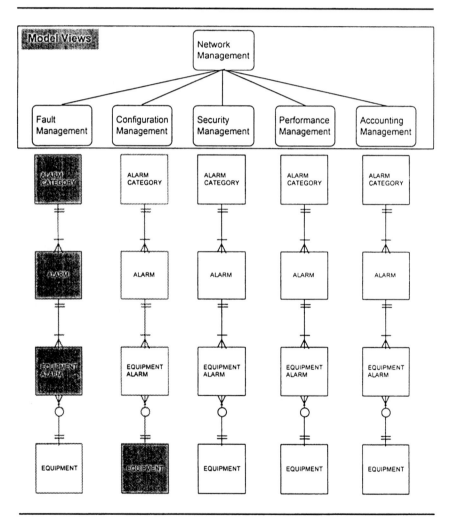

Figure 7.15   Metadata stewardship.

In a sense, this is another abstraction problem. Recall that data models were created to control existing information. The models provided a method for describing data required by the organization. The data models provided a common framework from which to discuss existing and required needs. In order to control these models, another layer is introduced, the meta-layer or methodology level. Here we define the control of our metadata.

The integrity of metadata may be maintained by the identification of a strategic data steward for each data model component. This will allow for high quality data to be structured, created, maintained, and consumed by other members of the organization.

Example

In Figure 7.15, the common entities across five model views are displayed. The shaded entities indicate the business area that maintains metadata control. It does not matter that occurrences of the shaded entities are being created, read, updated, or deleted across the Network Management functional areas. They are all using the same entity templates. Metadata control has been established; therefore, if another functional area would like to make a change to the structure of the entity, they must coordinate it through the Fault Management functional area (for ALARM CATEGORY, ALARM, and EQUIPMENT ALARM) or through Configuration Management (for EQUIPMENT).

Metadata control is shown in this diagram at the entity level. It should also occur at the attribute level. In a normalized data model, attributes within an entity usually are owned by differing business functions. Only one area in an organization should be assigned metadata control for any data model object.

7.5   MODEL VERSION/DATE

Every data model shall be assigned a model version/date.

Discussion

The model version/date records the version number and/or date on which the last changes to the model were completed. Other dates also may be recorded, including approval or review dates. The modeler should refer to applicable configuration management and change control procedures for proper version identification and file/document marking.

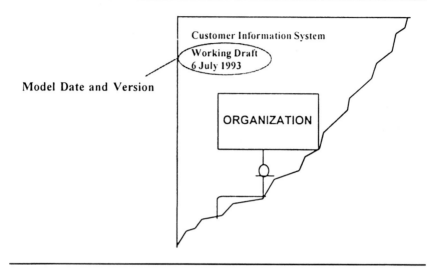

Figure 7.16   Model date and version.

Example

The cut-away of a data model diagram page in Figure 7.16 depicts clear marking of the date and status of a data model for a Customer Information System.

7.6   MODEL SOURCE OF MATERIALS

Every data model shall maintain the source materials used in the construction of data model objects.

Discussion

On any project, a data modeler or modeling team must first identify what sort of materials need to be gathered and where to gather them. This data-gathering activity can be accomplished in a variety of ways, including facilitated sessions with individuals, evaluation of existing business plans, cross referencing to any process models that have been created, examination of current systems, or even shadowing a subject matter expert.

Once a representative collection of documentation has been gathered, the data modeler can then start the process of constructing entities, attributes, and relationships. As each data model object is placed into the model, it should be marked in such a way that can be traced to its source. This will lend credibility to the structure of the model, provide the reviewer with a mechanism for evaluating the soundness of the model, and allow the organization to examine the impact of business decisions of their information systems.

Example

The analysts who have built the model fragment in Figure 7.17 will have an extremely easy time validating their model. Every data model component is linked to a source of materials that can be validated and verified if any questions arise.

This technique will help the organization keep the models "alive." The business plan or other materials change. As the sources change, the data model can be enhanced to include new data requirements, or deduct those components no longer required. The linkage from the source to sink provides the organization with a mechanism for performing impact analysis. As a goal or strategy is contemplated, the organization can determine the impact on its current or future information system components. This will allow the organization to make more informed IS investment decisions.

7.7 MODEL TEAM MEMBERSHIP AND ROLES

Every data model shall identify the members of the modeling team and identify their roles in the development of the model.

Discussion

It is good practice to include individuals who participated in the development of the model as points of contact. In some situations this may not be possible—therefore, careful attention to documentation of model components during development will be absolutely critical to long-term management of the model. Reference to the point of contact should include a current address or phone number to which inquiries may be directed.

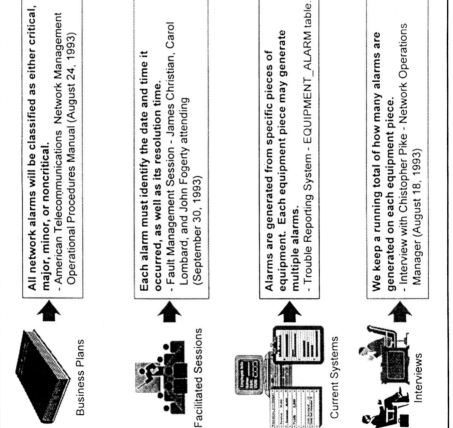

Figure 7.17 Model source of materials.

William Zane - Project Manager

Responsible for the management of both the project team and the customer. Mr. Zane developed the project plan, provided required materials to QA, and delivered the final product to the customer.

He may be reached at (703) 555-1212 x123.

Carol Freeman - Data Modeler

Responsible for the development of the data model. Ms. Freeman provided the facilitation and recorded the model in IDEF1X notation. She was the on-site representative from our firm and acquired the necessary buy-in from the client. She may be reached at (703) 555-1212 x652.

Kevin Gambrell - Process Modeler

Responsible for the development of the IDEF0 Functional Model. Mr. Gambrell used the data model as a basis for event identification, and constructed process models to respond to such events. His interaction with the customer was limited. Mr. Gambrell also provided supported to the data model effort, with weekly Quality Assurances.

He may be reached at (703) 555-1212 x657.

Figure 7.18 Model team membership.

Example

The data modelers who prepared the model, as well as the Quality Assurance Reviewer, will be quite pleased with the meticulous detail provided in figure 7.18. All personnel on the project, their responsibilities, and a contact number are provided. If it is a large modeling effort, the detail for the data model may become even more granular. Roles and responsibilities per model view or per data model object may be established.

8

Normalization Rules

Normalization has gotten something of a bad rap from many data modelers. It has been misunderstood, misapplied, and misrepresented so often that the point of normalization and its origin in common sense ideas about how to organize and group sets of dependent items has been lost. Normalization, and the normal forms that are used to test the organization of attributes into entities, are no more complex than many of the organizing schemes that we use in everyday life—the Dewey decimal system in the local library, the postal addressing system, the way products are arranged at the local grocery. As Date suggests, normal forms are a formalization of common sense, intuitive notions of how to organize information (1986). In fact, the normal forms might be referred to more accurately as "formal norms."

The problem with normalization is that the rules have usually been communicated using language that is intimidating to the average information systems professional. Becoming proficient at normalization also takes practice—there is simply no way to provide examples that cover every conceivable situation an analyst might encounter. As a data modeler, you need to study normalization concepts and work hard at applying them until you feel completely comfortable with your level of proficiency. Nothing else you do while building data models will contribute as much to the eventual creation of sound database designs.

Before continuing our discussion, we need to introduce one of the important concepts of normalization—functional dependency. Every action taken to normalize a data model is either directly or indirectly tied to functional dependence. Date (1986) provides a formal definition:

> Given a relation R, attribute Y of R is *functionally dependent* on attribute X of R—in symbols, R.X → R.Y (read "R.X functionally determines R.Y")—if and only if each X-value in R has associated with it precisely one Y-value in R (at any one time). Attributes X and Y may be composite.

Establishing functional dependence is about defining primary keys (and candidate keys). Most everyone who works with databases is familiar with the concept of a primary key. According to normalization theory, values in a database table should be functionally dependent on the value of the primary key. We will explore this relationship in detail in the normalization rules later in this chapter.

In order to assure that a data model is normalized, each attribute must be placed into an entity where it is functionally dependent on the entire primary key, and *where it is also not functionally dependent on any other attributes in the model*. If no such entity exists, then an entity must be created to hold the attribute. If an attribute has been placed in an entity where it does not meet these criteria, then it must be moved, and that movement may cause the modeler to "decompose" the contents of the original entity into two, or under limited conditions more than two, entities. Conversely, it may cause the modeler to create one entity where two existed before, as a result of recognizing functional dependence (see the Balanced One-to-One Relationship rule). Thus, normalization is not a process. It is a test to determine whether an attribute is properly positioned in the model based on the normal forms.

Five normal forms have gained general acceptance among the data management community. They are referred to as First normal form, Second normal form, and so on up to Fifth normal form. Numerous other normal forms have been defined based on special situations or complex data types. We do not explore these here, although you are encouraged to explore them as you encounter situations where they might prove beneficial.

Testing for normalization is not an "all at once" exercise. Neither is it a sequential process (e.g., work from First normal form up to Fifth in an unnormalized model). It will occur incrementally, as a modeling team works its way through the business domain in a process of discovery. When you begin the modeling effort, you will not know all of the attributes required by the business (e.g., the Universal Relation) (Kent, 1981). The modeling team's objective is to discover and define the attributes—to establish the boundaries of the domain—during the course of developing a data model. The only exception to this is a reverse engineering exercise, where the data elements contained in the existing program and data structures define a "complete" domain for the system (assuming that the exercise is limited to the automated system and the data products it generates). Normalization aids in the discovery process as well as giving a consistent structure to the end product.

8.1   BENEFITS OF NORMALIZATION

There are benefits of normalization that contribute directly to the quality of a data model. Normalization

- **Aids in the discovery process.** By applying the normal forms, and using the results of that application to pose questions to the business experts, the data modelers often uncover new requirements or rules that might have been overlooked without the analytical rigor of normalization.
- **Ensures precise capture of business logic.** The use of normal forms is dependent on one critical component—the knowledge of business rules and logic. Without that, even experienced data modelers cannot build models that accurately and completely reflect the logic of the business domain. Only the domain experts can—and should—determine whether a functional dependency exists between two attributes. We have found that even during reverse engineering exercises, with large sets of data element values to work with, it is virtually impossible to fully reconstruct the dependency logic without the participation of business experts.
- **Minimizes redundancy.** One of the precepts of normalization is "one fact in one place" (Date, 1986). This is useful on many levels. The most obvious benefit comes from improved database designs. Those designs that minimize redundancy while retaining referential integrity result in more efficient, more reliable databases. Second, at a conceptual or logical level, minimized redundancy aids the enterprise data administrator(s) in efforts to ensure that a business concept is defined once and used in a consistent fashion by all stakeholders.
- **Minimizes requirement for use of null values.** Introduction of null values in a database can cause problems in access and use of data, particularly using aggregation operations such as SUM (Date, 1986; Korth and Silberschatz, 1986). From a logical perspective, the presence of a null value indicates that the organization of attributes into entities is incomplete. There is some additional business fact

that has been overlooked that separates those instances that have a value for the attribute from those that do not.

- **Prevents loss of information or introduction of unintentional results.** The organization of attributes into separate but related entities must be done with care. Improper decomposition of information in a database design can lead to unintentional results when data is accessed (Korth and Silberschatz, 1986). The objective of normalization is to create a logical data scheme that minimizes or eliminates the potential for unintentional results. We will explore this in greater detail in our normal form examples.
- **Aids in model management and integration.** We must retain enterprise awareness when creating data models (remember our discussion on quality in Chapter 1). When combined with an aggressive data management program, adherence to a set of normal forms increases the likelihood that models created by separate modeling teams can be integrated and managed effectively.

8.2 BUSINESS NORMAL FORMS

Clive Finkelstein introduced a set of Business Normal Forms that closely parallel the formal normalization rules established under relational theory (1989). Finkelstein created these forms in order to support the notion that users should be directly involved in building data models, but that the formality and arcane language used in conjunction with traditional normal forms made them undesirable for use by individuals whose primary interests are managing a business and using data, rather than building databases. The premise behind Business Normal Forms is an important one. In order to build quality data models, the data analyst must find ways of ensuring that business experts participating in modeling sessions can successfully portray their requirements using the model. The business participants must have a degree of knowledge sufficient to allow them to *directly* interpret a data model.

In the past, the data analyst served as an interpreter, interviewing subject matter experts, building a working draft of the model, reading back the results to the subject matter experts, then refining the model. In many cases, the business participants never saw the model, or saw only simplified fragments. It was left up to the data analyst to determine whether the model accurately reflected the business rules. This dual role—that of expert data modeler and pseudo business expert—forced the data analyst into a difficult position. It also ensured that the data modeling was less objective than it should have been. The data analyst had less time to concentrate on his or her area of expertise (modeling), and assumed responsibility for knowledge that rightfully belonged to others (business experts).

Finkelstein's Business Normal Forms prescribe not only a condition, such as existence of a repeating attribute in an entity, but also a cure, a resolution strategy, for each condition. There are five Business Normal Forms (1BNF through 5BNF), and while there are some subtle and obvious differences in comparison to the traditional normal forms (1NF through 5NF), the results achieved are similar—a data model in which every attribute is placed in an entity where it is fully functionally dependent on the primary key.

We will stick to the traditional normal forms for our rules, but will refer to Finkelstein's work when it adds an interesting dimension. If you are a practicing data modeler, we encourage you to explore Business Normal Forms in more depth. Finkelstein has written extensively on their definition and use (1989, 1992).

8.3 READING THE NORMALIZATION RULES

We have established separate rules for each of the normal forms as a convenient means of discussing the characteristics of each. However, be aware that some normal forms imply adherence to other forms. For instance, a model that is in Boyce-Codd Normal Form (BCNF) is by definition also in First, Second, and Third normal form. This will become apparent as we explain the examples in the following set of rules.

8.4 FIRST NORMAL FORM

Every data model should be in First normal form (1NF).

Discussion

First normal form is formally defined as:

> A relation R is in first normal form (1NF) if and only if all underlying domains contain atomic values only. (Date, 1986)

In order to assure that a relation (entity) is in 1NF, each attribute in the entity must meet the criteria outlined in the Atomic Attribute rule. If an attribute exhibits non-atomic properties, take steps to reduce it to an atomic state:

Decompose composite domains to the single concept level, creating additional attributes as needed to record data requirements.

Alternatively, according to Finkelstein:

Identify and remove repeating group attributes to another entity. The primary key of this other entity is made up of a compound key, comprising the primary key of the entity in which the repeating group originally resided, together with the repeating group key itself, or instead another unique key based on the business needs. The name of the new entity may initially be based on a combination of the name of the repeating group and the name of the entity in which the repeating group originally resided. It may be later renamed according to its final attribute content, after . . . normalization is completed (Finkelstein, 1989).

As Date points out, a model that has components that are only in 1NF, and have not been normalized further, has a logical structure that is undesirable. First normal form structures still contain redundancies that can lead to problems in database operations (e.g., INSERT, UPDATE, DELETE). The reader is referred to Date (1986) for further reading on this topic.

Example

Assume that a hypothetical enterprise wishes to offer a series of one day TRAINING COURSEs to its employees (Figure 8.1). It publishes a schedule of the courses, providing a description of each, and a list of dates on which each course is offered. Figure 8.2 depicts the resulting database table if we were to populate the TRAINING COURSE entity in its unnormalized state using one implementation strategy. Note the redundancy introduced in order to accommodate the repeating offering dates for each course. Obviously, any change to a course description, for instance, will have to be made in each database record for that course, requiring much unnecessary processing, and increasing the risk that a record might be overlooked or minor differences in the descriptions occur. The primary key is not unique in the table shown in Figure 8.2, violating a fundamental rule.

A second implementation strategy for the unresolved repeating attribute is depicted in Figure 8.3. Observe that the implementation of the repeating attribute is based on the current known maximum number of

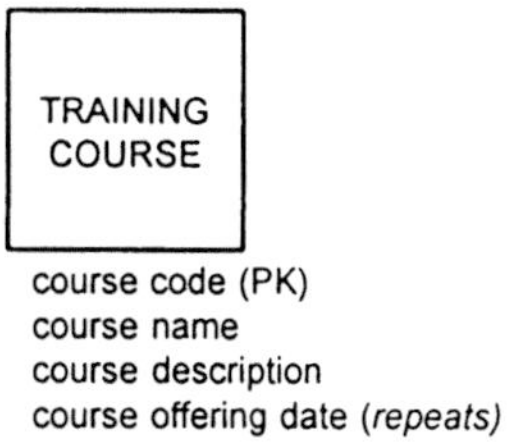

```
┌─────────────┐
│             │
│  TRAINING   │
│  COURSE     │
│             │
└─────────────┘
course code (PK)
course name
course description
course offering date (repeats)
```

Figure 8.1   Unresolved 1NF pattern.

Course Code	Course Name	Course Description	Course Offering Date
PC001	Introduction to PCs	An overview of PC fundamentals for beginners only.	01/11/94
PC001	Introduction to PCs	An overview of PC fundamentals for beginners only.	01/18/94
PC001	Introduction to PCs	An overview of PC fundamentals for beginners only.	02/01/94
OS001	Introduction to PC Operating Systems	An overview of commonly used PC operating systems, including features, commands, and limitations.	02/02/94
OS001	Introduction to PC Operating Systems	An overview of commonly used PC operating systems, including features, commands, and limitations.	02/04/94
TC002	Intermediate Telecommunications	A study of telecommunications as it applies specifically to computer networking.	03/01/94
TC002	Intermediate Telecommunications	A study of telecommunications as it applies specifically to computer networking.	03/18/94
TC002	Intermediate Telecommunications	A study of telecommunications as it applies specifically to computer networking.	03/22/94

Figure 8.2   One implementation strategy for unresolved 1NF entity.

Course Code	Course Name	Course Description	Course Offering Date		
PC001	Introduction to PCs	An overview of PC fundamentals for beginners.	01/11/94	01/18/94	02/01/94
OS001	Introduction to PC Operating Systems	An overview of commonly used PC operating systems, including features, commands, and limitations.	02/02/94	02/04/94	NULL
TC002	Intermediate Telecommunications	A study of telecommunications as it applies specifically to computer networking.	03/01/94	03/18/94	03/22/94

Figure 8.3   A second implementation strategy for non-1NF entity.

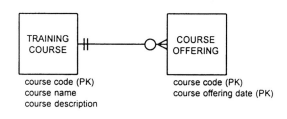

Figure 8.4   Resolved 1NF pattern.

offerings for any one TRAINING COURSE. Courses with fewer offering dates have NULL entries and the database schema will have to be modified if we ever have a course with more than three offering dates.

Following the 1NF resolution method outlined in our earlier discussion, we create the model fragment shown in Figure 8.4. Note that the repeating attribute, *course offering date*, has been moved to a new entity COURSE OFFERING, and has assumed a role as part of a compound primary key. Figures 8.5 and 8.6 portray the database tables used to implement the resolved 1NF. Note that the repetition of *course name* and *course description* has been eliminated now that the repeating attribute *course offering date* has been moved to the new entity. Updates to either of those two attributes for a TRAINING COURSE can be achieved in a single record, rather than across multiple records. Furthermore, COURSE OFFERING now provides an effective mechanism for handling any number of offering dates per TRAINING COURSE.

Course Code	Course Name	Course Description
PC001	Introduction to PCs	An overview of PC fundamentals for beginners only.
OS001	Introduction to PC Operating Systems	An overview of commonly used PC operating systems, including features, commands, and limitations.
TC002	Intermediate Telecommunications	A study of telecommunications as it applies specifically to computer networking.

Figure 8.5   Sample table of TRAINING COURSE resolved for 1NF.

Course Code	Course Offering Date
PC001	01/11/94
PC001	01/18/94
PC001	02/01/94
OS001	02/02/94
OS001	02/04/94
TC002	03/01/94
TC002	03/18/94
TC002	03/22/94

Figure 8.6   Sample table of COURSE OFFERING resolved for 1NF.

8.5   SECOND NORMAL FORM

Every data model should be in Second normal form (2NF).

Discussion

Remember that normal forms are designed to place attributes in an entity where they are functionally dependent on the whole primary key. When compound keys (keys that are comprised of more than one attribute) are encountered, you must confirm that all non-key attributes placed in the entity are determined by the entire set of key attributes, and only those key attributes.

Second normal form (2NF) is formally defined by Date (1986) as:

A relation R is in second normal form (2NF) if and only if it is in 1NF and every non-key attribute is fully dependent on the primary key.

To resolve entities that are not in 2NF, follow the steps described by Finkelstein (1989):

Identify and remove attributes into another entity which are only **partially** dependent on the primary key and are also dependent on one or more other key attributes, or which are dependent on only **part** of the compound primary key and possibly one or more other key attributes.

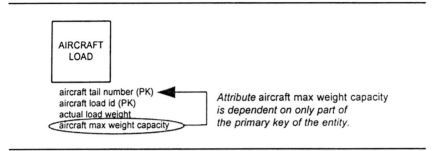

Figure 8.7   Unresolved attribute dependency on part of a compound key.

Examples

Assume that our enterprise is an air cargo operation, running loads of freight on its fleet of aircraft. The enterprise wants to track how much of its capacity it is using, so information is required on each aircraft's capacity and the actual weight of each load. The enterprise computes a varying maximum weight capacity for *each aircraft*, based on its age, configuration, past maintenance history, and other factors (not shown in our model fragment). Figure 8.7 depicts the entity as originally modeled.

In order to resolve the dependency problem, we follow the steps outlined by Finkelstein, and the result is a 2NF model structure shown in Figure 8.8.

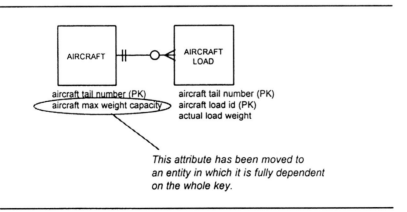

Figure 8.8   Second normal form resolution.

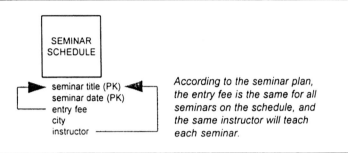

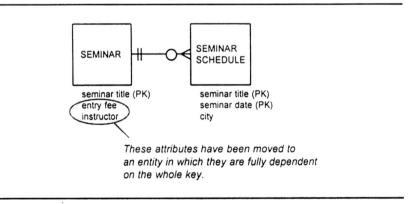

According to the seminar plan,
the entry fee is the same for all
seminars on the schedule, and
the same instructor will teach
each seminar.

Figure 8.9   Unresolved dependencies on primary key parts.

Our second example involves a consulting firm that is sponsoring a series of seminars around the country. Each seminar features a special instructor who is uniquely qualified to lead the seminar. The entry fee for each seminar title is different, but once established, it does not vary by date or location. Figure 8.9 shows the model fragment in its non-2NF state.

To bring the model to 2NF, we apply Finkelstein's prescription, moving the attributes that were dependent on only part of the primary key—*entry fee* and *instructor*—to a new entity with *seminar title* as the primary key (Figure 8.10). As you can see, the model is now in 2NF. Note that it is also in 1NF. The SEMINAR SCHEDULE entity is a repeating set of attributes for our new SEMINAR entity.

These attributes have been moved to
an entity in which they are fully dependent
on the whole key.

Figure 8.10   Second normal form resolution.

8.6   THIRD NORMAL FORM

Every data model should be in Third normal form (3NF).

Discussion

Third normal form (3NF) involves the resolution of transitive dependencies. It is defined formally by Date (1986) as:

> A relation R is in third normal form (3NF) if and only if it is in 2NF and every non-key attribute is non-transitively dependent on the primary key.

In order to resolve 3NF patterns as they arise during model development, follow Finkelstein's (1989) steps:

> Identify and remove into another entity those attributes which are dependent on an attribute(s) other than the primary (or compound) key.

Database tables that contain transitive dependencies will be subject to potential update anomalies. We provide an explanation of these with our example.

Example

Our example involves an AIRCRAFT owned by an overnight package carrier (Figure 8.11). The carrier needs to maintain information about an aircraft's maximum range and operating altitude in order to assure that it is properly deployed along the company's routes, and that it can operate within safety limits. Furthermore, the company maintains a service history for each aircraft, and must know the date on which it first entered service. While the latter information, *aircraft service entry date*, is clearly unique to each aircraft, our first two pieces of information are actually characteristics of the design of the aircraft. All aircraft of that design (designated by model number) will have the same operating characteristics. Therefore, *maximum range* and *maximum operating altitude* are not functionally dependent on *aircraft tail number*, but rather on *aircraft model number*, which is in turn functionally dependent on *aircraft tail number*, the primary key of the entity.

Assume for the moment that we leave the entity as it is defined in

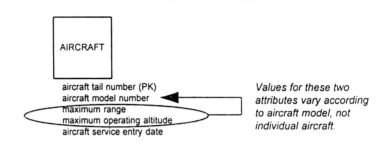

AIRCRAFT

aircraft tail number (PK)
aircraft model number
maximum range
maximum operating altitude
aircraft service entry date

*Values for these two
attributes vary according
to aircraft model, not
individual aircraft.*

Figure 8.11   Unresolved transitive dependency.

Figure 8.11. We execute our CREATE TABLE instruction, and begin to populate and use the table. What kinds of problems could we encounter? Figure 8.12 provides a sample set of table rows that we can use in our analysis.

Assume that our package carrier wishes to maintain a list of general characteristics of various aircraft models, such as *maximum range* and *max operating altitude*. The operations planning department wants to know what aircraft models will suit its needs in the future, and is interested in aircraft designs that the company has not purchased. Because the primary key of the table is *aircraft tail number*, information cannot be inserted on aircraft models for which an *aircraft tail number* is also not available (remember, no null values for primary keys). Furthermore, look at the redundancy that exists in the *maximum range* and *maximum operating altitude* columns.

Suppose the company wants to delete the aircraft with tail number UN1023 from the table. Not only is the information about that specific

aircraft tail number (PK)	aircraft model number	maximun range (miles)	max operating altitude (feet)	aircraft service entry date
UN5137	AX-700	5,000	30,000	10/27/91
UN4278	BY-900	9,000	32,000	12/3/90
UN1777	BY-900	9,000	32,000	04/25/88
UN5343	AX-700	5,000	30,000	08/31/87
UN1023	AX-500	10,000	35,000	02/15/84

Figure 8.12   Sample table for AIRCRAFT.

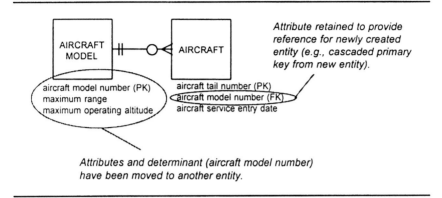

Attribute retained to provide
reference for newly created
entity (e.g., cascaded primary
key from new entity).

AIRCRAFT
MODEL

AIRCRAFT

aircraft model number (PK)
maximum range
maximum operating altitude

aircraft tail number (PK)
aircraft model number (FK)
aircraft service entry date

Attributes and determinant (aircraft model number)
have been moved to another entity.

Figure 8.13   Resolved transitive dependency.

aircraft deleted, but also the information about the AX-500 aircraft model—the fact that it can fly as far as 10,000 miles and as high as 35,000 feet. Finally, what if the company needs to update information about a particular aircraft model, such as the maximum range? It will have to update the record for each aircraft of that model type; otherwise, it will be faced with an inconsistent set of data.

To resolve these problems, the non-3NF entity should be decomposed into two entities as shown in Figure 8.13, using Finkelstein's procedure.

As you can see from Figure 8.14, the resulting database tables eliminate the insertion, update, and deletion anomalies of the non-3NF tables.

8.7   BOYCE/CODD NORMAL FORM

Every data model should be in Boyce/Codd normal form (BCNF).

Discussion

Date (1986) provides the following formal definition of BCNF:

A relation R is in Boyce/Codd normal form (BCNF) if and only if every determinant is a candidate key.

We have already defined a *determinant* as any attribute on which another attribute is fully functionally dependent. The principal difference between BCNF and 3NF, of which the former is a stronger defini-

Aircraft Model

aircraft model number (PK)	maximum range (miles)	max operating altitude (feet)
AX-500	10,000	35,000
AX-700	5,000	30,000
BY-900	9,000	32,000

Aircraft

aircraft tail number (PK)	aircraft model number	aircraft service entry date
UN5137	AX-700	10/27/91
UN4278	BY-900	12/3/90
UN1777	BY-900	04/25/88
UN5343	AX-700	08/31/87
UN1023	AX-500	02/15/84

Figure 8.14   Tables based on 3NF model.

tion of the latter, is that BCNF shifts emphasis from primary keys to candidate keys. Thus, BCNF allows the modeler to deal more effectively with cases involving multiple candidate keys, composite candidate keys, and overlapping candidate keys (Date, 1986).

In practice, it is rare to find an entity that is in 3NF that is not also in BCNF. Following Finkelstein's steps for resolving 3NF will also resolve BCNF, provided the strategy is followed for *all* attributes, including candidate keys.

8.8   FOURTH NORMAL FORM

Every data model should be in Fourth normal form (4NF).

Discussion

Fourth normal form (4NF) is based on the principle of *multi-valued dependency* (MVD), which is defined by Date (1986) as:

Given a relation R with attributes A, B and C, the multi-valued dependence (MVD):

$$R.A \rightarrow \rightarrow R.B$$

holds in R if and only if the set of B-values matching a given (A-value, C-value) pair in R depends only on the A-value and is independent of the C-value. As usual, A, B and C may be composite.

The formal definition for 4NF, also from Date (1986):

A relation R is in fourth normal form (4NF) if and only if, whenever there exists an MVD in R, say $A \rightarrow \rightarrow B$, then all attributes of R are also functionally dependent on A. In other words, the only dependencies (FDs or MVDs) in R are of the form $K \rightarrow X$ (i.e., a functional dependency from a candidate key K to some other attribute X). Equivalently: R is in 4NF if it is in BCNF and all MVDs in R are in fact FDs.

Key characteristics of 4NF can be summarized as:

*   Fourth normal form applies only to entities with three or more attributes (note the definition of MVD).
*   Resolution of Fourth normal form MVDs results in the creation of two new entities (as did our resolutions for 1NF, 2NF, 3NF, and BCNF).
*   4NF eliminates a fair amount of redundancy, easing potential for update anomalies and reducing space requirements.

Let's look at one more important aspect of 4NF, one that was identified by Finkelstein in the development of his Business Normal Forms. Assume that we have three attributes, A, B, and C, in an entity R, and there is a multi-value dependence as follows:

$$R.A \rightarrow \rightarrow R.B | R.C$$

which can also be interpreted as:

For each instance of R.A, there may be multiple instances of R.B, and the value for R.B is independent of that of R.C (remember our definition of MVD). Therefore, R.B is not atomic with respect to R.A since R.B contains repeating values for every value of R.A.

By now, the reader should begin to recognize the similarity to 1NF. In normalizing MVDs, Date suggests a conversion from the unnormalized (i.e., not in 1NF) form of the entity into a normalized (1NF) form, then resolution into two new entities to eliminate MVDs. However, if we return to our discussion of 1NF, we find that Finkelstein's resolution of 1NF also serves to remove MVDs from an entity (1989). Both approaches result in the same model constructs, and we are not suggesting one over the other. The example should illustrate the similarity between 4NF and 1NF resolution.

Example

Our example is a much simplified version of a model used to manage airline flight crew schedules. During the course of their analysis, the modeling team generated a sample instance table (Figure 8.15) in an attempt to understand the relationships among aircraft assignment attributes.

As the reader can see from the table, the following assumptions hold:

- For a given aircraft, there are many potential crew members.
- A given crew member can fly on more than one aircraft type.
- A given aircraft is individually configured to transport many (but not all) types of cargo, and each type of cargo can be transported on more than one aircraft.
- The crew members and cargo type are independent of each other. In order to schedule crew members, we do not need to be concerned with the cargo type.

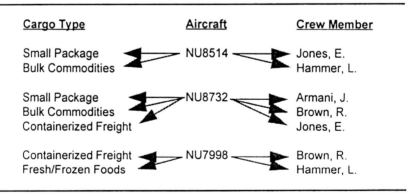

Figure 8.15   Sample instance table.

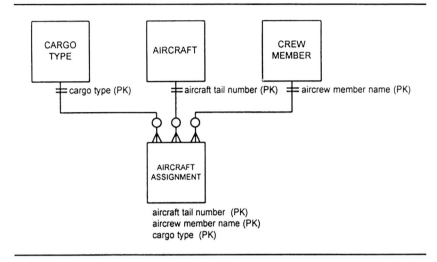

Figure 8.16   Unresolved 4NF pattern for AIRCRAFT ASSIGNMENT.

In other words:

aircraft tail number → → aircrew member name
aircraft tail number → → cargo type

Let's look at a model fragment that captures the model components we have been discussing. Assume that the modeling team identified the CARGO TYPE, AIRCRAFT, and CREW MEMBER entities, then attempted to model the complex relationships among the three which we have described above. The results of that effort are shown in Figure 8.16. We have introduced only the primary key structures, and have kept those as simple as possible for the example.

Resolution according to 4NF rules results in the creation of two entities to replace AIRCRAFT ASSIGNMENT (Figure 8.17). In accordance with the accepted resolution strategy, we decompose AIRCRAFT ASSIGNMENT into two separate entities: AIRCREW ASSIGNMENT and AIR CARGO ASSIGNMENT. Recall that one characteristic of our multi-value dependencies in this example is that crew member relationship to aircraft is independent of the air cargo relationship to aircraft. Therefore, there is no direct relationship between our two new 4NF entities.

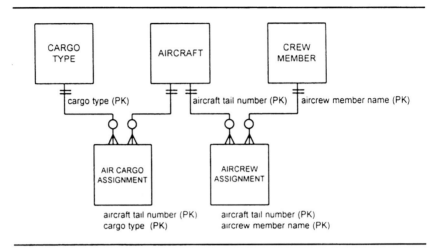

Figure 8.17   Resolved 4NF pattern.

8.9   FIFTH NORMAL FORM

Every data model should be in Fifth normal form (5NF).

Discussion

Fifth normal form (5NF), also known as Projection-Join Normal Form (PJ/NF) is founded on the notion of join dependency. One of the clearest explanations of 5NF that we have encountered comes from Finkelstein (1989):

> The decomposition of a relation (entity) into other relations is called *projection*. These projected (or decomposed) relations can be combined together based on common keys. This is called a *join*. Join dependency therefore means that a relation, after projection into three or more subset relations, must be capable of being joined again on common keys to form the original relation. A relation that can be projected to three or more relations is called *n-decomposable*: this is a characteristic of join dependency.

Once again, Date (1986) supplies some clarifying definitions:

Relation R satisfies the **join dependency** (JD)

    $* (X, Y, \ldots, Z)$

if and only if R is equal to the join of its projections on X, Y, . . . , Z, where X, Y, . . . , Z are subsets of the set of attributes of R.

What are the characteristics of a 5NF relation?

- Nonloss decompositions into *more than* two projections (e.g., other entities) based on functional dependencies or multi-value dependencies. Remember that the other normal forms we have studied thus far result in the creation of two entities where one existed before. 4NF, for example, results in decomposition of a relation containing multi-valued dependency into two projections (other entities). So one gauge of correct 5NF projection is the creation of three or more entities where one exists.
- For an entity to be in 5NF, projections must be based not only on the primary key, but on all candidate keys in the entity. The interesting thing about 5NF is that you may have difficulty identifying all of the join dependencies. Join dependencies are generalizations of multi-value dependencies, as MVDs are generalizations of functional dependencies. Therefore, by ensuring that all entities in a model are in 4NF, you will have very likely brought it close (if not all the way) to eliminating any entities that are not in 5NF. As Date (1986) suggests, entities that are in 4NF but not in 5NF are probably "pathological" in nature (his term), and are probably going to be relatively rare in practice. Our advice is to not worry too much about finding non-5NF entities, since they will most likely be resolved during the course of resolving other types of dependencies.

Examples

Assume we have an entity ORG SERVICE LOCATION, with only three attributes (all primary key attributes, and therefore all candidate keys):

    organization name (PK)
    service type (PK)
    location id (PK)

Let's further assume that our entity has the set of known values shown in Figure 18.18.

organization name	service type	location id
AAA Service Company	plumbing	Plant A
AAA Service Company	electrical	Plant B
XYZ Service, Inc.	plumbing	Plant B
XYZ Service, Inc.	electrical	Plant A

Figure 8.18   Sample set of values for ORG SERVICE LOCATION.

The issue that 5NF is designed to address is: "Given an entity (with at least three attributes, such as ORG SERVICE LOCATION) that *can* be n-decomposed, *should* it be decomposed?" Let's examine this issue one step at a time, using Date's discussion (1986) as a guideline.

We can decompose then re-join ORG SERVICE LOCATION as shown in Figure 8.19.

As the reader can observe in Figure 8.19, the re-joined ORG SER-VICE LOCATION, created from the 3-decomposed entities, results in the creation of another instance (tuple) that was not in the original ORG SERVICE LOCATION (i.e., XYZ Service, Inc. providing electrical service to Plant A). Recall from our discussion that an entity satisfies a join dependency if and only if it is equal to the join of the projections of entities created from a subset of its attributes. In effect, the decomposition has introduced what Date (1986) refers to as the "connection trap." The inference of the ORG SERVICE LOCATION decomposition and join is:

XYZ Service, Inc., provides electrical services
Electrical services are provided to Plant A
XYZ Service, Inc., serves Plant A

Therefore, XYZ Services, Inc., provides electrical services to Plant A.

However, this was not our intention, if we assume that our original entity ORG SERVICE LOCATION captured the desired combinations of values, in which XYZ did not provide electrical services to Plant A (only to Plant C). We may state our original assumption more generally as follows: Even if an organization provides a service, and the service is provided to a location, and the organization serves the location, it does *not* necessarily mean that the organization provides the service to the location.

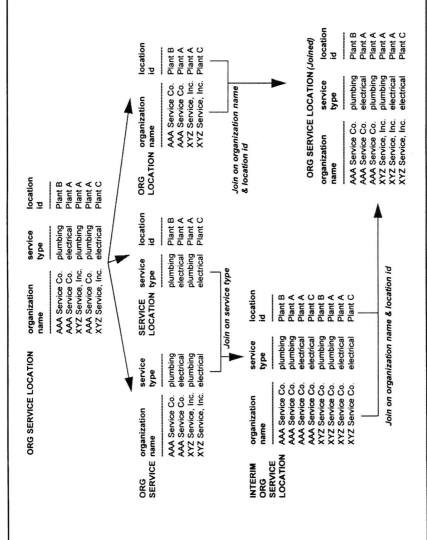

Figure 8.19   Decomposition and re-join of ORG SERVICE LOCATION.

283

The re-joined set of values introduces an incorrect instance of the entity. Therefore, we can be confident that our original ORG SERVICE LOCATION is in 5NF, and need not be decomposed.

A second example will illustrate a case in which the decomposition is warranted. We have a group of athletes that train for and compete in running events at a series of track meets. For this example we will impose the following assumption:

> If an athlete trains for an event, and the event is scheduled at a track meet, and the athlete plans to attend a track meet, then the athlete will compete in that event at that track meet.

Remember that this type of assumption did *not* hold in our first example. This rule is critical in understanding why our initial, unnormalized model in Figure 8.20 is not in 5NF.

Based on the stated business rules, we can decompose the non-5NF entity ATHLETE RACE SCHEDULE into three 5NF entities, ATH-

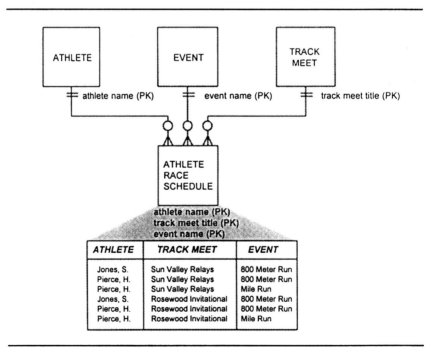

Figure 8.20   Non-5NF entity and table.

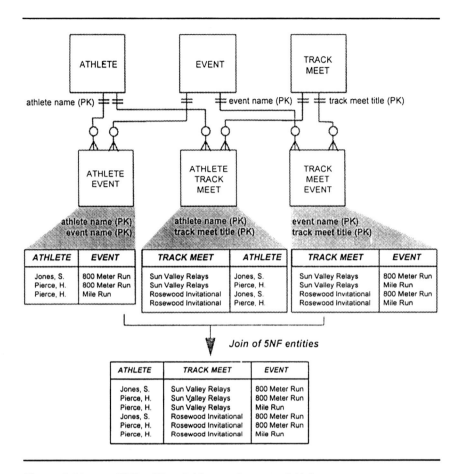

Figure 8.21   5NF entities, tables, and successful join.

LETE EVENT, ATHLETE TRACK MEET, and TRACK MEET EVENT, as shown in Figure 8.21. Sample tables have been provided for each, based on the original non-5NF table values. Note that a natural join of the three tables results in non-loss of data.

What if we had chosen not to decompose the original ATHLETE RACE SCHEDULE entity? Figure 8.22 illustrates the potential for problems in the non-5NF structure. There is nothing to prevent us from adding a row with Jones, Rosewood Invitational, and Mile Run. However, Jones does not train for the Mile Run (see ATHLETE EVENT entity in

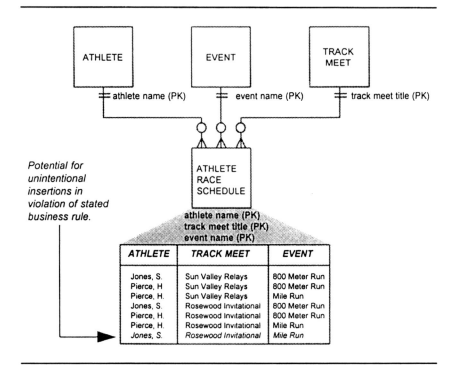

Figure 8.22   Non-5NF entities may lead to erroneous data insertion.

the 5NF model fragment), and therefore should not be scheduled. The non-5NF model does not allow us to properly represent the rules in order to prevent athletes who do not train for an event from being scheduled to race in it at a track meet (Figure 8.22).

8.10   NORMALIZATION SUMMARY

We have examined each of the five prevalent normal forms in detail, and have discussed general concepts of normalization. Before we leave this topic, there are some additional thoughts about normalization that we have found to be important.

• **There is no one best way to apply normal forms.** You may follow more of a sequential, organized (classical or synthesis) normalization approach if you are performing reverse engineering of data files, forms, or other information that is already in a structured but unnormalized form. At the same time, you may be working with teams of domain experts, discovering additional requirements piece by piece, working those into your model, placing every attribute one at a time in its proper place based on functional dependencies.

• **Normalization is a series of tests, rather than a process.** The process component of normalization lies in the resolution strategies that you employ to bring a model from an unnormalized state to the target normal form state. But each time you add attributes to the model, you need to evaluate, to test, whether the placement of each attribute is in conformance with normal forms.

• **Normalization requires domain-specific knowledge.** Domain experts (generally interpreted as "business people") need to be involved in the modeling process, and they need to participate in validating normalization assumptions. If you are going to build a properly normalized model, you must understand the functional dependencies, and generally the only people who understand those are domain experts. Sure, you can observe existing systems or processes, read policy and procedure manuals, analyze forms. That will take a long time, and will get about 80 or 90 percent of the information you need (yes, we are ever optimistic). What about the other 10 or 20 percent? And what about *changes* to business rules, or examination of alternative requirements? Get the business experts and users involved in normalization, at least enough to validate the model if you have created it without their direct involvement. Normalization is not a difficult concept to grasp; in fact, most business people that we've worked with pick up on the concepts very quickly, and understand the value and implications of the normal forms. Of course, if you explain normalization using the formal definitions, you will probably alienate your experts and have to fight an uphill battle from that point forward.

• **Normalization is dependent on a thorough analysis and correct interpretation of business rules.** A data model is a representation of the real world concepts within the scope of the model. Normalization is a key strategy for ensuring that your model is conceptually correct.

• **High-quality data models are built by applying normalization continuously as each model component is added to the data model.** In other words, normalize "on the fly." You can build your model so that at any point it meets the normal form criteria you have established. By ensuring that every attribute added to your model meets the functional dependence test (i.e., is fully functionally dependent on the primary key, the whole primary key, and nothing but the primary key [Kent, 1993]), you can ensure that your model maintains its normalization integrity, and you can avoid having to go through a messy normal-ization exercise later that will most likely result in substantial changes to your model. Our advice is "normalize now."

REFERENCES

Date, C.J. *An Introduction to Database Systems, Volume I.* Reading, MA: Addison-Wesley, 1986.

Finkelstein, Clive. *An Introduction to Information Engineering: From Strategic Planning to Information Systems.* Sydney: Addison-Wesley, 1989.

Finkelstein, Clive. *Information Engineering: Strategic Systems Development.* Sydney: Addison-Wesley, 1992.

Kent, William. "Consequences of Assuming a Universal Relation." *ACM TODS 6*, No. 4 (December 1981).

Kent, William. "A Simple Guide to Five Normal Forms in Relational Database Theory." *Communications of the ACM* 26, No. 2 (February 1983).

Korth, Henry F. and Silberschatz, Abraham. *Database System Concepts.* New York: McGraw-Hill, 1986.

Best Practices

The Best Practices section shows data modelers problems that do not fit "neatly" into other areas of the book. It was originally conceived to show data modelers how to handle situations that are familiar to all of us. We hope it helps.

9.1   MODELING LOGICAL VERSUS PHYSICAL OBJECTS

Discussion

One recurring data modeling question concerns the distinction between logical model objects, and physical model objects. In practice, we often see TROUBLE TICKET, INVOICE, or REPORT entities in our data models. These are physical objects and the modeling team must determine whether they are appropriate for a particular application domain. Attributes are plagued by this same dilemma; when we describe domain entities, we often provide a description of the entity and an entity code. The existence of these objects leads to much emotional discussion.

From a purely business perspective, such entities and attributes are superfluous to the business community. Businesspeople are accustomed to a particular monthly report or the information codes, but the entities and attributes are not essential to running the business. The requirement is for the organization to present information or distinguish between certain entity types.

Examples

In the first example, an assumption has been made about how customer problems will be implemented, that is, by a trouble ticket. This physical representation of the information is a bit premature in a logical data model. The idea is to capture the required information components and *then* determine the appropriate vehicle for capture and dissemination.

The model in figure 9.1 has been reexamined by the quality reviewer and the following changes were implemented to allow it to reflect the "true" information requirements. The TROUBLE TICKET entity has been removed from the data model and the information on the ticket has been modeled. This is presented in Figure 9.2.

In Figure 9.3, a *customer status code* is provided as well as a *customer status*. The data modeler has made an assumption about how the customer status will be implemented—as an encoded field of some type. This usually is a result of existing codes that the business community is familiar with.

Figure 9.4 presents the results of the model after the analyst has removed the *customer status code* attribute. This creates a more "logical" model. This is one method for the resolution of the problem.

An additional resolution is presented in Figure 9.5. Here, *customer status* is rolled into the CUSTOMER entity and is displayed as an enumerated data type. The diagram presents the results of the model above, after the removal of *customer status code.*

Are we interested in
the trouble ticket itself
or are we interested
in the information that
is maintained on the
trouble ticket ?

TROUBLE
TICKET

trouble ticket number (PK)
problem
problem category
problem date
problem time
time to repair
customer name
customer phone number
technician assigned
technician level

Figure 9.1   Physical object—Entity level.

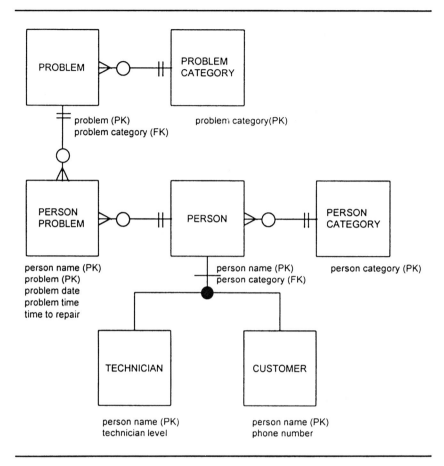

Figure 9.2   Physical object—Entity level resolved.

As a third example, attributes that exist on reports and screens can be modeled as data, but a REPORT, SCREEN, OUTPUT, or an INPUT entity should be questioned. In general, avoid including physical characteristics in a logical data model. Physical characteristics include any connotation of technology (hardware or software), physical location (databases, files, reports, forms, or tables), organization (data steward), or application (systems, applications, or programs).

The only time that technology-dependent items should be modeled is if the business area involves the management of systems, equipment, or technology, and if characteristics and information about those items are needed. A good example of technology-dependent modeling is an information system repository model—often referred to as a "meta-model"

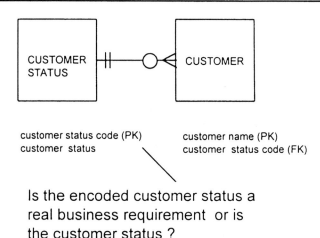

customer status code (PK)   customer name (PK)
customer status   customer status code (FK)

Is the encoded customer status a
real business requirement or is
the customer status ?

Figure 9.3   Physical objects—Attribute level unresolved.

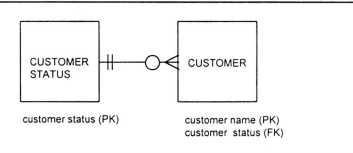

customer status (PK)   customer name (PK)
                            customer status (FK)

Figure 9.4   Physical objects—Attribute level, possible resolution.

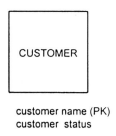

customer name (PK)
customer status

Figure 9.5   Physical object—Attribute level, enumerated data type
resolution.

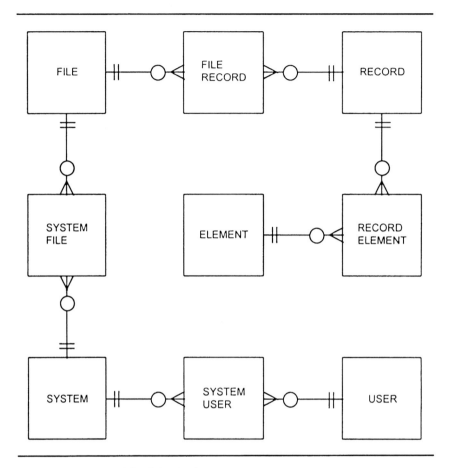

Figure 9.6   IRDS minimal schema.

in which such entities as SYSTEM, DATA STRUCTURE, SCREEN, or REPORT might be included as objects to be managed. Figure 9.6 shows a subset of the Information Resource Dictionary System (IRDS) minimal schema. This attempted to manage heterogeneous data dictionary environments.

9.2   AGGREGATION

Aggregation will be applied in bill of material or similar situations.

Discussion

Aggregation is the ability to represent an object in whole, without losing reference to its constituent parts. A personal computer system is made up of a monitor, a processing component, and a keyboard. The processing component can then be broken down into a cpu board, memory board, a disk drive, and a host of other items. Many problem domains are best understood by breaking an item apart and reviewing it in part and then in whole. The data modeler must understand how to use this mechanism to the best of his or her ability (see Figure 9.7).

Aggregation is often referred to as the bill of materials problem. In most manufacturing organizations a bill of materials structure is essential to help identify: which parts are used in different products, and what products and parts are made of. Identifying every part as an entity can lead to redundancy and a general misunderstanding the process. By applying the concept of aggregation appropriately, a flexible structure is created that is understandable to all subject matter experts.

Example

The first aggregation pattern we will describe is the bill of materials problem. Figure 9.8 contains a PRODUCT, which is made up of many PARTs, which in turn is made up of many COMPONENTs. This pattern is seen when we model organizations—organizations are made up

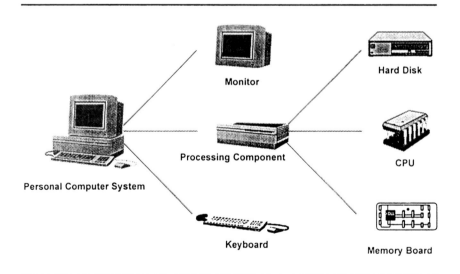

Figure 9.7   Aggregation.

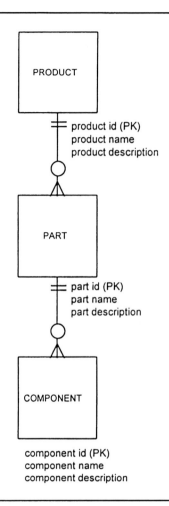

Figure 9.8   Aggregation relationship.

of groups, which are then made up of divisions, which then may have departments—or other similar areas. The problem with this description is that there does not appear to be a distinction between the three items. Clearly we need to know the components of a PRODUCT, but how could we remodel this area so there is not as much repetition?

The move to the model shown in Figure 9.9 represents a new way of thinking about products. A COMPONENT and a PART must be viewed by the organization as salable commodities. If we can sell a PC, why can't we sell the keyboard or the monitor or the disk drive indepen-

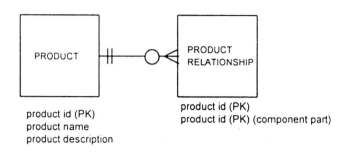

Figure 9.9 Revised aggregation relationship.

dently? If this is agreed to by the enterprise, then the model below will suffice and provide a more stable structure for the organization's products. The PRODUCT and its makeup can be derived through the PRODUCT RELATIONSHIP entity.

Aggregation is not the same as generalization. Recall that generalization is called *a kind of* or an *is a* relationship. Aggregation is referred to as *a part of* relationship. Both are critical for communicating requirements, but they represent different ideas.

9.3 LEVELS OF ABSTRACTION

A data model should maintain a consistent level of abstraction.

Discussion

A frequent problem observed in data models is an attempt to mix and match levels of abstraction. This problem manifests itself in a variety of ways, but most often it can be detected by looking for an entity or entities with relationships to *every* other entity in the model.

Data modeling is a technique for describing the relationships between the data (information) components of an organization, therefore, an occurrence of data (information) should be the lowest level of abstraction. We'll call this the Data Level. The other levels of abstraction are created to help manage this environment.

An entity, such as PERSON, VEHICLE, or STOCK, attempts to assemble or collect similar occurrences into a group and describe its constituent parts. This is the level of abstraction most data modelers concern themselves with. The next level of abstraction is the Meta-Model or Methodology level. The description of how entities, attributes, relationships, and other model parts interact are described at this level. The final level of concern is the Meta-Meta-Model or Repository Level.

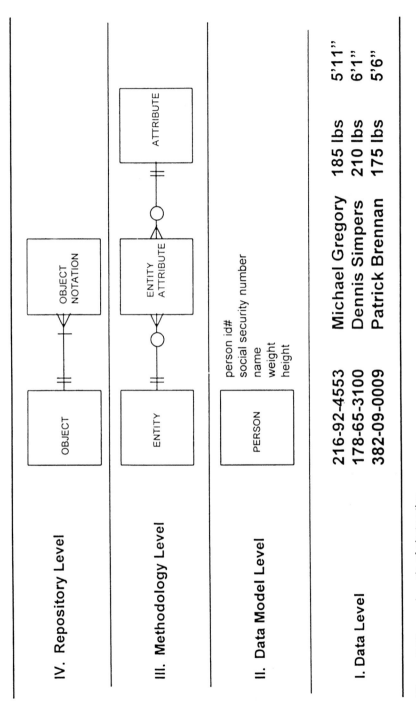

IV. Repository Level

OBJECT

OBJECT
NOTATION

III. Methodology Level

ENTITY

ENTITY
ATTRIBUTE

ATTRIBUTE

II. Data Model Level

PERSON

person id#
social security number
name
weight
height

I. Data Level

216-92-4553	Michael Gregory	185 lbs	5'11"
178-65-3100	Dennis Simpers	210 lbs	6'1"
382-09-0009	Patrick Brennan	175 lbs	5'6"

Figure 9.10   Levels of abstraction.

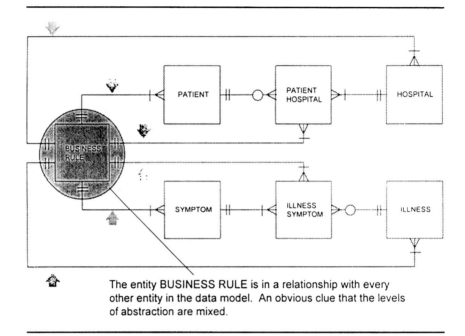

The entity BUSINESS RULE is in a relationship with every other entity in the data model. An obvious clue that the levels of abstraction are mixed.

Figure 9.11   Mixed levels of abstraction—Illegal.

Examples

The most common abstraction problems occur between the Data Model and Methodology levels. In the example shown in Figure 9.11, the entity BUSINESS RULE participates in a relationship with every entity in the data model. The modeler has attempted to show the linkage between a business rule occurrence (a policy, procedure, etc.) and objects created in the data model. This is an abstraction mismatch.

As a further test, draw the occurrence tables for the entities in question and ask if this is what we wish to represent. The mapping the modeler is looking for in this example is maintained at the meta-model level.

As with every rule (see Figure 9.12), there are exceptions. Most data models do in fact mix between levels. Domain, Type, Rule, or other entities that are provided to control occurrences or provide guidance for the population of occurrences are legal abstraction mixes. In the example below, the FACILITY CATEGORY entity is used to "control" the population of subtype occurrences for FACILITY. In other words, the values for the supertype discriminator of FACILITY are maintained in an entity. Be careful with the use of abstraction; it is a powerful concept and can be misused with relative ease.

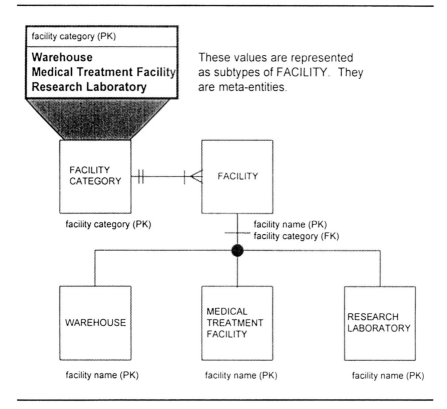

facility category (PK)

Warehouse
Medical Treatment Facility
Research Laboratory

These values are represented
as subtypes of FACILITY. They
are meta-entities.

FACILITY
CATEGORY

FACILITY

facility category (PK)

facility name (PK)
facility category (FK)

WAREHOUSE

MEDICAL
TREATMENT
FACILITY

RESEARCH
LABORATORY

facility name (PK)

facility name (PK)

facility name (PK)

Figure 9.12   Mixed levels of abstraction—Legal.

9.4   MODELING COMPLEX DATA TYPES

Discussion

The power of technology is doubling every two to three years, making available more than just static information pieces. Multimedia has raised the quality bar for data modelers. We must broaden our perspective to include those items heretofore referred to as complex data types.

Complex data types are those that take advantage of the new technologies we have been provided: digital video, sound, or any other mechanism that provides input to one of our five senses. The problem with most data models is they ignore some potentially valuable input because they feel the discussion of data types is a system design issue. We concur, to a degree. The line between analysis and design has always been fairly blurry and users are now requesting complex data that they could not have requested in the past. The inclusion of a fingerprint for an FBI system or a driver's license photograph for a Department of Motor Vehicles system is an essential requirement that must be captured during analysis.

There is no difference between modeling a complex data type and any other information piece. The real difference is the thought process of the data modeler—he or she must open his or her mind and think more creatively. Instead of requesting recurring reports from business users, viewing existing screens, or examining file layouts, the data modeler should shadow the business users and look for opportunities to package information into useful formats.

Example

In the example below, analysis has been performed in the endangered species domain. The analyst captured the ENDANGERED SPECIES, its LOCATION, and some additional non-key attributes, like the total number remaining and the estimated number in specific locations. This information is presented in Figure 9.13.

This same domain was modeled a bit differently by a data modeler who understood the value of complex data types. The change is small, but substantial. A depiction of the species, which visually describes the threatened creature, has been included in the model (see Figure 9.14).

In addition to the endangered species depiction, complex data types were placed in the model for ENDANGERED SPECIES LOCATION and LOCATION. This will allow the subject matter experts to see the habitat,

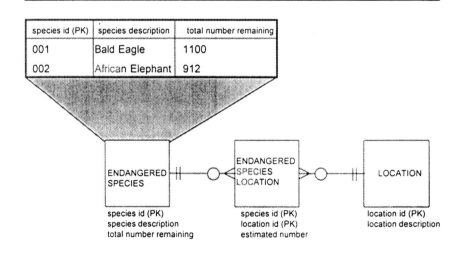

Figure 9.13   Without complex data types.

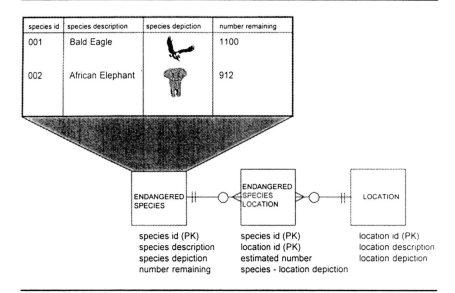

species id	species description	species depiction	number remaining
001	Bald Eagle		1100
002	African Elephant		912

ENDANGERED SPECIES

species id (PK)
species description
species depiction
number remaining

ENDANGERED SPECIES LOCATION

species id (PK)
location id (PK)
estimated number
species - location depiction

LOCATION

location id (PK)
location description
location depiction

Figure 9.14   With complex data types.

as well as the species in existence in the habitat. We believe this is a more complete analysis effort than the model without complex data types. Please note that we have not specified an implementation technology, we have simply described a visual requirement. This is no different than requesting a specific process or a unique piece of information.

9.5   A NOTE ABOUT SYNTAX

Discussion

No discussion of data modeling is complete without mentioning syntax. All of the data modeling notations used throughout the universe must comply with a formal set of rules. These rules identify what is permissible and what is not permissible. We have presented our rules in a hybrid format so they can be equally enforced in IDEF1X, Chen, Finkelstein, Martin, or any others. A model that adheres to syntax alone is no guarantee of a quality model.

Examples

In IDEF1X, a generalization structure can be complete or incomplete. A complete generalization structure contains two horizontal lines and

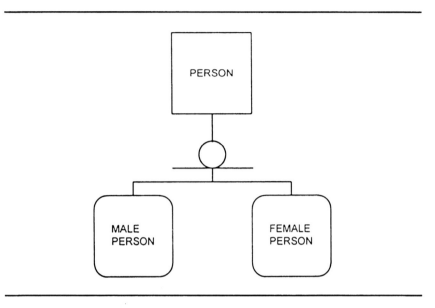

Figure 9.15   Incorrect category structure.

indicates there are no more valid subtypes. An incomplete generalization structure contains one line and indicates there may be more subtypes. In Figure 9.15, a PERSON can be either a MALE PERSON or a
FEMALE PERSON. There is no other valid sex. This would represent a
complete generalization structure. However, the data modeler has neglected the syntax and elected to show it as an incomplete structure,
identified by one horizontal line.

   This is corrected during the Quality Assurance review by an alert
data modeler. Two vertical bars are placed beneath PERSON to represent a complete generalization hierarchy (see Figure 9.16).

   As a second example, In IDEF1X there are two relationship types :
identifying and non-identifying. An identifying relationship is indicated
by a solid line; it means that the primary keys of the parent are cascaded into the child entity and participate in the primary key of the
child. A non-identifying relationship is indicated by a dashed line; it
means that the primary keys of the parent are cascaded into the child
entity and do not participate in the primary key of the child. Therefore,
the migrated keys must support the nature of the relationship between
two entities and a relationship type (identifying or non-identifying) shall
not be defined contradictory to the use of the migrated keys in the child
entity. This would violate the syntax of IDEF1X.

   In the example in Figure 9.17, keys migrated to support an identi-

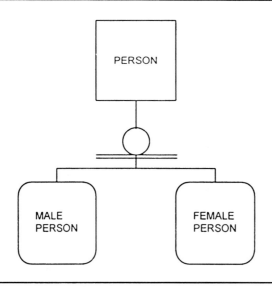

Figure 9.16   Syntactically correct generalization hierarchy.

fying relationship must become part of the primary key in the child entity. There are no possible exceptions.

Figure 9.18 shows keys migrated to support a non-identifying relationship. Syntax demands they shall NOT become part of the primary key in the child entity.

The rule itself is self-explanatory. Use of attributes in a child entity

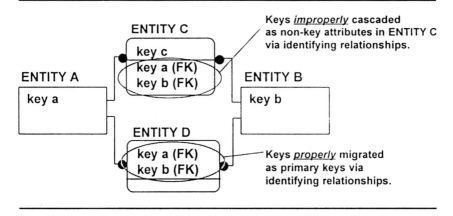

Figure 9.17   Keys migrated via identifying relationships.

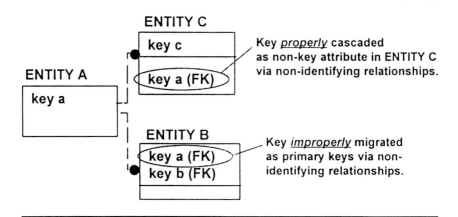

Figure 9.18   Keys migrated via non-identifying relationships.

that are migrated from a parent entity must be consistent with the relationship along which they were migrated. Since attributes that are part of the primary key aid in identifying the entity, then those that were migrated must have necessarily migrated from identifying relationships. The child entity is actually dependent on its parent(s) for its identity; the parent entity becomes an extension of the relevant information set that can be used to describe the child entity. As a result, the child entity cannot be fully identified and defined independent of its parent. This logic does not hold, of course, for non-identifying relationships.

9.6   MODELING MULTIPLE IDENTIFIERS FOR AN ENTITY

Discussion

There exist a number of objects in the world for which there are multiple identifiers. A person may have a social security number, driver's license number, passport number, employee id, and perhaps, a number of other identifiers that allow an organization to uniquely identify that individual. An organizations has a similar dilemma; it may have a vendor id, customer id, or an identifier that describes it as an alliance partner to another organization.

In most organizations, these identifiers are components of distinct systems that maintain similar information about a person or organization. Customer information, vendor information, and alliance partner information will contain unique components, but they will also contain core data that must be shareable and consistent. The problem for the data modeler is how to indicate their similar role of these identifiers in the data model and provide a mechanism for the control.

Examples

In Figure 9.19, each identifier is assigned its own subtype to describe its role and to show that the identifier only applies in certain instances—a driver will have a driver's license number, an employee will have an employee id, a U.S. citizen will have a social security number, and a person who is traveling abroad will have a passport number. This will resolve the multiple identifier problem and the data model will communicate to business experts; however, there is no control of the identifiers.

All of the identifiers serve the same role and could be considered to be in the same domain. The method used in this example ignores the similar role of these attributes. Control of identifiers is more difficult.

Figure 9.20 is a simpler model. It maintains the same information as above, but the degree of control is increased. All identifiers for an individual are maintained in the IDENTIFIER entity. This is a meta-entity that maintains all unique identifiers for a PERSON: social security number, employee id, passport number, and any others desired. If additional identifiers are introduced, they can simply be added as an

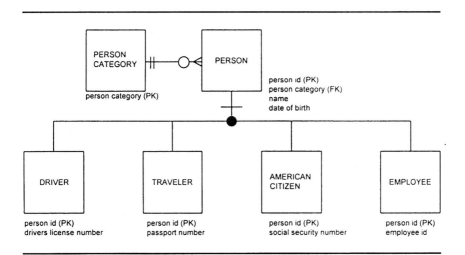

Figure 9.19   Multiple identifiers for a PERSON—One resolution.

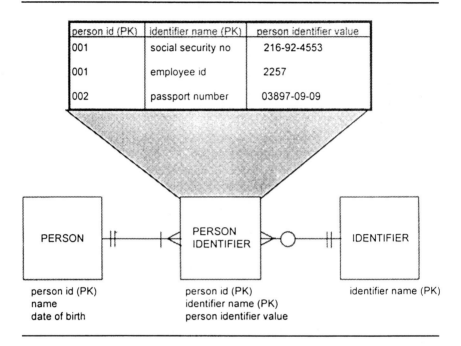

person id (PK)	identifier name (PK)	person identifier value
001	social security no	216-92-4553
001	employee id	2257
002	passport number	03897-09-09

PERSON

person id (PK)
name
date of birth

PERSON IDENTIFIER

person id (PK)
identifier name (PK)
person identifier value

IDENTIFIER

identifier name (PK)

Figure 9.20   Multiple identifiers for a PERSON—Possible resolution.

additional occurrence without impact to the model. This model fragment may not communicate to business users as well as the previous model, but it certainly will be easier to maintain. All relationships that may be introduced to the subtypes in the previous model—a DRIVER drives a CAR, an EMPLOYEE works for an ORGANIZATION—will be maintained as optional relationships from PERSON. The person identifier value attribute maintains the value of each identifier as applies to an individual.

9.7   MODELING LOCATION

Discussion

There are almost as many ways to model location as there are data modelers. It is a concept that seems so simple on the surface, yet leads to many different personal opinions. The problem with LOCATION is that there are so many possible location objects, and then there are many permutations of these objects. For example, a location could contain x and y coordinates, room number, apartment number, PO Box, street address, city, state, country, bed number, or a number of other possibilities. To complicate matters, the number of valid combinations of these objects is seemingly infinite. The following methods are presented to promote discussion.

Examples

The first method of modeling location is straightforward. A LOCATION is described with an artificial key, *location id*, and then a number of non-key attributes including *street address, city, state, zip code*, and *country*. PERSON LOCATION REASON describes the connection between PERSON and LOCATION. Is it a mailing address, billing address, home address, or work address? This allows us to distinguish among addresses. Figure 9.21 describes this method.

This is a rather simplistic attempt at modeling a LOCATION. It assumes all LOCATION occurrences have a *street address, city, state, zip code*, and *country*. Post office boxes, building numbers, room numbers are ignored in this model. Foreign locations and nonpostal schemes are ignored.

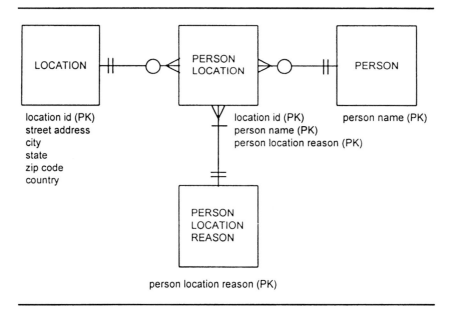

Figure 9.21   Location—Questionable method.

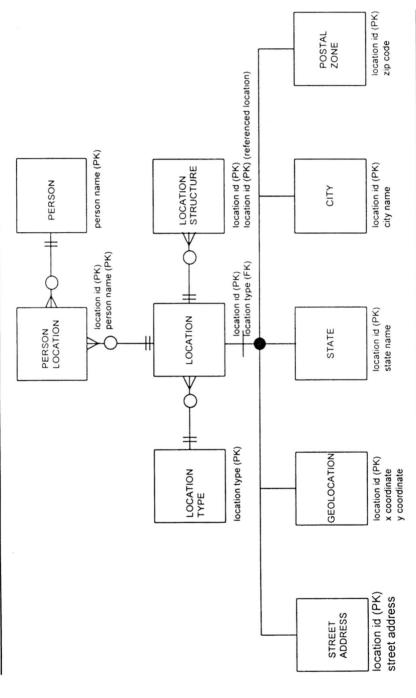

Figure 9.22 Location—One method.

As a second example, Figure 9.22 describes a method of modeling LO-CATION that is straightforward and flexible. As a new location object is discovered, it is simply added as a subtype. In the example below, we have CITY, STATE, STREET ADDRESS, ZIP subtypes. LOCATION TYPE contains the valid values for the subtypes. LOCATION STRUCTURE shows the hierarchical relationship between locations—cities within states, street addresses within cities. If we wish to discover where a PERSON lives, we simply extract it from the PERSON LOCATION entity.

This is a structure that is easy to implement and flexible. Post office boxes, room numbers, building numbers and other mechanisms for identifying locations can simply be placed in the generalization structure. Nonpostal schemes for identifying locations are included as subtypes, such as GEOLOCATION.

In Figure 9.23, a more abstract method is utilized. A LOCATION is a coordinating mechanism. It contains no attributes other than an artificial key. It is associated with other entities in the data model to determine their location. A POSITIONING OBJECT identifies categories of locations such as a street, state, longitude, latitude, zip code, and so on. It is used to identify a COORDINATE. A COORDINATE is a symbol representing a place. It helps humans find where a specific place is. For example, it may be 2000 15th Street or Germany or 113 degrees longitude. Thus, a LOCATION can have many COORDINATES and a CO-ORDINATE can have many LOCATIONS. NAVIGATION is a framework for interpreting a COORDINATE. Instances of NAVIGA-TION could be postal, grid, and the like. NAVIGATION identifies the different systems for identifying locations. Every POSITIONING OB-JECT is supported by one or more methods of NAVIGATION. A NAVI-GATION POSITIONING OBJECT entity allows many NAVIGATIONs to be associated with many OBJECTs.

9.8 MODELING BUSINESS (OR LEGAL) PARTY

Discussion

A business party is a generalization problem that is very often faced by the data modeler. It occurs when a business rule requires the participation of two seemingly unrelated entities. For example, a customer may be either a person or an organization. A legal party may be either a person or an organization. The enterprise maintains information about all of these entities and the data modeler is faced with a dilemma. How can they represent the similarities between the two entity types, while still maintaining their independence?

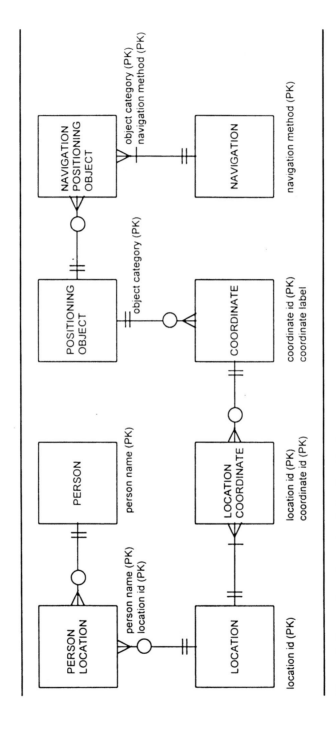

Figure 9.23 Location—An abstract method.

Examples

There are a number of techniques for solving this problem, but they all depend on the organization's business rules. The examples we present below use CUSTOMER to explain the concept, but it is equally applicable to PATIENT (for animal and human patients), LEGAL PARTY (for organization and person), or any other occurrence of this situation. Let us say that we were asked to review the model in Figure 9.24. What would our understanding of the organization be?

It appears the business rules are *our customers consist of organizations and individuals willing to buy our product* and *we view every organization and person as a customer.* This construct is consistent with the business rules, but may become cumbersome when we begin to model the complex relationships between an ORGANIZATION and a PERSON, that is, a person may be an employee, a contact person of, or any other relationship. These relationships will be described by two identical primary keys, and may be less communicative than another structure. In addition, these associations require additional attributes and they will be difficult to show in this structure.

In the first example, we introduced CUSTOMER as a supertype of ORGANIZATION and PERSON. In Figure 9.25, we introduce CUSTOMER as a subtype of both ORGANIZATION and PERSON. This is an implementation we have seen quite often in practice, but do not

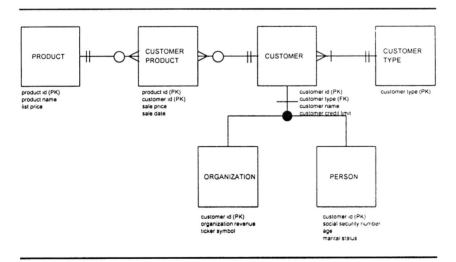

Figure 9.24   Extremely questionable customer structure.

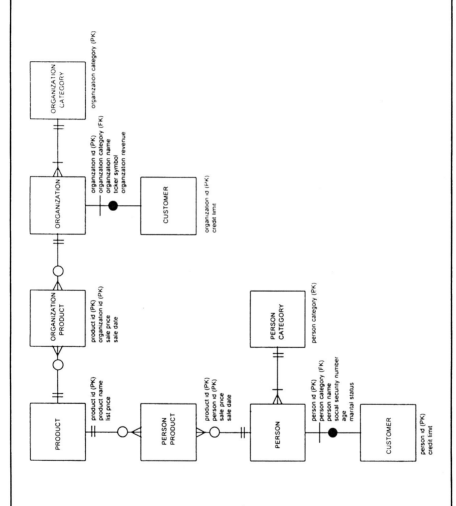

Figure 9.25   Potential customer structure.

recommend. Although this allows ORGANIZATION and PERSON to retain their independence, it also introduces redundancy into the model.

Homonyms have been introduced in the model at the entity and attribute level. CUSTOMER is a subtype of two supertypes, and *credit limit*, *sales price*, and *sales date* have been introduced into the model in two different places. In addition to the redundancy, the model does not precisely explain to the reviewer what a CUSTOMER is.

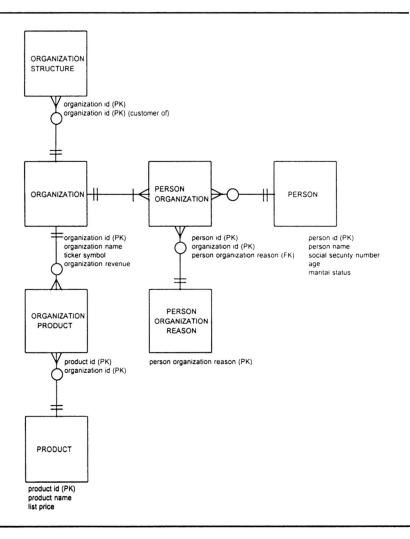

Figure 9.26   Customers represented as relationships.

As our third example, customers are often described as relationships. A customer is someone or some organization that purchases a product or service from our organization. If a customer did not require any additional information, such as a credit limit, it might be modeled as a relationship. Figure 9.26 shows how such a model might be constructed. There is a recursive relationship between an ORGANIZATION and another ORGANIZATION. This is described by the ORGANIZATION STRUCTURE entity. The second *organization id* is aliased to show that the one organization is a customer of the other. There are multiple reasons for an ORGANIZATION and a PERSON to relate. One is the customer relationship. This value would be contained in PERSON ORGANIZATION REASON as a static value.

The problem with this model is it is difficult to add customer specific attributes. We have identified a customer as being no different than any other relationship between two entities. Additional attribution will require the creation of CUSTOMER entities.

Figure 9.27 is our preferred structure for modeling CUSTOMER. The first item to notice is the lack of duplication among the entities and attributes. There is only one CUSTOMER and the *sale price*, *sales date*, and *credit limit* contain only one occurrence. This model emphasizes the independence of CUSTOMER, ORGANIZATION and PERSON. As this model grows more complex, it will be easy to develop relationships between ORGANIZATION and PERSON because they are not subtypes of CUSTOMER, nor are they supertypes of CUSTOMER. This is a clean implementation of the concepts.

This model recognizes the importance of treating PERSON and ORGANIZATION as separate principal entities, while allowing CUSTOMER to contain significant things common to both.

9.9   MODELING DELETE RULES

Discussion

We have already discussed whether a foreign key can be optional or accept nulls and what should occur on an attempt to update the primary key of the target of a foreign key reference. Both are restricted operations. One question that remains is what should occur on an attempt to delete the target of a foreign key reference. This is known as a *delete rule*.

Example

Is this a question that analysts need to be concerned with, or is this a question for the database designers to struggle with? Once again we are

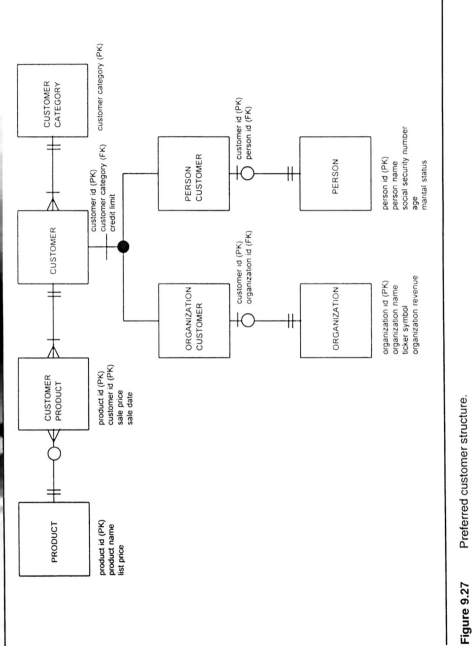

Figure 9.27   Preferred customer structure.

315

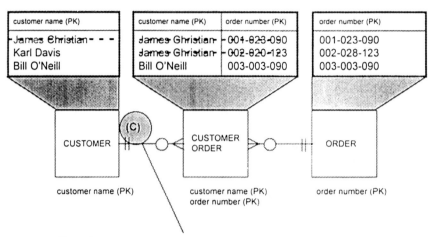

The (C)ascade delete rule would eliminate the occurrence of James Christian from the CUSTOMER and CUSTOMER ORDER entities.

Figure 9.28 Cascade delete.

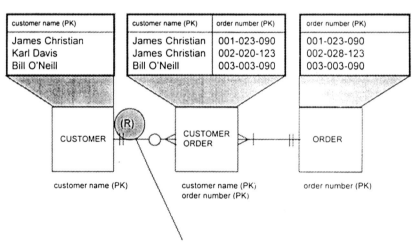

A (R)estrict delete rule would not eliminate the James Christian occurrence because there are associated orders. If there were not, the occurrence would be deleted.

Figure 9.29 Restrict delete.

faced with an analysis versus design question. If the analyst elects to ignore this question, the database designer would choose between *Cascade* and *Restrict* delete rules. If the database designer were to choose the Cascade option (Figure 9.28), the CUSTOMER occurrence would be deleted along with any associated ORDERs. If we delete the occurrence of James Christian, it will cascade to CUSTOMER ORDER and remove associated orders—001-023-090 and 002-028-123.

This is a quite a different result than the Restrict option (see Figure 9.29). In this case, the CUSTOMER occurrence would not be deleted if there were any associated ORDER. Is this a decision we should leave in the hands of our designers? We suggest not. These are decisions that the business experts need to resolve.

The specification of delete rules is an important part of the complete analysis package that should be dictated to the designer, not left to his or her discretion. This is a business decision to be made by the subject matter experts in the organization. Too often, the consequences of seemingly trivial decisions are lost orders and increased maintenance for the information system professional.

9.10   MODELING A PERSON'S NAME

Discussion

A name is defined by Webster's dictionary as, "a word or words by which an entity is designated and distinguished from others." A person's name is an interesting data modeling problem because it can be very simple like the first example or complex like the third example. The data model will reflect the business requirements for an individual or organization identifier.

Example

The first approach to modeling a person's name is the most commonly used method. It uses an artificial key to identify the person, *person id*, and *person name* is included as a non-key attribute. This technique is described in Figure 9.30.

This approach is useful as long as we are only interested in the current name of the person and do not care about the history of the name. For example, if the person is married or changes his or her name for political or religious reasons, the model will only capture the new name.

The second example, Figure 9.31, is a model fragment that corrects some of the difficulties we encountered with a more simplistic approach. The model below captures all occurrences of the person's name and iden-

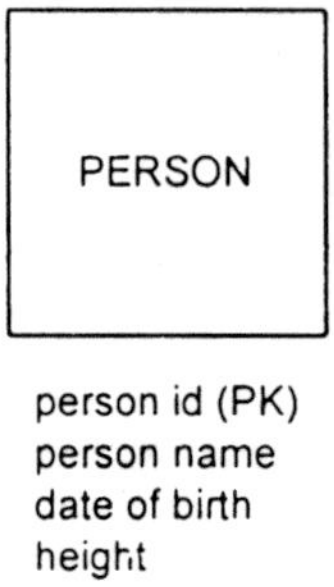

PERSON

person id (PK)
person name
date of birth
height

Figure 9.30 Person name—Approach 1.

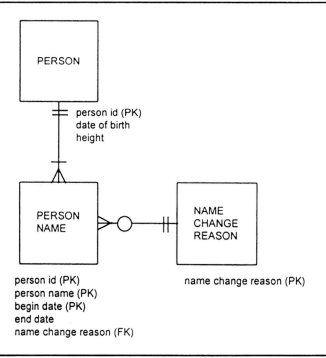

Figure 9.31 Person name—Another approach.

tifies the reason for the change. In addition, for example, if a woman marries, then divorces and reuses her former name, the addition of *begin date* as a component of the primary key will handle the transaction.

This model captures many more details about an individual's name, but may not be complete for all business requirements. For example, surnames, titles, nicknames are not included. In some applications, this may be extremely important information.

In our third example, Figure 9.32 attempts to correct the situation by decomposing *person name* into its constituent parts. The name of a person is captured in the *person name* attribute. In addition, we have broken down the name into four component parts. These parts (fore-name, middle name, surname, nickname) are described by the *name category code*. This model is also concerned with the mode of use pertaining to a designation. This is represented with the *name usage code*. Here we can capture how the name is used. It may be an alias, a preferred name, or some other designation.

Granular levels of detail can easily be achieved with the data models. The key point is to define how much data is enough for to satisfy a business requirement. If only the current name is needed, there is no need to go to this level of detail.

9.11   MODELING TIME

Discussion

In general, well defined, widely recognized (within the business area) or independently managed periods of time having meaning for members of the enterprise and used in managing the enterprise have characteristics and attributes that result in the need to model them as entities. Examples of such time periods include Fiscal Year, Calendar Year, Fiscal Month, Day Shift, 3rd Shift, and designated holidays. The following criteria, confirmed by questions posed to the business experts, should aid in determining whether a time period exists.

- Is there a clearly defined start date/time and end date/time for a subject time requirement?
- Do I have a requirement(s) for collecting or aggregating information according to predefined periods? This will typically be derived information captured in an intersecting entity between the time period and the subject about which the information is being gathered: for example, a fiscal year to report organization performance measures or a daily period to capture information on the stock market.

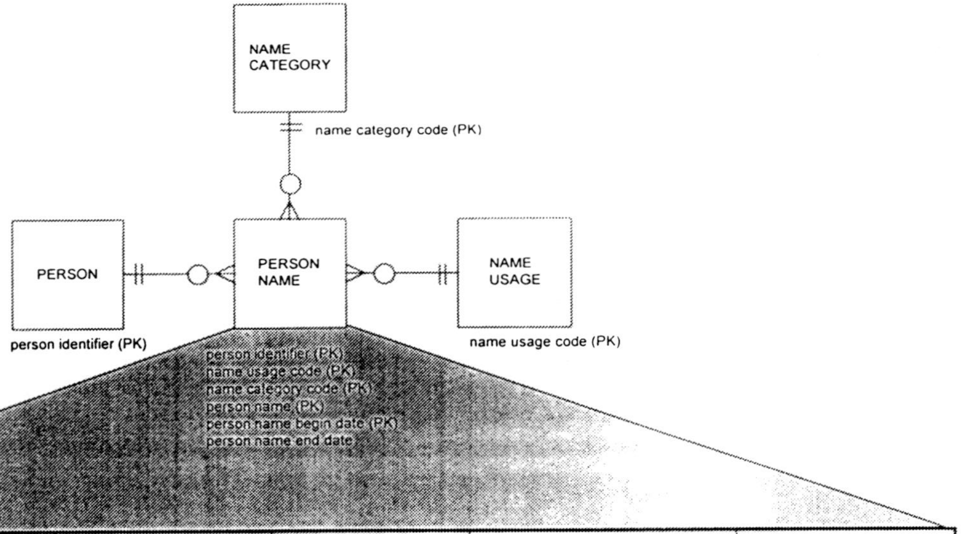

PERSON

person identifier (PK)

NAME
CATEGORY

name category code (PK)

NAME
USAGE

name usage code (PK)

PERSON
NAME

person identifier (PK)
name usage code (PK)
name category code (PK)
person name (PK)
person name begin date (PK)
person name end date

person identifier (PK)	name usage code (PK)	name category code (PK)	person name (PK)	person name begin date (PK)	person name end date
0000001	social name	surname	Smith	01/01/62	
0000001	social name	forename	John	01/01/62	
0000001	social name	middle name	Jacob	01/01/62	
0000002	preferred name	forename	Missy	09/03/67	
0000002	social name	surname	Freeman	10/16/66	01/06/91
0000002	social name	surname	Reingruber	01/06/91	06/03/92
0000002	business name	forename	M'Liss	06/03/91	

Figure 9.32 Person name.

- Is the period a generally recognized period used to plan, manage or control the enterprise or its performance?
- Is the period predictable, such that the characteristics of an individual instance can be planned in advance?

If the answer is "yes" to all questions, a TIME PERIOD entity is probably in order.

If the answer is no, then the period falls into a category of time that might be referred to as "ad hoc" periods, which are generally very specific in use, and do not adhere to the characteristics described above. An example of an "ad hoc" period might be "task duration." Periods of time that are not predictable should be modeled with time stamps.

Examples

The example shown may appear somewhat complicated at first, but it is based on some fairly straightforward ideas. There are four clusters in this model fragment, and we will discuss each of them individually.

1. TIME PERIOD ROLE allows the enterprise to identify a time period that falls into more than one category. Assume we wish to categorize our periods into groups like "corporate fiscal period," "calendar period," or "monthly period." In the absence of the TIME PERIOD ROLE, only one TIME PERIOD CATEGORY may be applied to each TIME PERIOD.
2. TIME MEASURE CONVERSION allows us to convert from one measure to another. Weeks are time periods that can be measured in days (7), hours (168) or minutes (10080). The time measure conversion factor will convert one time measure to another.
3. TIME PERIOD STRUCTURE allows one time period to relate to another category. A calendar period is made up of twelve monthly periods. The TIME PERIOD STRUCTURE allows these monthly periods to relate to the appropriate calendar period.
4. TIME PERIOD MEASURE allows the organization to capture a time period in a specific measure. For example, a Monday through Friday time period may have a duration of one hundred and twenty hours.

The second example depicts a subset of a data model used to fulfill a business requirement by a nonprofit association's marketing department. The requirement is to record the number of times the association is mentioned in a particular news media (i.e., newspaper, television network news, television local news, radio news, talk show, etc.).

In the third example, we demonstrate the concept of an "ad hoc"

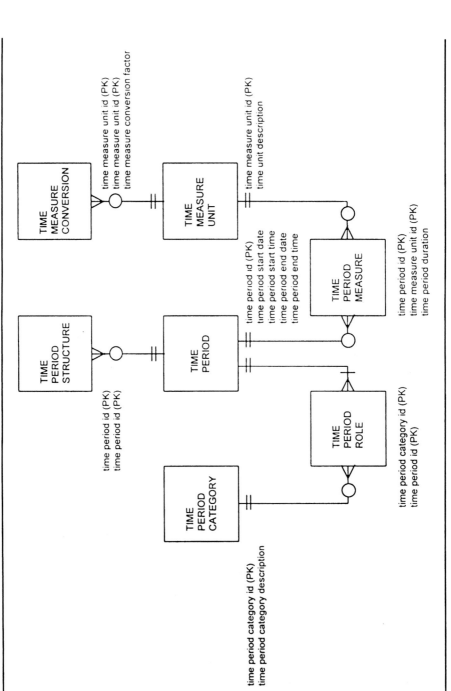

Figure 9.33 Model subset with time period entities.

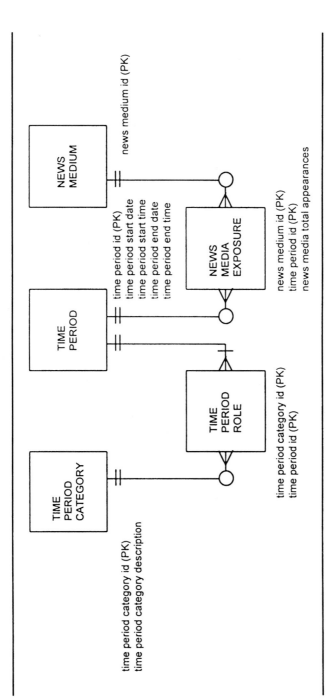

Figure 9.34   Time period used to capture time dependent information.

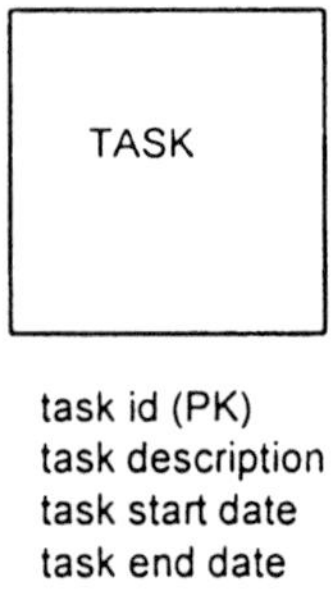

```
        ┌──────────────┐
        │              │
        │   TASK       │
        │              │
        │              │
        └──────────────┘

        task id (PK)
        task description
        task start date
        task end date
```

Figure 9.35   Time period without time period entity requirement.

period, which is meaningful to the business but which does not meet the other characteristics of time periods described above. In the example, the duration of the task represents a time period, with defined start and end dates. However, since each task will have a duration, and these may vary continuously, we do not consider the task duration a recognized time period that would cause us to uniquely identify and track it.

9.12   MODELING PROCESS VERSUS DATA

Discussion

Distinguishing between process and data model components is sometimes complex. During data-gathering activities, process components are sometimes unknowingly introduced in the data model. They do not add value to the model and usually obscure meaning. They are not data pieces, but usually reflect changes in an entity state.

Modeling processes in a data model occurs most often during reverse engineering efforts. The state of a data structure is captured with indicators or flags. Applications read the indicators to determine a conditional logic path to follow. Analysts examine these files and capture them incorrectly as attributes in the logical data model. These process components provide no business meaning independent of the application. They identify state changes and provide no value to the enterprise.

Example

On the stock exchange, quotes for securities are placed by a variety of wholesale firms, called market makers. At any one point in time, the highest bid and the lowest offer in a security is known as the inside quotation. If the *inside indicator* was captured in the data model, this

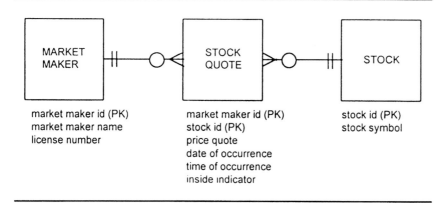

Figure 9.36   Unnecessary process flag.

may be a violation. The *inside indicator* is showing a quote that is at the "inside state." This information is not necessary in the logical data model (Figure 9.36), *unless other information will be derived from it.* As a rule of thumb, avoid entities and attributes that are designed to show changes of state unless there is additional data associated with them.

The *inside indicator* is only required if we are using it to drive out additional data requirements. A valid data model component would contain information derived from this indicator. Examples (Figure 9.37) may include the *number of inside quotes* made by a MARKET MAKER or the amount of *time spent at the inside.* This valuable business information could be consumed by the enterprise for regulatory purposes.

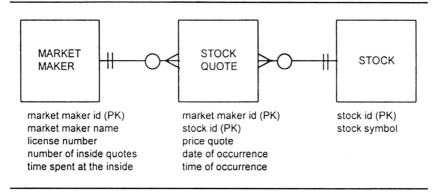

Figure 9.37   Process flag resolved.

CASE Tool Supplement

INTRODUCTION

Data models are excellent tools to define and control organizational information resources. The semantic language used to define data models is almost always produced with CASE tools. Imagine an organization without these products—the task of creating and maintaining an enterprise model would consume an inordinate amount of time and resources. We have included this supplement to provide buyers with criteria to evaluate and select CASE tools. Vendor offerings are not discussed. The sections below discuss CASE, its benefits, criteria for selection, and future trends.

WHAT IS CASE?

Computer Aided Software Engineering, or CASE, means different things to different people in the industry. CASE is as necessary to an analyst or a designer as a stove and a saucepan is to a chef. It is a critical component of the analysis and design tool kit. If we break apart CASE into its component parts, we gain insight into its meaning and use.

Computer Aided implies the use of information technology. CASE may help an analyst construct a business model, simulate activities occurring in the enterprise, or generate C++ code. The main point is that technology is applied to ensure that an arduous task is completed in a more timely and effective manner.

Software implies CASE is used during the software development process. In other words, CASE will apply automation to a particular task or activity in the lifecycle. This is a bit more restrictive than the authors would like, but it does have significance. CASE was originally used in exactly this capacity. Drawing data flow diagrams, entity relationship diagrams, and ensuring structured analysis and design rules were being followed was, and is, an excellent application for CASE. These activities are labor intensive: by off-loading these procedures to an application program, more time can be spent applying thoughtful analysis.

The disagreement we have with the term is the idea it is only for software. Business process improvement projects look to ensure the "right" processes are automated. This does not always conclude in a new software development project. Many improvement opportunities are changes to existing manual processes or the elimination of non-value-added activities. This type of analysis is also supported by CASE. This is, perhaps, why the term Computer Aided *Systems* Engineering is more applicable.

The *Engineering* component implies that CASE applies or enforces scientific and mathematical principles to planning, analysis, design, and construction activities. This is how we hope to improve the quality of our finished products. The same rigor we apply to other activities, such as building a house or designing a car, must be applied to an increasingly valuable resource, software.

Now, if we revisit the term, we can provide a suitable definition. ***CASE is the application of technology to a part or parts of the system development process. This encompasses planning, analysis, design, and construction activities.*** For convenience, we will further categorize CASE into two areas (Figure A.1): Upper CASE and Lower CASE. Upper CASE automates activities in the planning and analysis phases. Lower CASE automates activities in the design and construction phases.

WHY DO I NEED CASE?

CASE offers *potential* benefits to all who use its services. When CASE was first introduced, it was hailed as an information systems "silver bullet." Users expected this to be the answer to increase programmer productivity, produce zero defect software, resolve the software crisis, and any other IS problem. Well, it is a step in the right direction, but there are other forces that determine its ultimate success. CASE, *prop-*

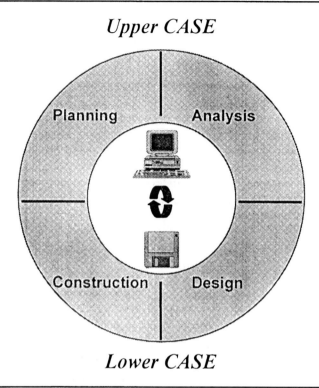

Upper CASE

Planning   Analysis

Construction   Design

Lower CASE

Figure A.1   CASE categories.

erly introduced, is a tool that can help us meet our industries development challenges and provide significant organizational benefits.

- CASE can help to *increase team and personal productivity.* No longer does the analyst need to manually level data flow diagrams, cross reference data and process models, or ensure all data model objects meet the minimum tests for completeness. These tedious activities can be handled quickly by an Upper CASE product. In addition, Lower CASE products may generate schemas, create database triggers, and generate some, most, or all of the program code. This allows analysts and designers to spend more time on tasks requiring a high level of cerebral input.
- CASE can help to *ensure timely delivery of high quality business sys-*

tems. By automating many of the manually intensive tasks, team members can focus on other activities to ensure the product is delivered on schedule. Automation of tedious tasks, combined with rule enforcement, can ensure the delivered product meets quality standards. Engineering connotes a high degree of rigor built into a process. CASE can provide the quality and completeness checks that guard against improper methodology application. The enforcement of these rules will produce higher quality analysis artifacts, which in turn will be consumed, and used to produce higher quality end products.

- CASE can help to *protect our investment in legacy systems.* Reverse engineering tools can abstract the designs from existing applications and allow analysts to better understand an existing environment. Organizations can then make more informed decisions regarding new information systems projects.
- CASE can help to *empower users.* Today's business users possess more sophistication than any other generation. They will not be satisfied articulating their requirements to an analyst and having a system arrive at some point in the future. They are willing and eager to contribute to the process. They want to redesign their business processes, lay out their screens, or offer insight into the activities that lend themselves to automation. Business users want to communicate their requirements and become a part of the process. Prototyping tools and interactive CASE products allow them to do so.
- CASE can help to *respond to changing business conditions.* The only certainty in the business environment is change. The organizations that adapt quickly will succeed, those that can't will fail. A properly constructed CASE environment can provide linkage from environmental assumptions to business plans, to business models, to information systems. In this environment, an organization can quickly identify changes and quickly adapt to the new conditions.

CASE is an exciting technology that offers potential benefits to all who employ its services, however, it must be introduced properly to ensure that a compatible environment is established and maintained. The productivity gains and efficiency increases are not guaranteed with the purchase of CASE. Planning and managing for change is a critical success factor for any organization contemplating its use.

THE CASE ENVIRONMENT

In the previous section, we prefaced the benefits of CASE with the word *potential*. There is a high degree of dissatisfaction with CASE. These problems result from CASE failing to deliver on its promise (overhype from vendors), and problems with other participants in the CASE environment. Figure A.2 identifies some of the major components: people, organizations, problems, and methods. CASE must interact with all of these components in a reasonable manner to increase the probability of project success. Let's look at each of these items in turn.

The first question from an analyst should always be, *what is the real problem I am trying to solve?* The introduction of CASE will not make an accounting problem go away or correct a faulty organizational structure. CASE will provide to the analyst a tool for organizing thoughts and viewing a problem in a structured manner. If the problem cannot be solved

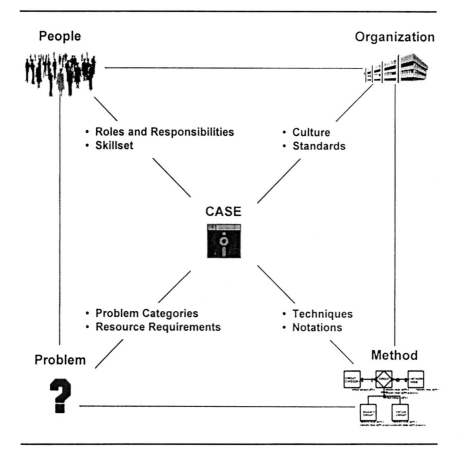

Figure A.2   CASE environment.

with thoughtful analysis or is obscured by the method employed by the CASE product, there is little hope for project success.

The skill set of project personnel is a contributing factor to CASE success. If project personnel do not understand the methods, the problem domain, or the organizational processes, they will fail. Making sure the right people are involved in the process and empowered with the proper roles and responsibilities is a critical barrier.

All CASE products support at least one Upper or Lower CASE method. In the planning and analysis phases, this may be Yourdon/Constantine, Finkelstein, Rumbaugh, or Booch. In the design and construction phases, this may be C++, Smalltalk, or a specific DBMS. Not all methods are equally applicable to every problem domain. A certain degree of paradigm matching must occur between the problem, the method, the organizational processes, and the people. If our organization was building an information resource management program, we would most likely use a CASE product that supported one of the Information Engineering paradigms. We would not use a process-centered approach like Structured Systems Analysis and Design Method (SSADM) or some of the current Business Process Improvement techniques.

The organization itself may play quite a large role in the successful CASE project. Every organization has its own culture. This culture may be conducive to change, or it may prohibit new ways of doing business. The introduction of CASE is a major change for an organization. Existing information system development processes should be reviewed to determine exactly what activities can be streamlined or improved with CASE.

CASE must interact with other components of the environment. This complex tapestry determines the ultimate success or failure of the CASE effort. CASE itself does not ensure success or determine the ultimate failure of any project. This is determined by the CASE environment. An individual's planning, analysis, design, and construction skills will never be replaced by CASE. They are meant to be compatible. CASE products should supplement an analyst or designer, not attempt to remove him or her from an area of expertise.

HOW DO I CHOOSE A CASE PRODUCT?

CASE is a candidate tool for all planning, analysis, design, and construction activities. Sophisticated tools (or so the vendors claim) are a substantial investment for an organization to make. Proper care should be given to their selection. Evaluation criteria should include the methodology supported, the level of integration, usability features, and the vendor.

The most important feature of a CASE product is the *methodology supported*. Consistency (McClure, 1989) between the process and CASE is the key. This consistency can help simplify CASE tool selection. An organization embarking on business process improvement initiatives should look for a tool that contains the same activities being performed. It should be process focused and contain techniques for activity-based costing, simulation, and other BPI components. On the other hand, an organization shifting its development resources to an object-oriented paradigm should look for C++, Smalltalk, or an Eiffel code generator.

This selection checkpoint applies to both Upper and Lower CASE products. Upper CASE tools are available to support a wide range of methods. Some of the tools that were originally designed to handle only structured or information engineering methods have been extended to support some of the emerging object-oriented methodologies. Lower CASE products should be mapped to the development system hardware and software present or planned. Compatibility with implementation languages, operating system characteristics, and other development tools is essential.

Integration is the vehicle that will allow CASE to reach its full potential. An integrated environment extending from planning through construction is not available unless an organization is willing to wholly commit to a vendor and its approach. Technology to implement a Best of Breed or Plug and Play approach is years away. Figure A.3 describes the multiple dimensions of integration: data, presentation, and control integration. The problem is increased exponentially when the lifecycle phases are introduced. Seamlessness between planning products and construction products introduces additional complexity into the integration dilemma.

- *Data integration* refers to the sharing of common data between CASE products. This is a factor of the underlying meta-models. If we are using an Integrated CASE product, the degree of data integration should be high. This is sensible because the vendor is supplying the process and we would hope that all of the artifacts created are consumed by other activities in the lifecycle. If our organization is not willing to commit to a single vendor, the degree of data integration will decrease. Lack of industry standard interchange formats and a willingness of vendors to support them will continue to make data integration a difficult task.
- *Presentation integration* refers to different tools executing with a common set of controls or display information. An example of presentation integration is the look and feel of a MOTIF or Windows user interface, regardless of the executing application or the type of

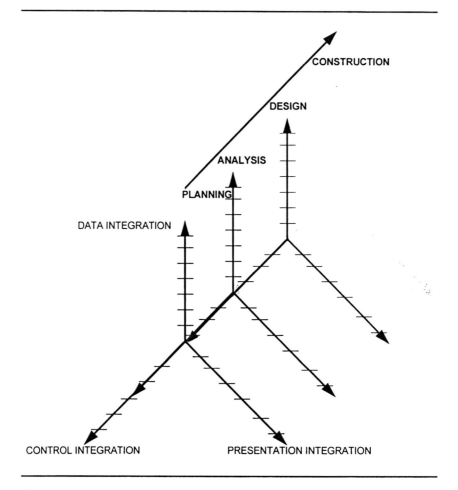

Figure A.3   Integration dimensions.

platform, the user interface is consistent. Presentation integration is not a significant barrier in the CASE industry.

• *Control integration* refers to the ability to command different CASE tools and their access to data. This will allow the products to coexist and interoperate efficiently. Repository standards, such as AD/Cycle or the National Institute of Standards and Technology's Information Resource Dictionary System (IRDS), require a great deal of control integration. These meta-CASE products must maintain strict access by users of any kind to the underlying meta-model.

Integration is the key to effective utilization of CASE. A requirement for a common interchange format to seamlessly translate all information from one CASE product to another is essential. Industry groups, such as the Electronic Industry Association's Common Data Interchange Format (CDIF) or the European Computer Manufacturers Association's Portable Common Tool Exchange (PCTE), are convening to come up with a representation format. In the interim, most of the existing tools will produce import/export files. These files can be mapped between one CASE tool and the other.

Usability is a measure as to the convenience and practicality of a CASE product. The automation of tedious tasks is a central theme behind CASE. An analyst or designer wants to alleviate his or her workload, not add to it. Product selection should look at a number of usability features including human factors criteria, reliability, the quality of output, and the documentation.

- The human factors approach to evaluating CASE looks at the conformance between the analyst and designer tasks and determines how well the product supports those activities. For example, a data modeler does not like to waste time laying out a data map—an automated model generation facility that reduces the number of crossed lines and presents the models in a readable manner would enhance the modeler's productivity. Other criteria would include support for model completeness and quality checks, and model management facilities. The basic question that needs to be answered is, "Am I spending less time on these tasks with CASE or additional time?" The answer should be obvious.

- *Stability* is a key factor in the selection process. The end user should not spend any time recovering from software errors or any other problems introduced through the tool. Patches and bug fixes are unacceptable in a CASE product. If CASE is going to reduce our system's development lead times, we need to ensure it can stand the challenge and not introduce additional complexities into the process. Quality is key.

- Our customers, internal and external, evaluate our efforts on the quality of the material they receive. This may be a data model, an entity report, a section of code or a screen prototype. The quality of output produced by the CASE product should be camera ready.

There are many dimension to usability. Each of the items detailed above can be exploded in greater detail. Asking the vendor for a thirty-day evaluation copy is the easiest technique for guaranteeing the product will help, not hinder, the analyst.

The CASE *vendor* is a critical, yet often overlooked evaluation factor. Can you describe any of the organizations you have purchased products from? There are over one thousand vendors staking their claim in the CASE market. Not all will survive the upcoming shakeout. Changing paradigms and new approaches will strengthen some organization positions and weaken others.

- The vendor should provide *hot-line support* for its product. Questions that cannot be resolved through existing documentation must be handled with some type of assistance center. An end-user should never have to delay execution of an activity because of an unresolved issue. The assistance center can be used to report errors, make suggestions, or seek clarification on issues.
- The vendor should create an *information-sharing environment* with the customer. Future directions, size of the firm, and other pertinent data should be discussed freely. There is no sense in buying a product from a firm if it does not intend to support the product in the future or if it is moving in a polar direction from the customer.
- *Formal classroom training* should be offered by the vendor. The training should, at a minimum, contain sections on the underlying methods and notation and hands-on product training. The firm should gear its CASE study toward an existing project. This will help jumpstart the project.
- Many projects are doomed from the outset because there is no reliable individual or individuals to lead the initial process. Vendors offering *consulting services* can provide the know-how to accomplish the task at hand. In addition, the consultants can perform in a mentoring role to project team members, so that on the next project they do not require as much support. Eventually, the project team will be able to function on its own.

One final note on evaluating the vendor. It is extremely important to gather as much background as possible. Contact other organizations who are using the product, find out the level of support they have been provided, and how freely they have received information from the vendor. The purchase of a product should signify to both parties the beginning of a two-way partnership. The customer should feel comfortable with the vendor and its direction and the vendor should solicit improvement ideas from the customer.

FUTURE TRENDS

There are upcoming changes for the CASE industry and we are seeing evidence in today's products. The environment of the future is going to blur the distinction between analysts and end-users. Increasing use of artificial intelligence for model analysis, multimedia technology for usability, explicit support for reuse, metrics for project management, and an increased use of natural language facilities will allow tomorrow's end-users to create their own applications.

- *Artificial intelligence* is on the comeback trail. After years of being oversold, expectations have been readjusted and appropriate application domains discovered. One such domain is CASE. Facilities for enforcing methodology rules and suggesting appropriate actions based on acquired facts are being built into the products. AI facilities can help with the syntactic and conceptual aspects of quality assurance and defect removal.
- *Multimedia* can no longer be described as an emerging technology. It's here. The blending of text, video, sound, and other technology to stimulate our senses is being incorporated into CASE. Methodology advisors are available to us today that contain digital video, hypertext, and other technologies for self-education and training. The continued exploitation of new technologies will continue at warp speed.
- *Reuse* is the principal benefit associated with the object-oriented paradigms. The ability to reuse artifacts from all phases of the lifecycle is a critical need. The CASE environment will explicitly provide its users with an ability to search for, identify, and modify components for reuse. The introduction of class libraries is an example; however, we will see a much more concerted effort to reuse planning and analysis components.
- *Natural language* is capable of capturing all the descriptions necessary for a complete model of an enterprise or information systems. The English language interrogatives (who, why, when, where, what, and how) succinctly define these descriptions. The problems of using natural language to capture them include rigorous unambiguous capture and automated interface with CASE tools. Customers or other nontechnical personnel can more readily understand, validate, and describe their own models with minimal support from technicians in terms of natural language. They can access and maintain these models using currently available COTS natural language query tools. Specific domain modeling technicians find that the quality of natural language models developed by the owners and users of information

systems exceeds the quality of the models they extract via facilitation or interviews. Significantly better quality activity models, data models, organization models, dependency models, geotechnical models, and the like can be developed from the common natural language model than from independent efforts by specialized technicians. In fact, it will become practical in the near future to derive all of these specialized models from the common natural language model. Natural language offers a much more practical approach to a comprehensive repository and CASE tool than any products currently available or likely to be available in the near future.

- *Metrics* will be incorporated into many more products. They will be used to measure the status, progress and to estimate future work. Future CASE products will include a database to collect and analyze previous project metrics. These measures will cross the entire lifecycle and provide input to project management and project quality.
- *Templates* will be of increasing importance and we will see them incorporated into many more products. They will be used to expedite the construction of an analysis model or to compare an organizational process with the best practices in the industry. Templates will be developed for a multitude of application domains.

The basic need to solve organizational problems will always remain with us. In the future, the job of the analyst or empowered business user will require an additional level of sophistication in his tool kits. These tools are being constructed and will soon make their way into your organization. The analyst should keep abreast of these changes and determine how they could be applied to his or her area of responsibility. Technology is providing the organization with a powerful mechanism for change—we must determine its impact and carefully introduce it, now and in the future.

REFERENCES

McClure, Carma. *CASE is Software Automation.* Englewood Cliffs, NJ: Prentice-Hall, 1989.

Object Modeling Supplement

INTRODUCTION

We have included an object modeling supplement in this book for a number of reasons. The first is we believe object orientation will be the dominant software development paradigm of the future. As our systems grow and become more complex, object-oriented technologies can help us bridge the gap between legacy systems and new application demands. Consider the management of networks: An existing network is usually comprised of several different element managers each containing its own proprietary management system. Unless we migrate to a common platform, an expensive and usually unrealistic suggestion, we will have extreme difficulty in managing this environment.

Object orientation lends itself well to network management because we can treat the element managers as discrete objects. It doesn't matter if equipment is older or newer with SNMP or CMIP support. Each element manager is treated as an independent object, each possessing its own characteristics and behavior. Similar messages are sent to these devices and they are handled differently, yet appropriately, by the services each object supports. The trend toward distributed, heterogeneous environments provides additional momentum for the adoption of object-oriented techniques.

A data modeling methodology provides a solid foundation from which to move into object-oriented methods. While object-oriented techniques are quickly taking shape, it is a technology in its childhood. The economic justification for full-scale implementation is meager and the promise of reuse and improved delivery of systems remains elusive. Most organizations are applying some degree of object-oriented techniques to particular applications, but are foregoing dependence until the technology has had a chance to mature. An investment in quality data modeling puts an organization one step closer to solving business problems within this paradigm.

WHY OBJECTS?

In all other industries, we build products from ready-made parts. Each component is rigorously tested to ensure it meets quality guidelines and then it is aggregated with others to form a whole. Only in the information systems field do we continue to custom build. A direct result of handcrafted systems is the inordinate amount of time spent on maintenance (Grygo, 1990). Sixty to eighty percent (Yourdon, 1992) of information systems dollars are earmarked for maintaining and enhancing existing applications. Of course, while maintenance work is consuming our resources, requests for new information systems are piling up. This inability to respond to user demands is known as the *software crisis* (Verify, Schwartz, 1991).

Object-oriented techniques promise to deliver us into a new development environment. We will be able to proactively respond to the software crisis because our industry will begin to mirror others. Customization will occur on a much smaller scale because of the emphasis on reusability. When objects are created according to precise rules, they can be standardized. These components will be placed into a software library for reuse by programmers. As new application demands are voiced, these parts or software ICs (Cox, 1986) will be aggregated to form a percentage of the whole.

Confusion over requirements will be kept to a minimum. Every object in an application domain corresponds to an item familiar to the subject matter experts (SME). Analysts can interview or facilitate sessions with individuals familiar with the domain and identify the objects and their behavior. These objects can then be seamlessly translated, (Figure B.1), into a design and implementation environment.

Object-oriented techniques can significantly reduce the percentage of time spent on maintaining applications. Objects entered into the library will be tested to ensure they meet quality guidelines, and as such, should be fairly stable. When objects breakdown we need only fix that object. Objects isolate program functions from one another so that a change in one doesn't disrupt other objects. This is quite a difference

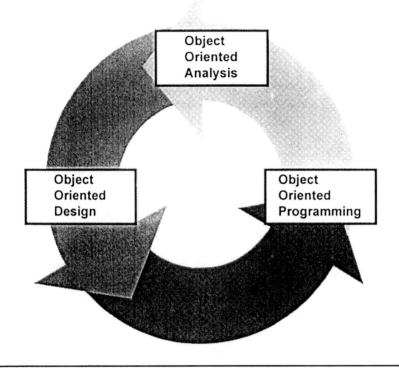

Figure B.1   Seamless transition.

from today's environment where a small change may have many undesirable side effects.

Are Data Techniques Object-Oriented?

In order to determine how to transition from data models to object models, let's look at the existing object-oriented (OO) methods and relate them to data focused techniques, such as information engineering (IE). We shall see that, although IE and OO have evolved separately over the past three decades, IE as a top-down technique and OO as a bottom-up technique, they share many ideas.

The object-oriented approach has its foundation as a programming environment. The first of these is Simula, which originated in the late 1960s (Simpers, 1991). Simula pioneered several of the key features of

OOA, such as inheritance and encapsulation. Smalltalk, another object-oriented programming language, was originally developed at the University of Utah in the early 1970s. This programming language combines the key features of Simula with the free, typeless style of LISP. Evolutionary refinements accomplished by the Xerox Palo Alto Research Center (PARC) through 1976 caused the language to evolve to its present form. Object-oriented programming products have proliferated in the past several years. The most popular of the object oriented development languages on the market today is C++, which is rapidly becoming the de facto standard in this area. However, not until the past decade has OO begun to mature from a basis for programming languages to object-oriented design and analysis techniques.

On the other hand, data-focused techniques stem from logical and theoretical database design concepts. They have their roots in mathematical relational set theory, applied to data by Ted Codd and his colleagues at IBM during the early 1970s for creating logical data representations. During the mid-1970s, the bridge from relational theory to practical business use was undertaken concurrently and independently by three companies: CACI (Europe), BIS (UK), and Information Engineering Services (IES) Pty. Ltd. (Australia), founded by Clive Finkelstein. The first two of these companies applied relational theory and normalization to the development of information systems analysis methods from a data processing perspective. Their efforts focused on how to solve problems in commercial database design. It was Clive Finkelstein's efforts that gave birth to Information Engineering (IE), which applied the relational theory and normalization techniques to strategic planning. Using IE, systems developers were, for the first time, able to translate user requirements directly to physical database design.

The primary purpose for emphasizing objects in OOA is to match the representation of these objects with how they are viewed in the real world. This is known as *abstraction*. The representation of real-world objects is accomplished through the identification of problem space objects, data about the objects, and processes. Assume we were constructing a simple model of an elementary school. There are a number of objects we would discover through abstraction. These include a TEACHER and a CLASS object. Both techniques, properly applied, would contain similar objects in their respective diagramming notations. The object model, however, goes one step further by defining the behavior of the objects (Figure B.2.). This provides additional insight into the elementary school domain. The analyst now knows not only the static information pieces, but also the operations of the object.

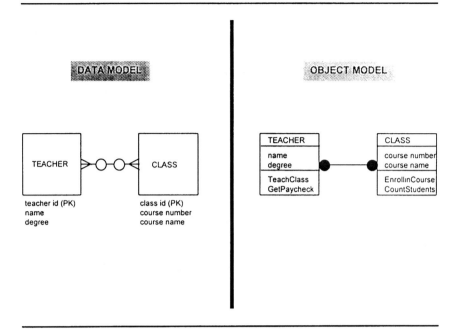

Figure B.2   Abstraction comparison.

Objects that are most recognizable to the business experts are used as the foundation during analysis. These objects form the basis for communicating the business requirements to every level of management and to the development teams. The ability to model a given business in logical terms, combined with the fact that these objects are named in terms familiar to the business experts, serves as a very powerful vehicle for the clear communication of requirements throughout the organization. Also, in direct correlation with the IE approach, OO emphasizes that the objects and their characteristics are used as the foundation from which to analyze the processes that access and manipulate the information. In comparison, IE represents data focused requirements, while OO represents data focused requirements.

This is the point of departure or the key paradigm shift. In IE, we are focused on identifying and sharing data across the enterprise. Functionality is described in terms relating to its operation upon data. This is not the case in the object paradigm. In OO, we are focused on describing the application domain in terms of object characteristics, and *object behavior*. Object-oriented analysis does not have the same end goal as

IE. IE is a data sharing approach, OO hides data in discrete objects and only provides the information necessary to complete an organizational scenario.

Inheritance is a key concept found in both techniques. It provides the ability to identify commonality among objects or entities within the problem space, while at the same time maintaining the differences pertaining to a subset of those object or entities. Using Figure B.3 as a guide, we can see inheritance in the data model. The CUSTOMER and EMPLOYEE entities inherit the data from PERSON. Object-oriented techniques extend inheritance by allowing data and behavior to be inherited. In the second half of the example, we can see CUSTOMER and EMPLOYEE inherit the data attributes and also the GetAge service. Another interesting point is the representation of STUDENT as a subtype.

In the data model, we subtype based on additional attributes or mandatory away relationships. This provides the reviewer with a static view of the differences in the entity types. Object-oriented techniques permit subtyping based on behavior. Even if an object looks the same—that is, it has identical characteristics—it may not act the same. Data modeling techniques lead us to believe a static view is all that is required to distinguish items in an application domain, object-oriented analysis looks at behavior as an additional differentiator.

Another basic concept in both OO and IE is managing complexity in the problem space by localizing volatile or incomplete requirements. Changes to any system are inevitable, as incomplete specifications are refined or as the business responds to new direction or markets. In any organization, it is essential to identify and manage these changes precisely and accurately. Within an OO framework, the ability to manage complexity in the problem space is addressed by *encapsulation*. Figure B.4 describes all of the information required to calculate a salary. Salary is determined for an hourly worker by the number of hours worked multiplied by the wage rate. The object model encapsulates or hides that complexity from the user by only showing a GetSalary method. Wage and hours worked are important, but only for the calculation of a salary. It is therefore germane only to the hourly worker object and is hidden from view.

An additional characteristic of the object-oriented paradigm is *polymorphism*. This is the ability of a method (or procedure) to behave differently on different objects. Figure B.5 shows two shapes, a CIRCLE and a RECTANGLE. Both objects have a Draw method. However, when it is invoked on CIRCLE it draws a circle and when it invoked on RECTANGLE it draws a rectangle. The method "draw" has within it the ability to recognize differences between the two types of objects and

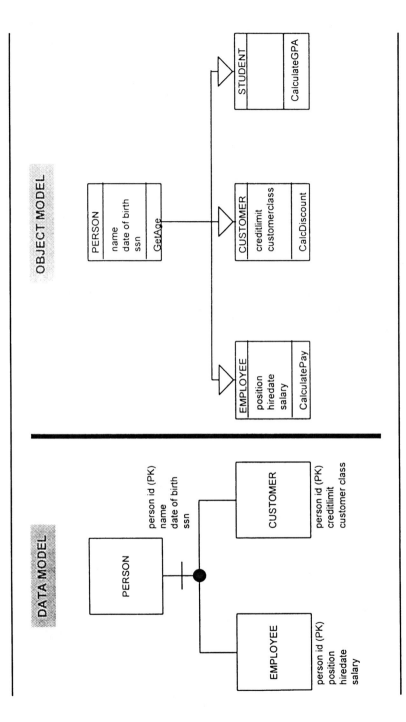

Figure B.3 Inheritance.

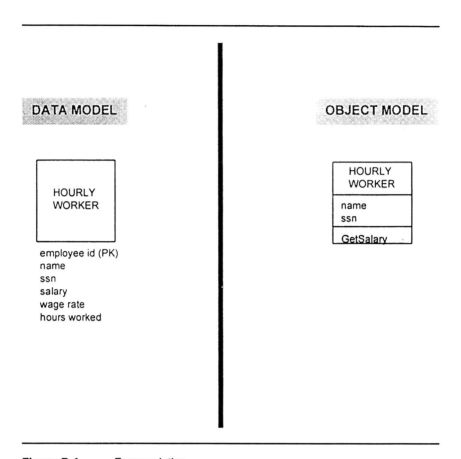

Figure B.4   Encapsulation.

could compensate by acting slightly different for one or the other. In the data model, there is no corresponding principle.

Information Engineering and other data focused techniques provide a clear transition path to object modeling. Both techniques recognize the importance of identifying data first and both techniques share similar principles. There are clear benefits to applying quality data modeling ideas to the object-oriented paradigm. The conceptual and syntax issues of completeness and correctness exist in both domains. The similarity between the two approaches will help a quality data modeling organization move forward.

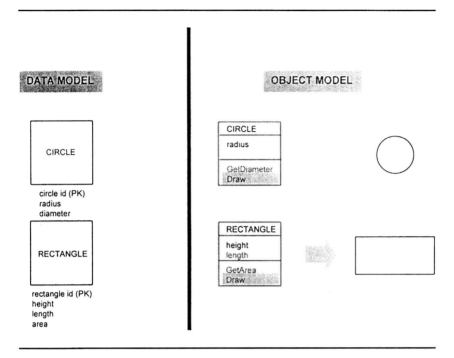

Figure B.5   Polymorphism.

THE FUTURE OF OBJECTS

There are a number of standardization efforts underway in the object-oriented community that will impact the future of these techniques. These efforts are critical to the adoption of the technology. The creation and subsequent adherence to the standards by industry organizations will exponentially increase the use of object-oriented methods. Organizations looking to adopt object-oriented techniques should pay close attention to the following activities.

• The Object Management Group was formed in 1989 with the purpose of creating standards allowing for the interoperability and portability of distributed (OO) applications. Most of the major players in the commercial distributed OO computing arena are among the several hundred companies that belong to the OMG. Figure B.6 describes the Object Management Architecture (OMA). It attempts

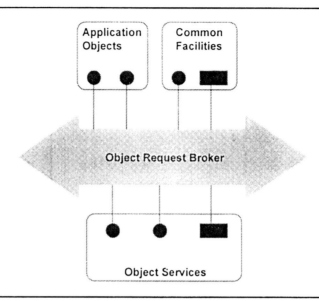

Figure B.6   OMG Object Management Architecture.

to define the various facilities necessary for distributed OO computing at a high level of abstraction.

- The Object Data Management Group (ODMG) standard for object
  databases, ODMG-93, is complete. This is primarily the work of five
  competing companies that offer object database products: Object
  Design, Ontos, O2 Technology, Versant, and Objectivity. This specification allows an application written to run unchanged on multiple
  ODBMS products.
- The Object Oriented Cobol Task Group (OOCTG), ANSI X3J4.1, is
  made up of twenty-five hardware and software vendors. This document spells out the changes to the existing COBOL 85 standard to
  include support for object orientation. Other language efforts include those for C++ (ANSI X3J16), LISP (ANSI X3J13), Ada, and
  Smalltalk.
- IBM is paving the way for reusable components with the development of their System Object Model (SOM). SOM is a model for
  sharing classes in a language independent format. In other words,
  classes developed in Smalltalk can be combined with those developed in Object Oriented Cobol, C++, or EIFFEL. SOM provides
  methods for updating, storing, and retrieving objects and updating
  all applications that use SOM objects.

The hype surrounding OO has often been compared to that surrounding Artificial Intelligence (AI) in the early 1980s. Only now that we have scaled down our expectations of AI are we finding domains for its use. Object-oriented techniques face a similar problem; organizations rushing to adopt should pay close attention to these industry consortia. They are the real indicators of the success of this technology. Vendors must adhere to the standards for interoperability and portability or object orientation will continue to flounder.

REFERENCES

Cox, B. *Object Oriented Programming: An Evolutionary Approach.* Reading, MA: Addison Wesley, 1986.

Grygo, G. "Object Oriented Technology Fills Leading Edge Niche," *Digital Review.* (July 30, 1990).

Simpers, P. "Information Engineering: A Business-Driven Approach to Object-Oriented Analysis," *Data Center Manager* 3, No. 4: 57–59 (July–August, 1991).

Verify, J. and Schwartz, E. "Software Made Simple," *Business Week*, 3233: 92–100 (September 30, 1991).

Yourdon, E. "The Decline and Fall of The American Programmer." Englewood Cliffs, NJ: Prentice-Hall, 1992.

Quality Review
Case Study

INTRODUCTION

This appendix presents the results of a sample quality assurance review, using a fictional company, its policies, and a data model built using those policies that purposefully has modeling errors and omissions. The objective of this appendix is to illustrate how an independent quality assurance review—using the proper tools and techniques—can be used to improve a data model. We discussed the quality review process at length in Chapter 2. Our emphasis here is on demonstrating what the results of a quality review would look like. The human resources subject area of the fictional company was selected because most everyone has a basic knowledge of the information and the types of policies that exist in commercial or government personnel or human resources departments.

When working your way through the statements, model, and findings, remember that it is virtually impossible to explain all aspects of even a small model fragment. As you probably know, the alternatives for modeling any given business situation are seemingly endless, and rely heavily on business experts' input. Since we built this example on our own, we have made some assumptions about certain aspects of the model that simply cannot be explained to every reader's satisfaction here. Our goal is to illustrate the potential that QA reviews have to increase the quality and utility of models, not necessarily to get every aspect of the model "right." Those areas of the model we purposely did not get right should appear in the QA Findings section.

THE SITUATION

ZYX Associates: Systems Consultants

A modeling team including business experts and data analysts has just completed a business-driven modeling exercise for ZYX Associates, a small but growing consulting firm specializing in information systems solutions design and development. The team used documented policies and plans to build a data model for the ZYX Associates human resources department. The model and supporting materials (a model review kit) is now being turned over for an independent quality assurance review.

Assume the business statements and model presented below are extracts from a larger human resources plan and data model.

BUSINESS STATEMENTS

The following business statements were included in the model review kit.

Performance Review Policy

All employees of ZYX receive a performance review annually, beginning on their first year anniversary. Employee performance is graded against a standard set of evaluation criteria, with an employee receiving a rating of 1 (excellent) through 5 (unacceptable) in each category. The categories are weighted, and an overall employee performance score is computed.

Bonus Plan Policy

Bonuses are awarded on an ad hoc basis to any employee who contributes significantly to the growth or well-being of the firm, attains substantial professional recognition by a national association or professional organization, or improves recognition of the firm within the industry or among potential clients. Bonuses are subject to income tax withholding. In order to be eligible for a bonus, an employee must be with the firm for more than six months. While not a firm rule, ZYX makes it a practice to award no more than three bonuses to any individual during a calendar year.

Policy on Hiring Relatives or Spouses of Employees

ZYX encourages the hiring of qualified professional and administrative staff members, including relatives, immediate family members, and spouses of current employees. However, an employee cannot have direct supervisory responsibility over any individual to whom that employee is related by birth, marriage, or as legal guardian.

Parking Space Policy

Employees will be assigned a numbered parking space for their personal use. At the request of the employee, parking privileges may be waived and the employee will receive a monthly stipend of $50 to cover public transportation expenses.

Health Benefits Policy

ZYX offers its employees and their dependents a choice of health care plans. An employee may select a new plan annually, and coverage under the selected plan begins on January 1 and ends on December 31. An employee may not switch plans during the year. New employees are covered beginning the date they are hired for the remainder of the calendar year. An employee may elect to not be covered by a plan. An employee's dependents are covered by whatever plan the employee selects.

THE DATA MODEL

The data model shown in Figure C.1 was developed by the modeling team to support the policy statements outlined above.

QUALITY ASSURANCE REVIEW FINDINGS

This section outlines a set of findings based on the business statements and data model. The far right column in table C.1 refers to applicable rules in Section II. The findings have been limited to those dealing with specific issues or problems in the model. Due to the abbreviated nature of this case study, we have omitted what we term "general findings," which address problems or issues occurring repeatedly throughout the model, usually indicative of some systemic problem that will need to be addressed through additional training, better modeling tool support, greater access to business experts, or creation of modeling standards or procedures.

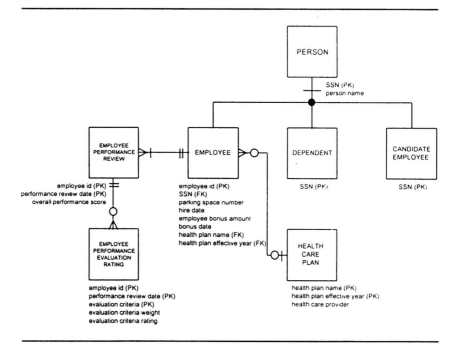

Figure C.1   The data model submitted for review.

Specific findings reflect either a syntactic problem, a problem translating the business concept correctly to the model notation, or model constructs that do not completely support the business statement(s). You should expect to have many more specific findings than general findings in a typical review.

In order to make the findings easier to follow in relation to the model, *attribute names* have been italicized, and ENTITY NAMES have been capitalized. Table C.1 outlines the specific findings of the review. You will need to refer back to the policy statements and data model in order to follow the findings.

THE DATA MODEL REVISED

Based on the findings and recommendations presented in Table C.1, a revised model has been prepared and is shown in Figure C.2.

Several aspects of the revision are noteworthy:

• The entity PERSON TYPE records the discriminator governing subtypes of PERSON (EMPLOYEE, DEPENDENT, and CANDIDATE

Table C.1.   Case Study Data Model Review Findings and
Recommendations

Specific Findings & Recommendations	Rule Reference(s)
1. The Health Benefits Policy statement refers to an employee's eligible dependents. However, the model does not contain any constructs (entities or relationships) that relate an employee to dependents.Recommendation: Consider creating a structure entity related to PERSON to relate dependents to employee(s).	• Recursive Relationship Rule
2. EMPLOYEE is a subtype of PERSON, yet has not inherited the primary key from PERSON (see item 3 below, however, before resolving this finding). When correcting this condition, note that *employee* id cascades to other entities in the model.	• Generalization Hierarchy • Primary Key Inheritance Rule
3. Use of SSN (Social Security Number) as a primary key for person may not be practical from a business perspective. Will ZYX have access to every individual's social security number, including dependents and candidate employees? What about individuals who do not have SSNs, such as infant dependents or persons who are not U.S. citizens? Also, social security number is considered private information, limiting its utility as a primary key. Also, use of abbreviations as attribute names should be avoided.	• Primary Key Characteristics Rule • Attribute Names Rule
4. There is no discriminator attribute for subtype PERSON. Add a discriminator to PERSON to control subtyping. Also, neither DEPENDENT nor CANDIDATE EMPLOYEE have any unique attributes or relationships. If none are discovered during further modeling sessions, these subtypes should be "rolled up" into the supertype.	• Subtype Discriminator of Rule • Subtype Justification Rule
5. A PERSON can be employed by the company and also be a dependent (ZYX Corp does not prohibit employing both spouses, or any other combination of family members; see related policy statement). As currently modeled, the subtypes of PERSON (EMPLOYEE and DEPENDENT) are mutually exclusive, thus preventing an employee from also being a dependent, and vice versa.	• Relaxation of Mutual Exclusivity Requirement Rule

Table C.1. *Continued*

Specific Findings & Recommendations	*Rule Reference(s)*
6. The Employee Parking Policy indicates that assignment of a parking space number is dependent on an employee's choice to drive or take public transportation, car pool, or some alternative mode of transport. Therefore, some employees will not have assigned parking spaces, and the attribute is optional. Also, there is no way to determine by the model if an employee is due to receive a $50 monthly stipend (except to read the *parking space number* attribute for each employee and accept only those that are null). To accommodate both the optional attribute and the identification of employees due the monthly stipend, add a discriminator in EMPLOYEE such as *employee commuting status* to differentiate between those that drive (and thus get parking spaces) and those that do not drive (and thus get a $50 stipend).	• Optional Attribute Rule • Subtype Discriminator Rule
7. The Performance Review Policy indicates that employees will receive a performance review on their first year anniversary with the firm. However, the relationship between EMPLOYEE and EMPLOYEE PERFORMANCE REVIEW is mandatory at both ends. New employees (with less than one year at ZYX) will *not* have received a review. Correct this to depict the optional nature of the relationship.	• No specific rule applies. This is a conceptual correctness issue.
8. The Performance Review Policy states that evaluation criteria ratings will be used during the review, but the relationship from EMPLOYEE PERFORMANCE REVIEW to EMPLOYEE PERFORMANCE EVALUATION RATING is optional. Should this be mandatory in order to comply with the policy?	• No specific rule applies. This is a conceptual correctness issue.
9. According to the Performance Review Policy, an *evaluation weight* is assigned for each standard evaluation criterion. This suggests that *evaluation weight* is functionally dependent on *standard evaluation criterion* (only) in EMPLOYEE PERFORMANCE EVALUATION	• Second Normal Form Rule

Table C.1.   *Continued*

Specific Findings & Recommendations	Rule Reference(s)
RATING, a dependence on part of the primary key. As a result, the entity is not in second normal form (2NF). Apply the resolution strategy recommended in the 2NF Rule to eliminate the partial dependency.	
10. There is an optional one-to-optional many relationship between HEALTH CARE PLAN and EMPLOYEE. While this is consistent with the Health Benefits Policy (employees may choose to waive coverage), it is results in migration of keys *health plan* name and *health plan effective year* that are optional foreign keys in EMPLOYEE. See item 11 below before proceeding with a resolution.	• Optional Foreign Keys Rule
11. The Health Benefits Policy suggests that the Human Resources Department will have to track at least two HEALTH CARE PLAN selections for each employee—the current year coverage, and an employee's selection for the next year. However, as modeled, the relationship from EMPLOYEE to HEALTH CARE PLAN has a degree of one. Based on the policy, the degree should be many. Note that this will result in a many-to-many relationship that will need to be resolved using an associative entity.	• No specific rule applies. This is a conceptual correctness issue. The Many-to-Many Relationships Rule applies to the resolution of the conceptual problem.
12. The Bonus Plan Policy suggests that an employee is eligible to receive more than one bonus that the Human Resources Department would be interested in tracking. This makes *employee bonus amount* and *bonus date* repeating attributes. Furthermore, employee bonus amount is functionally dependent on both the primary key of EMPLOYEE (remember our findings in items 2 and 3 above, however) and *bonus date*. In other words, EMPLOYEE is not in second normal form. Resolve by moving *employee bonus amount* and *bonus date* to another entity.	• First Normal Form Rule • Second Normal Form Rule

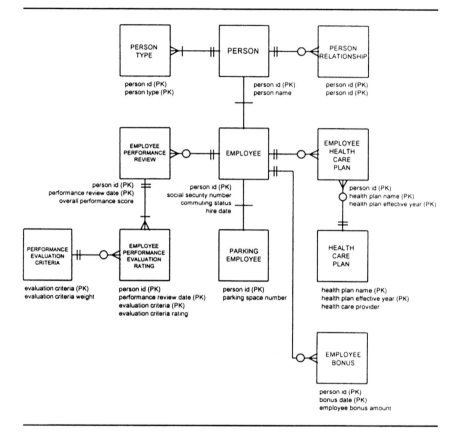

Figure C.2 One possible resolution of QA findings.

EMPLOYEE; the latter two were removed in accordance with a review finding). The person type attribute was repeating in PERSON, since according to the policy an individual could be both an EMPLOYEE and a DEPENDENT.

• The attribute *commuting status* in EMPLOYEE is a subtype discriminator governing PARKING EMPLOYEE.

• There are several policy issues that are still unresolved. We purposely did not address the issue of an employee reporting directly to his or her spouse, and we did not establish a policy governing whether two employees who are in the same family can select different health care plans. The current policy states that an employee's dependents are covered under his or her selected plan.

Index